Mary Selby is a doctor, married to another
doctor, with five small children. She lives in a
quiet Suffolk village where she once hosted
the village fête. *A Wing and a Prayer* is her
first novel.

# A WING
# AND A PRAYER

Mary Selby

**BLACK SWAN**

A WING AND A PRAYER
A BLACK SWAN BOOK : 0 552 99672 6

First publication in Great Britain

PRINTING HISTORY
Black Swan edition published 1996

Set in 11pt Melior by Deltatype Ltd, Ellesmere Port, Cheshire

Black Swan Books are published by Transworld Publishers Ltd,
61–63 Uxbridge Road, London W5 5SA,
in Australia by Transworld Publishers (Australia) Pty Ltd,
15–25 Helles Avenue, Moorebank, NSW 2170,
and in New Zealand by Transworld Publishers (NZ) Ltd,
3 William Pickering Drive, Albany, Auckland.

Reproduced, printed and bound in Great Britain by
Cox & Wyman Ltd, Reading, Berks.

*To Caroline, Fineas, Leonora,*
*Anastasia, Henrietta, Mei Ming*
*and China's children*

# Chapter One

St Jude, of course, was the patron saint of lost causes. If he had an opinion on the matter, it might well have been that he must have been last in the queue when the patronages were being given out. However, lost causes alone had clearly not been enough to keep him busy, so he had also given his name to the square Saxon church which anchored the village of Great Barking to the gently rolling South Suffolk hills.

Sunlight streamed through the huge church windows, glass glowing in shades of wine gums in the morning light. Sunbeams formed on the dancing dust specks, dust a mixture of age, furniture polish and bat droppings, and created streaks and shafts in the brightness, whilst lending a kind of dim haziness to everything else.

Despite the sun, it was cold inside. Jacob Bean had turned on the heaters on the Saturday evening as always, but the roof space avidly devoured every scrap of warmth. The air remained resolutely nose-freezing, a state of affairs not helped by the fact that the heaters were fixed, rather pointlessly, eight feet up on the walls. Hetty wondered if it was Mrs Groat who had swivelled them so that they pointed upwards at the roof. Perhaps she was hoping to toast the bats.

She smiled to herself, and in doing so caught the eye of Jacob Bean, who was both churchwarden and organist, as he returned from the Communion rail to the organ. He smiled back and winked conspiratorially. He always did. Hetty had no idea why, although she had often thought he might have confused her with some-one else, years ago, and never realized his mistake.

Alistair shifted slightly next to her and frowned sideways without actually looking at her. Hetty knew that this signified his disapproval at her exchange of glances with Jacob. For someone who really didn't give a hoot for religion, Alistair was terribly formal about church, and she was conscious of a surge of irritation. Hetty was genuinely very fond of Jacob, and could not honestly imagine that God would find it in Himself to disapprove of her exchanging smiles with him. Alistair, on the other hand, seemed to find it very easy to disapprove of her on the most tenuous grounds. It made her sad, when she thought about it, for it seemed to her to suggest that, after a quarter of a century of marriage, she no longer warmed him by her presence. Worse, she was beginning to feel that he regarded her more as a man regards an itch than a necessity. Hetty dismissed her depressing line of thought hastily – it would not do to cry during the service, it would embarrass Alistair.

Baby India Potter's wail echoed and amplified mournfully in the hush. Hetty wondered briefly whether a noise like that could bring the roof down if it struck the right frequency, rather like marching feet can cause bridges to collapse. Probably not, but what must those poor bats think of the noise? Did it hurt their ears, or could they even hear it? Hetty could remember very little of bat biology from her schooldays, but in any case it was a fairly safe bet that if the bats could live with the noises that Jacob and the congregation made, then India was unlikely to cause them any serious problems. Caroline Potter, two pews behind Hetty, jiggled the baby anxiously. It was not the first sound which India had made during the morning service, and the dis-approving eye of Mrs Groat had already homed in on

8

them. Mrs Groat's disapproval policed the church services at St Jude's, rather as the headmistresses of old policed school assemblies. She was a formidable woman, and it did not do to cause a disturbance. The baby grinned, showing her one and a half teeth, then belched obligingly but resoundingly. Caroline blushed as though she had done it herself. If only John were here to lend moral support – but then that would mean bringing the twins too, and that always made things completely impossible. The last time they had come to church *en famille*, Josh had hidden under the altar and Henry had eaten ten Communion wafers before the service began. Oliver Bush had had to break the others in half, in true loaves and fishes style, to ensure that there were enough to go around.

Caroline shuddered mentally, and wriggled physically at the same time, seeking comfort on the hard wooden bench. How many thousands of bottoms had wriggled here before her? She found the sense of the past in the village church deeply reassuring. It made her feel firmly anchored and a part of things, a thread in the endlessly weaving fabric of life, stretching back as far as history could see, and forward into the mists where the mind cannot follow. She wanted to feel that she was a thread in the life of this village, too, she really wanted to belong here.

The organ hummed back into life and briefly made the organ version of a fart, when Jacob hit the C foot pedal by mistake. The final hymn was rather obscure. Since Jacob, upon whom seventy years of living had bestowed more than his fair share of cataracts, was no more sure of its melody and rhythm than the rest of the congregation, it fumbled rather uncertainly through about three verses to a confused but heartily relieved 'Amen'.

The kneeling cushions, embroidered several years

9

ago by the good ladies of the village were, it seemed, designed to be just too small to support both knees at once. Hetty, balanced somewhat precariously on hers, tried hard to stop herself from wondering whether Mrs Groat and Mrs Bean had used some precise but devilish formula to construct them thus. No, not dear Mrs Bean, she was far too sweet and mousy. Mrs Groat, however, was surely capable of anything. Hetty reflected guiltily that she came to church for a cleansing of the spirit, which was not well served by such un-Christian small-mindedness. It was just that her mind did so tend to wander these days. Perhaps it was because of That Time of Life. *Imagine*, she thought, *a few hundred years ago I would have been considered an impossibly old hag.*

'The peace of God, which passes all under-standing . . .'

Caroline Potter sighed with relief as the proceedings drew to a close. It was hard to follow the service at all when India might want to breastfeed *at any moment.* Sarah Struther, her rather strong-minded and, in Caroline's opinion, feminist neighbour, had insisted that she should feed in church if she needed to: 'Heavens, woman, it's the house of God, not a Victorian parsonage. He designed them, He's hardly going to mind seeing them serve their purpose!' Caroline, how-ever, was not made of quite such stern stuff, and in any case it was not the opinion of the Lord she feared, but that of Mrs Groat. If the usual village gossip was anything to go by, then the unwrapping of her ample bosoms during the service would keep them talking for years; worse, she corrected herself, for generations. Yet leaving the service before the end, in order to feed India, would also involve drawing attention to herself hideously, something she could not bear to do. Alas, the house of God was also the domain of the Ladies of the Village, and upon them one's lifelong reputation could rest. Why, only yesterday she had heard Mrs Groat in the post office, discussing an incident involving the former postmaster and a pound of haddock, which had actually taken place in 1964. Mrs Groat, wife of the second churchwarden, Morgan, and self-appointed pillar of the church, appeared to Caroline to be the very personification of disapproval, and she found her intimidating in the extreme. It was odd, she thought, glancing over at Mrs Groat, that someone who looked so much like a gerbil could be so intimidating. Mind you, even a gerbil would be alarming if it were five feet tall and wearing a frightening green hat. Mrs Groat always wore hats for church, and they were always rather sharp-edged and threatening. This one, she felt, was a particularly scary green.

'Before you all depart . . .' The rector, realizing that he had forgotten – yes actually forgotten – to give out the most important notice the parish ever entrusted to him, was trying to attract the attention of his flock. 'There will be a preliminary meeting on Tuesday evening at the home of Jacob and Mrs Bean,' Mrs Bean beamed shyly at the assembled throng, 'in order to discuss the arrangements for this year's village fête. Everyone is most welcome to attend, and may I urge you to put on your thinking caps before then. The parish needs to raise an extra five hundred pounds to fund urgent repairs to the vestry, where we have a small patch of dry rot. We must not allow it to spread.' He raised his hands in vague benediction. 'I hope to see you all there.'

Hetty, following Alistair out of their pew, imagined that Mrs Bean did not share this noble wish. There were around thirty people in church, and the thought of them pressed shoulder to shoulder in the Beans' tiny sitting-room was rather alarming. Alistair could not even stand upright in there when it was empty. In a crowd, he would surely suffocate. Caroline Potter was struggling to put on her coat. Hetty saw herself there, a decade or so ago, and felt a wave of sympathy. Alistair had always left her to come to church with the children alone, too. It was only since becoming Chairman of the Parochial Church Council that he had apparently become so devout. She supposed that John Potter would be looking after the twins. He was one of those New Men.

She squeezed past Alistair, who was exchanging loud pleasantries with the Ormondroyds in his clear public school English. 'Can I lend a hand?'

Caroline, flustered and in a tangle, handed India over gratefully, inadvertently frustrating Mrs Groat, who had materialized at her shoulder in order to exclaim in an entirely false grandmotherly manner at the sweetness and charm of the baby. 'Thanks so much,' she said, 'I haven't worked out an easy way of doing that yet.'

'Brave of you to come,' said Hetty. 'I should know.'

'Church usually makes me feel calm and peaceful,' said Caroline, 'but now I'm worrying about dry rot. You don't think the wind could carry it to us, do you?' She and John had only recently moved into their cottage, and worried endlessly that their surveyor might have missed something terrible such as a family of giant, voracious deathwatch beetles, every kind of fungal rot known to man, or a hitherto unknown species of thatch-eating termite living in the roof. An old cottage, however much longed for, could be quite a daunting responsibility after a series of hospital flats.

'Sure to,' said Mrs Groat, who was still hovering behind Caroline, waiting to coo. Her tone was a mixture of sorrow and gloat. 'What's more, if the wind doesn't carry it, the bats will.' She turned away, distracted, to Caroline's relief, by the rector.

'Take no notice,' said Hetty in a loud whisper. 'Bats don't carry dry rot. It just floats around by itself. Always has. There's no reason why you should get it just because the vestry has.'

'Thanks.' Caroline smiled gratefully at Hetty, straightening her navy coat and lifting India from Hetty's arms. In her pram suit, the baby looked like a big pink marshmallow. Hetty looked around for Alistair, but he was still trying to make conversation with Sir George Ormondroyd, so she walked out of the church with Caroline.

Oliver Bush, rector of Great and Little Barking, was greeting his departing flock with more than his usual gusto. A cerebral rather than a practical man, he adhered firmly to the belief that one should not eat prior to taking the morning Eucharist. This morning he had considerably overestimated the necessary quantity of communion wine, and had consequently consecrated far too much for the numbers present. He had finished off the extra himself, as is the usual custom in the Church of England. He really had to get some new spectacles, he thought rather fuzzily, trying to focus on the pink thing which Mrs Potter was carrying. Really, life would be a whole lot easier if he could see what he was doing and where he was going . . .

Hetty and Caroline emerged out of the porch and into the bright morning light together. India had just possetted on the shoulder of Caroline's coat, and Hetty was mopping her up. It amazed her that Caroline always managed to look so smart. She always looked like a Laura Ashley model, from her domed velvet headbands to her navy wool tights and shiny buckled shoes. Hetty grimaced inwardly at her own red bun and scuffed brogues. Usually she just wore wellies, or her old sheepskin slippers. Could she wear a domed headband? She wondered fleetingly whether Alistair would like it, but decided that he probably wouldn't notice. She wasn't sure that he ever really looked at her these days. Perhaps no married couples did, not after twenty-five years. She knew what Finn would say, though. 'What's that growing on your head, Mum?' It was a variant on his latest joke, repeated whenever chance presented. At least it was better than last week's toilet jokes, which all seemed to centre on whether someone called Cartwright could hit the ceiling. Hetty had not got the point of those, but Finn was at the age when boys believe that everything they say is immensely funny.

'How do you stay so slim?' she asked Caroline.

Caroline was immediately embarrassed. 'I'm not really,' she said apologetically. 'It's just that I'm tall.' She actually felt rather awkward being slim, it was so much easier to be pregnant. Sometimes, even now, when her tummy rumbled she would pat it comfortingly, before remembering that the fluttering sensation was not a baby and must therefore be wind.

Hetty wondered why she couldn't accept the compliment. It sounded almost as if she didn't like being slim. John Potter obviously adored her, though. *As Alistair once adored me . . .* 'Why don't you come to tea?' she asked on impulse. 'I've been meaning to ask you ever since you moved in. How about Tuesday?'

'Oh, I don't know, I . . .' Caroline was flustered, trying to refuse.

Hetty, always intuitive, guessed why. 'Don't worry, the house is very child-friendly. I can cope with your twins. I have had four boys you know. Nothing can better the mess that they make. Now, I won't hear "no". Come at three thirty.'

'Do I hear tea?' The rector's wife was at her elbow. 'I'll tell you what, why don't you both come to me?' Rose took her role as Rector's Wife very seriously. Unfortunately, effusive friendliness did not sit easily on her narrow shoulders. Hetty secretly believed that Rose had never got over her sense of injustice towards the

Almighty, who, in His wisdom, had had her marry a man named Oliver Bush.

'No, you come to me, Rose, I've already baked.' Hetty could feel Caroline sighing with relief. This was understandable, as the rectory parlour was full of little china things which could be a dangerous delight to unfettered two-year-olds. Despite its large size, it was the kind of room in which it would be very unwise to swing a cat, and taking the twins there would have caused a serious breech of parish relations. Rose still believed that children should be seen but not heard, and that one could reasonably expect this of two-year-old twins. She would no more have moved her little china ornaments than give a child a drink in a plastic cup. Appearances were everything, she felt, and it was important that the rector's wife should present vicarage teas on good china.

'Good morning, good morning!' The rector had joined them, his myopia giving his smile an unfocussed quality. In fact, if you didn't know that he was a man of the cloth, you might imagine he had been drinking. 'So nice to see young people in church! What is the baby's name?'

'India. India Harriet Potter.' Caroline was proud of her baby's name. She herself came from the kind of old county stock who name most of their female children Sophie, so she felt that she had broken the mould of her background in a small but important way. India's name would not label her as a wearer of pearls and frilly blouses, as Caroline's own had done. Caroline had four cousins named Sophie, and had possessed the somewhat upper-crust name of Ffoulkes before she married John. She had found the accepted image of the brainless Sloane rather hard to shake off at university, and did not want her children to have the same problem.

'India?' Rose Bush's tone was both surprised and

disapproving, whilst her smile remained benevolent and her eyes crinkled delightfully.

'I must impose on you for some tea, introduce myself, as it were.' Oliver Bush spoke vaguely to the pink blob, not sure if she was old enough to be included in the conversation.

'You're too late, Oliver. I'm just arranging a little tea-party, and Hetty has very kindly offered to do the baking.' Rose was officious, vicar's-wife-ish.

Hetty crossed her eyes at Caroline, who pressed her lips together quickly. It was beginning to sound rather royal. Rose did not notice the exchange; she was wondering who else she should invite. It was fortunate that Hetty made such very acceptable Battenburg cake. It almost made up for that terrible lived-in look in her lounge.

Angela, Lady Ormondroyd was rather a scrawny woman, and she wore the kind of expensive, rather structured and brightly coloured suits that scrawny women who are very wealthy like to wear. She favoured strong colours, and was today wearing a rich royal blue which said 'Dior' loudly to those who spoke the language. Unfortunately for her, no-one in the congregation did speak that particular language, so the suit went largely unlauded. Only the rector noticed it, remarking loudly that it was splendid to see such vibrant colour in church, a comment which did not endear him to Angela. She was in rather a hurry to get away, and was annoyed to be accosted by Rose Bush, asking her to one of those awful village teas. She never understood why these people felt the need to embarrass her by asking. She could not believe that previous ladies of the manor had partaken of cosy little salmon sandwich teas with the village folk – although with George's mother, one never knew.

'So sorry not to see old Lady Ormondroyd here today,' Rose was intoning sweetly.

Angela gritted her teeth slightly. 'I'm afraid my mother-in-law is a little unwell today,' she said coldly. 'May I let you know about tea? I shall need to check my diary.' Her accent was near-perfect upper class English, most of her Texan twang having been mercilessly eradicated at great expense.

'Oh, of course,' said Rose, who never took a hint, being quite oblivious to them. 'I look forward to seeing you there.'

George was heading down the church path by now, and Angela was able to escape from Rose and her unwelcome invitations before the conversation became even more personal. The villagers seemed not to understand that she did not wish to have friends among them, only admirers. She did not realize that Rose was far too much of a snob to be able to spot another one.

Caroline walked the hundred yards or so home alone. Hetty lived in the other direction. The Ormondroyds shared the first half of her route, which took her straight past the Hall, but they had gone ahead, and she did not like to impose herself upon them, especially as they had not been formally introduced. She knew that she ought to introduce herself, that her family and her upbringing demanded that she should, and yet to do so would make her uncomfortable, for she knew what the Ormondroyds would be like. They would be like most of her aunts and uncles. Caroline had been born into the class of people who fill the society pages of *Harpers*, but with the kind of brains that such people prefer not to see in their female children. She had always felt the vague disapproval of her relatives, and as a result she rarely felt entirely comfortable with anyone – except John, of course.

The air was fresh and crisp as she picked her way

carefully through the remains of last autumn's dead leaves, which still formed a slightly treacherous mulch at the edge of the road. The Ormondroyds' geese had been honking boisterously all morning, as loudly as though the Gauls had just arrived, but India seemed to be soothed by the sound. Caroline automatically patted the baby's back as she walked. She came to the gates of the Hall. They were of wrought iron, so through them she could clearly see old Lady Sybil Ormondroyd, wearing her Sunday best and plainly heading for church. George and Angela were obviously remonstrating with her. Poor Lady Sybil. Of course she wasn't actually mad. John said that it was dementia, although the woman in the post office said that it had really come on very quickly last year, just after old Sir Hector died. Still, John should know best – she was his patient now, after all.

She reached her own front door, noticing with a sigh that someone's dog had been chewing the bay tree again, and there were dirty paw-marks on the white walls. She turned the handle.

'Mummymummymummy!'

'Enry got my bickie . . .'

The outraged howls of her two-year-old twin sons hit pain level as she stepped into the hall. There was a green potty with wee in it tilting dangerously on the hall step, and John was nowhere to be seen. Caroline guessed that he had gone to sit on the loo and read magic magazines as soon as he heard her coming up the drive. It was his refuge, just as St Jude's was hers. You couldn't really make demands of a man who was sitting on the loo. Most women, she knew, wondered what on earth their husbands did for so long in the lavatory. Caroline knew about hers. He practised card tricks.

Stepping over a crumbled biscuit and two empty crisp packets, she put India into a rocking baby seat and headed for the wee. Church was her break, her weekly slab of peace, her chunk of Englishness. Now it was over for another week, and already she felt in need of a stiff gin. Unfortunately she didn't actually like gin, but she had been brought up to believe that girls like her must always ask for 'G and T' and never, never ask for advocaat. It was a sign of the unshakeability of her allegiance to her upbringing that she drank gin, which tasted to her like aftershave, and had never even tried advocaat, which she would almost certainly have loved. She would have particularly loved it with lemonade, a cherry and a little cocktail umbrella – but that, of course, would mean social death.

'I did feel sorry for Caroline Potter in church,' remarked Hetty as she and Alistair walked up the hill to their house. It was in the opposite direction to the Potters', on the Forge Road – named after their house, once the haunt of the village blacksmith. 'She obviously wants to come and get to know people at church, but it's so hard when you've to manage a baby.'

Alistair said nothing, as so often seemed to be the case when she spoke to him these days, and she grew suddenly irritated. 'You're not listening, Alistair,' she accused.

'Mmmm?' he said, beaming with sudden alertness at the Ormondroyds' groom, who was coming towards them on a palomino pony. 'Good morning. Fine day.'

Lucy Bellingham displayed her dimples in the way which she practised every morning in front of the mirror. She had tried to deepen them with the tip of a pencil, but the resulting grey marks had proved rather difficult to erase. 'Hello there.'

The horse paused in order to dump a large spadeful of fertiliser right outside Hetty's gate, and Lucy rose obligingly in her stirrups. Hetty noticed with childish delight that Alistair was embarrassed by the horse, although his eyes were fixed on Lucy's rather horse-womanly thighs in her tight cream breeches. She must surely have been put into those surgically, thought Hetty. Probably, since she was one of *the* Bellinghams –her ancestry made even Sir George Ormondroyd's look positively plebeian – she was born wearing them and they just grew with her.

'I'll get a spade,' she said, half to herself, and headed off through the gate. When she returned for her prize, Alistair was still chatting to Lucy. Even though she ought to be accustomed to his attempts at mixing with the truly upper classes – they often brought good business, after all – Hetty felt odd, excluded. Alistair was paying real attention to the girl, and she found herself thinking that it was a long time since he had paid such sincere attention to her. Even during sex. The thought had crept in unbidden, surprising her, and she pushed it away, concentrating on getting the manure to the dahlia bed without leaving a trail of little clods. *Perhaps*, she thought, *no-one feels cherished at my age*.

Jonathan and Rory were in the drive, tinkering under the bonnet of Jonathan's car. Jess, the old golden labrador, dozed in the doorway, watching with half an eye.

'Did you boys remember to put the chicken in the oven?' she asked them.

'Oh Mum—'

'Don't worry. I guessed that you planned on us eating it cooked,' said Rory, appearing from under the bonnet with a streak of oil down one cheek.

'You're my hero.' Hetty headed indoors to wash her hands and prepare the vegetables. Jess the dog, who had found a pleasant patch of sunlight, raised an eyebrow in greeting, but dozed on. Hetty patted her briefly in passing, glancing back at the boys with a sigh. Of all of them, Rory was the one she feared for the most. The others were all so uncompromisingly male – even Finn, who was only twelve. Jonathan, back for the weekend from his vet school flat, was tall and handsome, booming and broad-shouldered. Luke was the local girls' heart-throb, captain of the under-fifteen cricket team and more self-confident than James Bond. Even Finn was a county swimmer, *and* he already had a girlfriend, at the age of twelve. They were all terribly hale and hearty except for Rory. Rory had never been the sporting type. He was quiet, artistic and musical. Music was his life – he loved opera, played the flute, and hoped to study music at university. Alistair couldn't understand it, didn't want to understand Rory. Worse still, he had recently begun to make veiled jibes at Rory's lack of a girlfriend. Hetty guessed that Alistair feared Rory might be gay, but was afraid to say so lest speaking his fear should give it substance. She had never discussed it with him; she knew he could be verbally cruel, and she feared his reaction if she brought up the subject. Funny, he wasn't always like that.

She sighed as she chopped carrots. Alistair would reject Rory if he were gay. He would take it as a personal slight, a betrayal of his own manhood. Yet she was closer to Rory than to any of the others. She could not bear the thought of losing him because of some rift with Alistair. Nor could she bear the thought of the heartache Rory would face if Alistair was right. Alistair had always said that she mothered Rory too much, but that was bunkum.

It struck her that nowadays she seemed to spend a lot of time reflecting on Alistair's less pleasant attributes, on how much he had changed over the years. How could the Hetty and Alistair of now possibly have evolved from the Hetty and Alistair of their Scottish

21

honeymoon, twenty-five years ago? Strange how, young and inexperienced, they had grown together through the early stresses and strains which had beset them: the infertility, the money worries, then eventually four young children. Yet now, with the practical problems of life ironed fairly smooth, now when they had so much, they seemed to be losing one another. Once there had been so much laughter and love, yet the distillate of that seemed now to be this untogetherness. Distillate, supernatant, ancient words from long-forgotten 'O' level chemistry flashed into her head. *How many years ago was that? Can I really be forty-five? I don't feel as though I've changed inside since my sixteenth birthday.*

Her vision blurred annoyingly, and the vegetable knife sliced neatly and cleanly into her thumb. Hetty cursed her self-pity aloud and Alistair, coming in through the back door, heard.

'Hetty, have you cut yourself?' He sounded concerned.

'It's nothing,' she said, feeling his sympathy to be tinged with a hint of condescension. 'It's just onions and a cut finger.'

'Oh. Is lunch long?'

'About six inches,' she answered automatically, remembering once on their honeymoon in Fort William, when they had laughed their socks off at the very same joke, then made love till the caravan rocked.

Alistair audibly repressed a sigh, a skill which he seemed to have honed to a fine art recently, and went into the lounge with the *Sunday Times*. It was Rory who, a few minutes later, came through to lay the table and stuck a plaster on Hetty's thumb.

## Chapter Two

Next door to the Potters, in the Old Post Office, the day had barely begun. Sarah Struther believed that neither convention nor habit should dictate the detail of her life. Therefore she arose with her appetite – for both life and food – and retired to bed when she had had her fill of the day. Today her appetite had arisen late, and she could hear the church bells striking twelve as she drank her coffee and liquidized Friday's *Financial Times* in the blender. It was not Sarah's own *Financial Times*, at least not originally. Sarah would no more have purchased the *Financial Times* than embarked upon the F-plan diet – nor, indeed, any other diet. The entire pile of *FT*s were the newsagent's leftovers for the week. He let her have them every Saturday, which saved him the trouble of having to dispose of them elsewhere. There were not, of course, very many spare ones each week, this being a part of what is commonly known as the gin-and-Jaguar-belt, but Sarah found them very useful. She was not a snob, but she had to admit that the tabloids were far inferior to the quality press when it came to papier mâché, and when Sarah wasn't making pots out of clay she was making them of papier mâché.

Sarah was a huge and glorious woman, striking in both her beauty and in what Rubens would have termed her voluptuousness. In fact, Rubens would have believed himself dead and in heaven had he been sharing her breakfast this morning, for she was not only exotic in her beauty, she was, as usual, quite naked.

23

Many smaller women would not have felt comfortable in such a state of undress, but Sarah was totally at ease with her body shape, and would no more have dieted than purchased the *Financial Times*. She was also Great Barking's most famous inhabitant. She was famous for her pots, to the extent that the *Sunday Times* had even sent a reporter to write a feature on her daily life. The article was in the paper this very day, which was why a copy of it lay, unopened, on her kitchen table.

She finished her toast, switched off the liquidizer, and stroked her white cat. 'What do you say, my darling? Shall we look?'

The cat, who was entirely accustomed to the status of more-than-human which she occupied, yawned, but had little else to say. Sarah read the article on herself thoughtfully. It was banal, but not untrue, and it featured a half-page picture showing several pots and herself in a coloured sari. She was not sure whether to be relieved or aggrieved that they had not been rude or provocative about her. The photographer, although polite, had clearly been insulted by her weight, in the way that some men are, yet the picture was not unreasonable. Perhaps the photographer had not had the final say in which shot was used. She smiled to herself. The young journalist who had interviewed her had not been offended by her weight, particularly not during the night during which he had been enveloped by her large, warm breasts. In fact, his performance had been delightfully enthusiastic once his colleague had left. Still, he could hardly have told the truth in his article. She doubted that 'Sarah Struther is a huge, sexy woman who eats men like me for breakfast, and who spends most of her day entirely naked' would have got past the editor. A shame really, for it would certainly have set Great Barking a-quiver. They would all have been crouching in their potting sheds right now, waiting for the fire and brimstone, and the vicar's wife would probably already be a pillar of salt.

There was a knock at her door. Sarah slipped on her kimono and opened it to find that skinny girl from next door standing on her step. Personally she thought that Caroline needed a bit more meat on her. Mind you, she did have twins. Sarah had some respect for women who had given birth, never having done so herself. She was, at thirty-five, becoming slightly aware of the shriek of biological sirens in her loins. She had always done what she wanted to do, drunk freely of life and pleasure, and enjoyed her freedom. She had never felt lonely, and a partner had never been an issue as she had never felt that she had met her mate, but occasionally now she was tempted to leave the plastic thing out when something came up, as it were. As long as he wasn't a Sagittarius, of course. She smiled encouragingly at Caroline. Looks could be deceptive; after all, look at Rose Bush. She looked for all the world like a kindly old grandmother.

'I'm so sorry to bother you.' Poor Caroline was clearly embarrassed at finding her only partially dressed.

'Don't be silly. Come in, sit down, have some coffee.' Before Caroline could explain that she only wanted to borrow an egg, she was seated at the table with the white cat on her lap.

Sarah's coffee was something else. She brewed it up in a little copper pot with a long handle, watching it carefully as the mixture rose, then collapsed gracefully in on itself. 'If you drink it in Turkey, it's Turkish coffee,' she said, in answer to Caroline's query, 'and in Greece it's Greek, so I suppose here it's Suffolk coffee. Mind you, I was taught to make it by an old friend in Larnaca, so it would be most accurate to say Cypriot.'

'It's lovely, I've never had it before. In Corfu, on our honeymoon, they gave us Nescafé.'

'You have to ask,' said Sarah, remembering Nicos, who had never needed asking. 'Have you settled in?'

'Yes and no.' Caroline smiled ruefully. 'I don't think we'll ever finish unpacking. I've been making curtains. Do you know, I actually thought we'd been quite bold until I saw all this. It's wonderful!'

Sarah's house looked like the inside of a shop in a Moroccan bazaar. It was warm and exotic, full of rich, glowing colours reflecting off small brass mirrors amidst huge green palms. It smelt of sandalwood and coffee beans. It drew you in and enveloped you in a world of incense, Ali Baba pots and magic carpets, so that you half expected to see a group of men in fezzes drinking tea and playing cards around an opium pipe.

'You could be an interior designer. I would love a house like this, but I just wouldn't know where to begin.'

Sarah, who was accustomed to compliments and never embarrassed by them, said, 'I didn't design it, it just evolved out of the things I like. The best designs are not designed at all, you know. They happen. This house is just an extension of me.'

'I wish I had your eye for things, though,' said Caroline, thinking of her brocade curtains and Liberty sofa – a wedding gift from her Godmother. They might be classics but they didn't exactly fire the imagination. Having only popped round for the egg, leaving India bouncing in her chair and John making a Lego castle for the boys, she now found herself reluctant to leave. There suddenly seemed to be so much to learn.

'You've plenty of time to make your house fit you,' said Sarah. 'You've only been here for a few months. I've lived here for years.'

'I hope,' said Caroline firmly, 'that we're here for good. We've lived in so many characterless hospital flats that settling down is really important. We've never had time to belong anywhere, you see.'

'That's important for us all,' said Sarah, sensing words from the heart, 'but villages are funny. Just by moving in you are already deemed to belong.'

'I hope you're right.' Caroline finished her coffee. She had not thought of it that way before.

'Of course I am,' said Sarah. 'Here, let me read your coffee grounds.' She swilled them round and inverted the cup. Caroline was not quite sure that she was being serious but decided that, given the decor, she probably was. 'Oh, I see a pregnancy. Were you planning another so soon?'

Caroline, who could not remember having done very much recently to make a baby even a remote possibility, blushed deeply in mingled hope and embarrassment. 'Oh, I'm sure I can't be, I—'

'Time will tell us what is in store,' said Sarah, deeply but logically. 'But here, take this as well as the egg. It's raspberry leaf tea – wonderful for morning sickness.'


'John,' said Caroline cautiously over the roast later, 'do you ever get the urge to be less conventional – you know, more outrageous?'

John spooned mustard onto his plate in a vast heap. He loved the grainy sort. 'Mmm, I often have an urge to cover you in chocolate sauce and lick it—'

'Oh, for heaven's sake, I didn't mean sex.'

'When I hear the word urge, I think of sex.'

'When you hear anything you think of sex.'

'Enry want ex, Mummy, Enry want ex.'

'Here, Henry, have some of this nice chicken.'

'Yosh chi-in, Yosh ch-in!'

Caroline forked some onto his plate, thinking it was

27

little wonder that they never had a chance for any serious discussions. She persisted. 'Sarah is unconventional, and her house is wonderful. She thinks I'm pregnant, you know.'

'What?' Now she had his serious attention.

'She read my coffee grounds.'

John's attention returned to the mustard. He was not the kind of man who took psychic forces seriously, for a man who can produce a rabbit from a hat does not like to think he can be easily deceived. After a moment he said, 'She's in the paper this week.'

'Really. Which paper? The Broomhill one?'

'No, the national press. *The Sunday Times*, no less.'

'Goodness!' Caroline shot into the lounge to find it. It lay, a heap of confetti, in the Lego castle. 'Oh no! The twins have had it.'

'Sorry, love,' said John. He was always so placid about everything. It was one of the things which she had fallen in love with – his calmness, his gentleness – yet sometimes she almost hated him for it. Then, of course, there were his looks. He had the most sexy eyes. In a dinner suit he was devastating. One of his patients had told the receptionist that the new doctor ought to be a paid stud, and the receptionist had told Caroline. *So why don't I feel like sex these days?* she thought. *Perhaps I should come off the pill; perhaps it's upset my libido.*

John said that it was because of India sharing their bed all the time. He'd suggested that they left India in bed and had a wild time on the carpet, but Caroline had read in an airport travel novel that you got your bottom burned that way. She did sometimes wish he'd get fired up over something, though, something other than being a magician or eating chocolate out of her navel. Yuk.

She wondered, suddenly, what Sarah did about sex. 'Do you find her attractive? She is beautiful.'

John smiled at his wife, for once not needing to protect her insecurity with a white lie. Henry leaned over and spat potato into Josh's dinner. 'The woman is a mountain. I like to know where I am with my women, you know, anatomically speaking.'

'Yeugh,' said Josh loudly.

'She has a beautiful face,' persisted Caroline.

'Too earthy,' said John, 'too fat.'

'Mummy, Enry spit,' said Josh, then, louder, 'Mummy enry spit Mummy!'

'I saw these instructions,' said Caroline to the twins, 'about babies. It said, "after unwrapping your new baby, do not throw away the packaging, as she may come in useful later." That's what I am. Baby packaging.'

Henry threw up onto the carpet.


Only a hundred yards away, the carpets of Barking Hall were as free of vomit as one would expect in a house where domestic staff are employed. The drawing-room was long, high-ceilinged and elegant. At its beautifully proportioned windows hung great brocade curtains, shielding deeply cushioned window seats and smoothly painted wooden shutters. A selection of soft sofas and chairs in primrose yellow and tawny rose gave the room a warm, glowing, friendly quality. It was awash with light and flowers, its occasional tables gleaming in the way that only tables in houses with servants can gleam. A fire crackled unobtrusively in the Adam fireplace, whilst above it a darkened oil painting depicted a long-dead ancestor and his wolf hound, proudly stanced and handsome, as only the rich can afford to be portrayed. Even the dog looked wealthy. It was the kind of room that welcomed the visitor, that greeted him warmly, sat him down for tea, and offered him a nice, home-made scone. Its occupants, however, seemed ill-fitted to its benevolent mood.

Sir George Ormondroyd and his wife Angela sat facing away from one another, drinking the coffee which Wilson had poured for them. George was deep in the *Sunday Times*, Angela was reading the social pages of *Harpers*. Their body language expressed a certain lack of interest in one another.

'That Struther woman from the Old Post Office is in this newspaper,' said George suddenly.

'Let me look.' Angela held the picture at some distance from her body, as though she might put on a few pounds by some kind of osmosis if she let it get too close. George said nothing. It was often easier that way, but he reflected, and not for the first time, that her voice had acquired a kind of tightness with age that made him think of a trussed and stuffed partridge. Having said that, lots of things made George think of game.

In the middle distance a whirring began as a variety of clocks prepared to strike the half hour. It was one of Wilson's jobs to make sure that no clock was ever out of synchrony, as a stray chime or bong had been known to upset Angela terribly. Wilson therefore habitually listened extremely carefully to the clocks, but one would never have guessed it from his unruffled expression.

He raised an eyebrow, just the required amount. 'Excuse me, sir.'

'Yes?'

'Lady Sybil is having breakfast and asked me to invite you to join her after your coffee.'

'Is she, by God? And where, might I ask, is my mother's companion?'

'Miss Hawthorn has gone to the doctor, sir.'

'On a Sunday?'

'She needed some stitches in her forehead, sir.'

'My God!' Angela's attention zoomed in. 'George, has your mother become violent?'

'No, madam.' Wilson's expression did not alter. 'Miss Hawthorn fell whilst retrieving Lady Sybil's kitten from the monkey puzzle tree.'

Both George and Wilson sensed Angela's disappointment, and she knew that they did. Heavens, wasn't it enough that there were bats in the church, defecating all over the family chapel, without a mad old bat living with them at the Hall, too? She had not wanted to take over this place when George's father died, and would never have agreed to do so if she had known that his mother would be part of the package. Angela came from a family who would not have hesitated to shut away any elderly relative – for her own good, of course – who developed the slightest sign of dementia, or God forbid, incontinence. Not so George. He and that interfering young doctor were in league, harping on about helping the old lady to stay in her own home. Help her live a normal life, they had said. How on earth could it be a normal life when she was several place-settings short of a full hamper? It was such a nuisance. An incontinent relative was social death at the annual Cartier polo day.

Angela shuddered. 'Sir George and I will speak to Lady Sybil,' she informed Wilson dismissively. 'Kindly thank the staff for an excellent lunch.'

'Thank you, madam.' Wilson had been trained at a special school for butlers, where they were taught to say 'Thank you, madam,' and 'Indeed, sir,' in Jeeves-like tones, without ever betraying an inner thought. In fact the college believed that they had successfully eradicated all inner thoughts. If they had known the kinds of things which Wilson's secret inner voice said to him as he acted out his Wodehousian role, they would never have given him a reference. *Silly cow*, he thought, now. *"Thank the staff"*. *Deluded Yankee nutcase, she is. Needs a good rogering.'*

There were, in fact, only two full-time members of house staff, of whom Wilson was one. The other was the cook, whose name had long-since sieved down to the apt but unimaginative 'Cook'. Angela Ormondroyd, however, always referred to her staff as though they were legion.

*We are legion*, thought Wilson, *Cook and I*, and he was reminded of the man at Capernaum who used those same words to Jesus when he was possessed. A religious man, was Wilson, despite his inner rebellion. He went out of the room and clicked the door shut with a careful sound which had once taken a week to perfect.

'Come on, then, old bean,' George loved to call Angela pet names to annoy her. It was his secret revenge. 'Let's go and see Mother.'

'George, we've just had lunch. I don't want breakfast with your mother,' said Angela, who had, as usual, eaten less than would satisfy a flea.

'Do you good,' said George, unperturbed. 'You could do with feeding up.'

Angela glared at his broad retreating back. *How could George possibly understand what a tiny woman like me needs to eat?* she asked herself indignantly. *Doesn't he realize that it takes years of habitual self-restraint to wear a Dior size eight?*

Sadly, the years had not been kind to Angela. Certainly she was well-groomed and had rigidly controlled any tendency she might once have had to put on a few pounds. Unfortunately, at the same time, she seemed to have squeezed her entire personality into a frame which was a size smaller than God intended, and in the process crushed all of the best bits out of existence, burying any real warmth and spontaneity she might once have possessed. Even more sadly, it was a

32

feature of this state of affairs that even if she had realized, she would not have cared a bean. She was, now, the kind of woman who did not weep at news reports of starving children in war zones, who was neither stirred by Puccini nor moved by epic novels. She would, however, have been quite hysterical had she known that her daughter Zoë was, at that very moment, having her nose pierced in High Wycombe, having sneaked out of school via the common room window.

George had long since given up hope of Angela ever possessing any real breasts again. She had been a good wife, he reasoned. She had given him a daughter, she was a good hostess, and as far as he knew she was not unfaithful. He could hardly divorce her for being an A-cup. He still fancied her, of course – George fancied almost anything that moved, provided that some sort of breasts were present, but she had made it very clear after Zoë's birth that she did not regard herself as being highly sexed, and that side of their marriage had never really got going again. George's basic politeness prevented him from troubling her as often as he would have liked, which was every night, at least, and they had settled into their present pattern of occasional, rather embarrassed encounters almost by default, each assuming that the other preferred to get things over with as quickly as possible.

They found Lady Sybil Ormondroyd sitting at the polished mahogany dining table, buttering croissants. 'Ah, George,' she said, 'sit down dear. I shall ask Cook to coddle an egg for you. Somehow I seem to have little appetite this morning.'

George took her hand gently, noticing its slight tremor, and feeling deeply protective. Her pale blue eyes met his grey ones questioningly. 'Mother, that's because you had lunch half an hour ago. Remember the

Châteaubriand? Cook prepared the broccoli just the way you like it.'

The old lady's eyes seemed to clear a little. 'Oh, of course.' She pushed her plate away. 'Where is Hawthorn?'

'Gone to the doctor, Mother.' Angela idly made fingerprints on the mahogany which Wilson had painstakingly polished that morning.

'Who are you?' demanded Lady Sybil, looking at Angela as one eyes a dog poo on one's quilt.

Angela glared. 'Angela. Your son's wife. As you know very well.'

Lady Sybil cackled. 'What a termagant. George, who is that girl? She's very ugly, and I think she might be American.'

'Now, Mother,' George tutted. Whilst Lady Sybil's powers of recognition came and went, in the case of Angela, whom she had never liked, they were more than usually absent.

'Now, George,' she waved a commanding finger at him, 'your father won't like her.'

'Father's dead, Mother,' said George, patiently.

'Of course I know he's dead,' said Lady Sybil stridently. 'He died on top of a French tart in a hotel in Harrogate.'

'She was on top,' muttered Angela to herself.

'Don't be disgusting, girl,' said Lady Sybil, proving that her hearing was not at all defective. 'That potter woman is in the newspaper. Your father left her money.'

'What?' Angela had not heard about this before, and the distribution of the family wealth interested her intensely. 'Why would he leave money to the doctor's wife?'

'No, not Potter. She who pots,' said George. *She of the breasts*, he thought, wondering what Angela would say

34

if she knew of his unfulfilled fantasy. Wouldn't offer to grow her own back, that was for sure. 'Yes,' he said aloud, 'he appointed her to administer the trust fund. The one for art in local schools.'

'Oh, that.' Angela lost interest, but had a little scorn to pour. 'What on earth do local schools need art money for? Equipment is wasted on state schools. All they need is a few pots of poster paint and some glue.' Angela wore her snobbery like a badge of office. Back in the States snobbery was impossible except for those whose direct ancestors had come over on the *Mayflower*. Texan oil magnates such as Angela's father had wealth and possessions in abundance, but not status. That was only acquired by marrying an English title. Having done this, Angela had taken the blessed opportunity to embrace snobbery with great enthusiasm. It was something of which she was immensely proud, and she would never realize that it opened far fewer doors than it closed.

'Shall you attend the village fête meeting on Tuesday, my dear?' George changed the subject adroitly. 'Mother always used to run the thing.'

'I certainly shall not,' said Angela.

'But the fête will be here at the Hall,' said George, genuinely surprised. 'It always is. I'm afraid, my dear, that by taking on the Hall you have acquired the fête.' He stroked his ginger moustache. It was, like most moustaches, far more gingery than the hair of its host – the hair, that is, which he still retained.

'Oh dear. You mean all those little people from the village will be trampling in the garden and thieving from the sheds?' Angela had never so much as pruned a rose, although she had occasionally arranged them, but she felt highly proprietorial about the garden. 'Surely we don't have to?'

'We do,' said George, in a voice that brooked no

argument, and it was then that Angela decided that tonight was to be George's lucky night. Not only tonight, but as many nights as it took to keep the fête away. If Angela had been a humorous woman, she might have made a joke about tempting fate, but as she was not, she did not. Not even to herself.

## Chapter Three

In the end, Tuesday's tea at Hetty's was a rather awkward affair. Rose – 'I knew you wouldn't mind, dear' – had taken it upon herself to invite Harriet Harbour, her oldest friend, who lived in the last house in the village. In addition, Angela Ormondroyd had turned up. No-one had been more surprised than Rose that Angela had actually deigned to come. In fact, if the truth was known, George had proved extraordinarily demanding on the physical front since she had begun her seduction on Sunday, and she was glad of a chance to get out of the house. It was all very well in the bedroom, but when she was checking the deep freeze to make sure that Cook had not filched the wild boar sausages, well, it was just too much.

It was really rather unfortunate, given Harriet's opinion of fox hunting, that the subject should have come up. Sir George Ormondroyd was Master of Foxhounds of the Barking Hunt, and the Boxing Day meet always gathered outside the Hall for sherry and ginger wine before galloping and hooting straight up The Street past Harriet's house to the open fields and woodland. Last year Harriet, aided by some of her music pupils, had painted a wonderful sign reading 'GOOD LUCK, MR FOX, MAY THEY ALL FALL OFF!' and had planted it on a post outside her gate. Harriet might be harmless, but it was somewhat galling to have loopy little old ladies sitting in moral judgement of one's traditional country fun, and the Hunt had been most offended.

'Sentimentality,' said Angela Ormondroyd, 'is the enemy of common sense. One should never be sentimental about country life. Country life is all about the survival of the fittest.'

Hetty found herself wondering how Angela would manage if the struggle for survival ever came her way, as it surely never had. She had been born, as the saying goes, with a silver spoon in her mouth – except that in Angela's case it had been an entire canteen. A sudden mental image of Angela being pursued across the Barking meadows by a pack of bloodthirsty hounds materialized to startle her, and she stifled a smile. Her imagination had always been rather pictorial, and on more than one occasion this had caused her to laugh quite inappropriately.

Harriet, caught unawares in the process of swallowing one of Hetty's sandwiches – awfully substantial with the crusts still on – felt herself start to blush as both Rose and Angela pinned her to her chair with their disapproving glares. 'Well, you know, it is rather cruel.' *Why shouldn't I speak my mind?* she thought. *My opinion is a valid one.* However, she shook inwardly as she mounted her small defence. 'I do know what foxes are capable of, but—'

'Well then, how can you possibly talk such utter nonsense?' Angela could kill a man at twenty paces with that tone. 'Do you know, my dear,' this to Caroline, who had observed the exchange with great sympathy for poor Harriet, but who lacked the nerve, as a newcomer, to join in, 'George has spent a positive *fortune* at his tailor as Master of Hounds. It must be good for the economy. All of those little men sewing. There must be thousands of jobs generated by hunting. All the grooms, the men who look after the dogs; why, the bill for the hounds last year . . .'

Harriet thought privately that the idea of Angela

38

having any concern whatsoever for the unemployed, whether rural or otherwise, was quite ludicrous. She switched off. There was no point incurring Rose's wrath by disagreeing with Angela. She had known Rose since they were children together at Great Barking school. Rose had always been rather a snob, but Harriet took the view that everyone has their faults, and she remained Rose's closest friend through thick and thin. There was also absolutely no mileage to gain from pointing out that, far from wanting the foxes wiped out, the Ormondroyds actually went to great lengths to ensure that there was always something to hunt. The occasional discovery of oven-ready chickens in ditches on the estate during periods of inclement weather was not something villagers were ever expected to mention. Silly Angela, silly George. She herself had actually made some friends amongst the pleasant, if rather hairy, young people with the odd dress sense who had congregated outside her house on Boxing Day last year. They had been most polite, and she had felt very sorry for them, their having no fingertips to their gloves in such weather. She had refilled their thermoses, adding a tot of whisky to each.

'I agree with you,' whispered Hetty to Harriet, under cover of passing her a scone. 'I think it's disgusting.' Harriet, thus reprieved from mass disapproval, relaxed a little.

'What do you think, my dear?' Angela's gimlet gaze bore into Caroline, who had lost track of the conversation. India was stirring where she had dozed off on the sofa, and Josh and Henry were alarmingly quiet behind it.

'I – um – well,' she hated being put in the position of having to disagree with anyone. 'I have hunted in the past, but now I don't think that I—'

'Good. I'm so glad to have found someone who

understands.' Angela had extracted what she required from Caroline. Caroline bit her lip, feeling a traitor to foxes everywhere. She had never been able to embrace without question the accepted opinions of the upper classes into which she had been born; she was far too prone to intelligent thought. *I'm like an arthritic knee*, she thought. *I don't fit in smoothly, I'm all knobbly and out of sorts.*

Hetty went off into the kitchen to refill the teapot. Really, she thought, the Ormondroyds were such difficult people to like. George was a pompous ass, and Angela was such a *snob*. She wished that Alistair didn't think so highly of them; but then, if the truth were told, it was probably George's reputedly excellent wine cellar that Alistair was thinking of. Not that he was ever likely to sample it, of course.

In Hetty's small, comfortable living-room, which Rose thought messy, Harriet thought charming, and Angela did not think about at all, Angela was preparing to leave.

'Shall we see you at the fête meeting tonight?' asked Rose.

Angela, who had been waiting for this cue, was conscious of having to draw a breath before she spoke. This was, after all, going to make a certain impact. 'I don't think so,' she said. 'You see, George and I will no longer be holding the fête at the Hall. We are having some work done on the gardens.'

Fortunately, the surprised silence lasted long enough for her to make a dignified exit, saying good-bye and an insincere thank you to Hetty on her way out through the kitchen.

'Well, well,' said Harriet, as the metaphorical thunderbolt faded away.

'Well!' said Rose.

Caroline said nothing, having yet to understand quite how sacred a tradition had been broken.

'We must speak to Sir George,' said Rose. 'Who would be the best person to speak to Sir George?' She looked at Caroline as though seeking inspiration.

'I don't know,' said Caroline, feeling horribly out of things. She picked up India for something to do. The baby opened her eyes and shouted 'nipple', in her own language. It sounded, of course, like a cry. Caroline furkled swiftly and expertly under her navy jumper and white blouse, then poked India somewhere up underneath. India began to feed at once, being well versed in this darkened ritual.

Rose, who later on had plenty of thoughts to express on the subject of visible breasts, was for once so taken aback that she could not think of a word to say. Harriet, however, exclaimed, 'Oh, I *do* admire young mothers these days. You seem to get on with things so capably.'

Caroline, who had agonized long and hard beforehand about attaching India to her dinner when in Hetty's house, was grateful. 'After twin boys, India seems quite easy,' she said.

Hetty, returning with the teapot, said, 'After twin boys I should think that most things seem quite easy.'

'But what,' said Rose, realizing that her chance to make a pointed remark about exposing oneself had long since passed, 'are we going to do about the fête?' She leaned far back into Alistair's leather chair, so that there was absolutely no possibility of an accidental glimpse of breast. 'The rectory garden is far too small since the tied houses were built on it, and there really is nowhere else.'

'Oh, surely Sir George will come around,' Harriet said. 'Sir Hector has only been gone for a few months, rest his soul, and it seems quite, well, disrespectful not to carry things on.'

Rose pursed her lips and accepted more tea from Hetty. 'A stupid boy, young George,' she said, and

Harriet knew that she was remembering the incident with the blunderbuss and the Christmas turkey. 'Easily led.' She stirred her tea as they all wondered what to do, reflecting sorrowfully that if the tied houses had never been built to house the two church wardens, she could now have offered to host the fête herself.

'Well, you could hold the fête in our garden,' said Caroline, with the innocent ease of one who does not understand that her words are the verbal equivalent of sitting in the Ormondroyd pew in church.

There ensued, as anyone who truly understands village life might have expected, a startled silence. Afterwards, when she was regretting it and wondering where on earth the impulse to offer had come from, Caroline blamed her mother. Her mother: pillar of the Women's Institute, Good Works In Court Shoes. That was where it had come from. *She's still exerting her influence on me, all the way from Dorset, making me conform to her standards*, she thought. *It has to be telepathy.*

'Are you sure?' asked Hetty. 'I mean, we'd all muck in, but it would still be a lot of work for you.'

Rose was torn between annoyance that a newcomer should be the one to step into the breech, and envy that she might actually pull it off and steal all the thunder. She, Rose, self-styled queen of the village fête – well, she was the only one still living in the village who had been its May Queen, even if it was forty years ago – might be diminished. She could accept playing second fiddle to the Ormondroyds, that was the natural order of things, but for her light to be dimmed under the bushel that was Caroline, well that was too much to bear.

'It really would be an awful burden for you, dear,' she said, 'and I'm not sure that your garden is big enough. Remember, you have never actually been to one of our fêtes. There would be all sorts of difficulties. Now I think—'

'Nonsense,' interrupted Harriet. 'It is a splendid idea. My dear girl, it would just show awful Angela that we don't all rely on her bounteous generosity.'

'Why Harriet,' said Rose in shocked terms, 'I didn't know that you were such a socialist.'

Harriet blushed the colour of boiled beetroot, but said nothing. And so things were left. They were not quite settled, but very nearly.


Afterwards, Rose walked home alone down the Forge Road, oblivious to the dappled greens of the hedgerow and the songs of the nesting birds. Spring filled the air in the way which excites gardeners all over the country, and sends them rushing to garden centres with their cheque books agape. Rose, though, felt deflated, usurped. Poor Rose. Her life had not gone as she had planned. She was a rector's daughter, and her father had been rector of this very same village. When she had married Oliver, her childhood sweetheart, she had vaguely expected their lives to follow a greater path. There had been the early struggles, first as a curate, then his first church in the suburbs of Coventry, then at last, and as though fate had planned it for her, the parish of Great Barking, and the very rectory in which she had grown up. Unfortunately, there it had stopped. Oliver had no ambitions towards higher office, and Rose had been forced to accept that she was not destined to be the wife of a bishop. Moreover, nothing is ever quite as we remember it to have been. The village of Rose's childhood had changed, as had the status of the vicar within it. She had expected tea on the lawn, long floral summers and the chance to be queen, but the modern Great Barking was a far cry from the church-centred village of her youth. Then, attendance at church had been effectively obligatory, the rector's family treated almost as equals by the occupants of the Hall, and with a slight reverence by everyone else. Now, in these days of falling church attendance, the parish was now combined with Little Barking and Bumpstaple, and it astonished her to realize that there were apparently people who frequented the post office who did not know that the rectory was still occupied by a real rector.

She reached her gate and turned up the drive. As she did so, a shaft of sunshine lit up the path before her, like a spotlight from heaven. She stopped, startled, and felt her spirits lift. All was not as bad as it seemed. After all, if the Hall was not to host the fête then she, Rose, was surely in a prime position to take charge of the whole affair. She would establish her authority this evening. What was more, after all these years, there would not be an Ormondroyd to open the fête. She, Rose, could take on this role. The whole village would be sure to turn out. They would all see just how capable and regal she could be. Then everyone who ever used the post office would know who inhabited the rectory, and would admire her immensely. Thus cheered, she entered the rectory with lightened step, and quite startled her husband with the enthusiasm of her greeting.


Great Barking lay in one of those gentle, rolling hollows peculiar to the very central part of East Anglia. In the days when Woolworth's stocked huge chocolate boxes with pictures of thatched cottages on the front, their photographers could have found material for two dozen milk chocolate assortments in the village. Apart from the church, the village boasted a post office and general store, a public house and the Hall. It also possessed, at the far end of Barking Road, almost as far out of the village as it was possible to be, a grey and ugly poultry processing factory. There was, sadly, no longer

44

a school, as it had been converted into The Old School House by a couple named Peter and Belinda, who sold antiques in Islington.

The village owed its preservation, untainted by the blights of more recent architectural style, to the succession of wealthy Ormondroyds who had inhabited Barking Hall for centuries. These privileged folk had, in a previous age, owned the entire village and all the land around it. Over the years, as farming practices changed, they no longer had need of all the tied cottages for housing the decreasing numbers of estate workers, and they had gradually sold them off. The Not In My Back Yard philosophy had led them to put heavy restrictions on the future use of any land which they sold, ensuring that almost no building had taken place in the village for over two centuries. The exception was the pair of tied church cottages in the grounds of the rectory, now rented to the Beans and the Groats. As the church had ancient rights over its land, and as God was widely held to be superior to the Ormondroyds, that had been outside their control.

The village cottages had, in recent years, been bought by the influx of doctors, lawyers, stockbrokers, estate agents and schoolteachers who now form part of the rich tapestry of country life everywhere. In the process they had been first enlarged and modernized, then stripped and restored. Outwardly they were little changed, largely because the owners had rushed to have them listed in the days when it was actually worth something to do so. But now, listing meant that they couldn't even put on a conservatory without permission in triplicate, and the generous grants once available for listed buildings had long since dried up.

If the village owed its time-warped beauty to the Ormondroyds, it owed its continuing life in these days of rural stagnation to the poultry factory. This rather insalubrious establishment was the main source of employment for the population of Broomhill, some four miles away. Without Broomhill Poultry, the town of Broomhill could not have flourished. It was not pretty enough for tourism. It had no railway link for commuters. However, on the decapitation and stuffing of chickens, its population thrived, and because of them, so too did the doctors, lawyers, stockbrokers and schoolteachers who served them but who preferred not to live amongst them. Instead, they lived in Great Barking. The estate agents flourished, too, for although the proceeds of stuffing chickens did not render the factory workers wealthy enough to enter the property market, estate agents always seem to flourish.

The factory rarely caused the village any trouble. There had only been the unfortunate occasion when one of its tanks overflowed and despatched five hundred gallons of chicken blood into the River Running (Mrs Groat had telephoned the rector in great terror, announcing the return of the Plagues of Pharaoh.) Otherwise, its shift workers dispatched themselves to and from Broomhill unfailingly at 8am, 3pm and 10pm without passing through the village at all, so it was only on the odd day when the wind was from the East, and the air particularly warm, that the villagers noticed the factory at all.

St Jude's church stood on a knoll overlooking a deep curve in the road, in a graveyard of yew, holly and several delightful privet bushes which had been trimmed into topiary shapes by the ever resourceful Jacob Bean. Sir Hector Ormondroyd had particularly liked the tall one, which Jacob had intended to resemble the tower of St Jude's. The growth at the bottom had insistently bushed out so that it resembled nothing more than a penis. Sir Hector had been the first to see this. He had, in fact, added a codicil to his will, requesting his burial beneath the penis, but since no-one at the time had understood what this meant, he was put in the vault with the rest of his deceased relatives.

The other houses in the village varied from white, timber-framed straw-thatched cottages, through pink, timber-framed reed-thatched cottages and thence back to white, timber-framed, straw-thatched cottages. One or two had tiled roofs, but over all, the village was an unemployed master thatcher's wet dream. As it happened, one had been around earlier in the year, leaving his card and surveying everyone's thatch. They had all been told that they needed completely rethatching in five years, which, strangely enough, was just the length of the thatcher's waiting list. It just went to show, as Harriet said frequently, that you never could tell. No-one ever knew quite what she meant by this, but it sounded profound.


Alistair complained that evening when Hetty reminded him that she was going to the fête meeting. 'It isn't even May yet. It seems ridiculous that it needs planning already.'

'It will be May tomorrow,' pointed out Luke, in the teenage tone that suggests that you really must have been ignorant not to have realized it.

'You know villages,' said Hetty, lifting the casserole onto the table. 'Here, you'll have to help yourselves. I'll have mine when I get back.'

'What is it, Mum?'

'Casserole, yuk!'

'Why can't we have a Chinese takeaway?'

'For God's sake, don't winge, Finn!'

'I did not winge. Rory, did I winge?'

'Yes, you did. Shut up and get some dinner.'

'Do you have to play mother, Rory?' That was Alistair, sharply.

Silence. Hetty, putting on her coat in the hall, felt a stab of pain for Rory. *Bastard*! she thought, uncharacteristically, for she had only ever sworn in the second stage of labour. Suppressing the urge to ask Rory to come with her, and thus make things worse, she set off the hundred yards or so down Forge Lane to the Beans' house. Halfway there, discovering that she was crying, she gave up and went home.

Caroline also complained. 'But you're not on call tonight. It's Richard's night. I'm supposed to be going to the fête meeting.'

'I'm sorry, love, I swapped it ages ago so that I could go to the Magic Circle meeting tomorrow.'

Caroline wanted to shout that it wasn't fair, that his things always took priority over hers, but she could not, for she knew that he was not an unfair man. He had booked his evening first. She could not hold him to blame for her own lack of organization. Besides, those who marry GPs are not allowed to complain, they have to see their husbands' calling as noble, and accept that the patients always come first, even the ones who actually deserve to be boiled in oil.

'Never mind,' she said. 'I'm sure they won't miss me anyway. Shall I put the kettle on?' As she passed the telephone, it rang. 'Hello, Caroline Potter speaking.'

'Isn't that the bloody doctor, then?' She sighed, thinking, not for the first time, that if it weren't for patients a doctor's lot could be quite a happy one. Then she smiled, remembering the man who had rung to say he couldn't manage it tonight, in the middle of John managing it perfectly well and with great enthusiasm. The call had given them the same problem, at least for about half an hour.

\* \* \*

Caroline was wrong to think that she would not be missed. In the absence of Angela Ormondroyd, and bearing in mind Angela's bombshell of earlier that day, it seemed that a new venue for the fête was indeed required, and that Yew Tree Cottage might do very well. The combined ladies, together with Oliver Bush, Morgan Groat and Jacob Bean, who made up the Fête Committee, made Thanking The Potters the first item on their agenda.

'So, we can do everything in the usual way,' said the rector, beaming. He felt wonderful today. Such a contrast to that seedy feeling that he always experienced on Mondays. 'The bunting, the trestle tables, the portable toilet.'

Rose, who had felt real pain in putting the offer of Yew Tree Cottage for the fête to the committee, butted in. 'Yew Tree Cottage does have a downstairs lavatory,' she said. 'I'm sure it would be an improvement on that thing.'

There were general murmurs of approval at the Potters' plumbing arrangements as they sipped their tea in Mrs Bean's small best room. Jessie and Jacob Bean had lived in the tied cottage for longer than most people could remember, with the Groats as their neighbours. Their cottages were mirror images of one another. Their interesting quality, however, lay not in their similarities but in their differences. Whilst the Beans' house was decorated without a thought either to fashion or to colour co-ordination, a jumble of checks and patterns which many an interior designer sweats gallons to emulate, the Groats' home was smartly thought out, fully accessorized and not terribly welcoming. It was a reflection of the differences between the occupants: white-haired Jessie Bean was a sweet and gentle soul in her sixties, to whom hospitality had always been far more important than appearance. Mrs Groat, ten years younger and about as welcoming as a bed of nails, believed the opposite, and would quite probably have spent her last penny on furniture polish even if it meant having no dinner for a week. It was fortunate, therefore, for the assembled group, that they sat around Jessie Bean's pine table with the red gingham cloth, rather than around Mrs Groat's polished mahogany veneer upon which their assorted china cups would have rested in fear and dread.

Morgan Groat had had little say in the decor of his house. Indeed it was a feature of his life that he had never had very much say in anything. When not out with his fishing rod, he was a church warden, and indeed he was partially responsible for the penis in the churchyard. He had been secretly eroding it, without Jacob's knowledge, as he was under the impression that it was meant to be the Eiffel Tower. This had had the unfortunate effect of shaping the base so that it bore even more of a resemblance to a pair of testicles than it had before.

Rose, officially in the chair, decided to inject some order into the agenda. Apart from herself and Oliver, the Beans and the Groats, the committee consisted of Carol Sheldon, a beautician who owned a chihuahua called Nigel, Harriet and of course Hetty and Caroline, who both seemed to be absent. 'The question is,' she said officiously, 'do we accept? After all, the Potters may not really know what they are taking on.'

'Oh, I think it's delightful of them to offer. To refuse would be churlish,' said Harriet, disliking Rose's obvious pique. 'Don't you, Oliver?'

'Indeed I do,' said Oliver, peering at Harriet over his half-moon spectacles, and Harriet blushed, as she always did when he looked at her. Harriet could not remember a time when she had not adored Oliver.

Mrs Groat, however, had just thought of a far more

serious question. 'Rose, dear,' she said, in the restrained tones of one enjoying the fact that she is about to drop a bombshell and therefore needs no vocal dramatics, 'who on earth will we ask to open the fête?'

There was a short silence. Rose waited. It would not do to volunteer, although she had every intention that the honour should fall to her. Let them argue about it for a while. Rose had presided over too many village committees to imagine that they might ever reach a consensus.

'Surely old Lady Ormondroyd. She has always done it in the past.' Jacob fumbled for his teaspoon as he spoke.

Mrs Groat sighed heavily into the awkward silence which ensued. No-one wanted to be the one to point out to Jacob that Lady Sybil's marble count was distinctly on the low side.

Jacob who, like many partially sighted people, was very finely tuned to atmosphere, frowned his surprise. 'She did it last year, didn't she, Jessie?'

Jessie was forced to explain what they all knew. Jessie resembled nothing more than a rather anxious church mouse, always chewing her lip and looking as though she were poised for flight. She did not like to speak badly of anyone. 'She did, dear, but that was before Sir Hector's death and since then, well, she hasn't been herself.'

'Totally out of it,' Carol Sheldon whispered to Morgan on her right.

Jacob, whose path through life was uncluttered by the distractions of other people's lives since he barely saw them, nor took much notice of them, unless he happened to play the organ at their funerals, was genuinely surprised. 'Is she ill?'

'No, dear, not exactly.' Poor Jessie was desperately uncomfortable. 'She just forgets things, people—'

51

'Dementia,' said Mrs Groat in lugubrious tones. Mrs Groat had never let it be said that she was one to beat about the bush – and indeed, no-one had ever said it. She was the kind of person who spoke her mind and counted not the cost to others. 'The woman is as nutty as a fruit bat. She could not possibly open the fête. Since Sir Hector's death she has become a danger to herself. Hit the sherry bottle, *I* think.'

'Well perhaps, as the fête will probably not be at the Hall . . .' began the rector rather desperately.

'She could no more open the fête than open Parliament,' pressed on Mrs Groat, who by now had really warmed to her subject. 'Her geese would make a better job of it.'

Harriet stirred uncomfortably. It really would not do for Mrs Groat to carry on like this. 'Greta, really, I do think you are exaggerating.' Mrs Groat stopped in mid flow and caught her breath. Carol Sheldon had not known that she was named Greta. It was a name Mrs Groat hated for its proximity to the surname Groat. Why, it was almost as bad as being named Rose Bush. Even Morgan had stumbled over it during their wedding service. Carol was bound to poke fun at her now.

Carol, who had detested Mrs Groat ever since she had referred to Nigel as a peke, enjoyed her discomfiture. 'Do you think, *Greta*,' she said sweetly, 'that the Ormondroyds might change their minds if we asked Angela to open the fête?'

Harriet said that if Angela Ormondroyd was going to be difficult, then the fête would be better off without her, whether she changed her mind or not.

'Well, I'm not sure,' said Jessie placatingly. 'We wouldn't want to *offend* the Ormondroyds.' Dear Harriet seemed so radical lately.

'One must not forget,' added Oliver thoughtfully, 'the

52

size of their charitable contributions to the church. If it were not for Sir Hector's bequest, we could not have repaired the roof this year.' He felt a little guilty for bringing money into it, remembering the biblical story about the old woman giving her last coin. It was not, after all, the size of the donation, but how much it meant to the giver which was important.

'Shame he didn't wait to snuff it till after we found the dry rot,' muttered Mrs Groat, but fortunately the only people who heard her agreed with her entirely.

There was a brief silence while Oliver's comment was digested. Mrs Groat broke it. 'So who shall we ask?'

'Don't you think,' said Harriet, 'that it might be a good idea to ask someone completely different? I mean, we do have our own local celebrity in the village.'

Rose and Mrs Groat spoke together, equally alarmed. 'You don't mean—' 'Do you mean—'

'Sarah Struther is a well known figure in artistic circles,' said Harriet. 'She was in the *Sunday Times* this week.'

'She is a bit odd, though.' Carol Sheldon was jealous of Sarah's dramatic beauty, appalled by her size and insulted by the fact that she was not currently hiding in an attic living on celery sticks and powdered milk shakes until she became more presentable. Carol ran her own beauty salon – 'Carole' – in Broomhill, and if too many women had shared Sarah's attitude, she would most likely have gone out of business. She wore her own, shoulder-length hair in a bouffant bob, the top of which was regularly lightened artistically. Her suits were always in the colours which the colour analysis woman had told her she should wear, and she never, never wore horizontal stripes. Daring, exotic and outrageous were words which one did not utter in the same breath as her name, and most of her clients, whatever their appearance on entering her salon, left it looking rather like her.

'Odd is the word,' said Mrs Groat. 'I've heard a few things—'

'A little eccentricity does not hurt at all,' said Harriet, who was very proud to know Sarah.

'More tea, Vicar . . .' Jessie was desperate to change the subject before the revelation concerning the suntan and Sarah's breasts should be aired in front of Oliver.

Poor Morgan Groat had seen them as he cut past Sarah's kitchen window on his way back from the river. There had been no white bikini line. The woman must have lain naked in the sun for hours. Morgan Groat remembered the incident well. In fact, if his name had been George Frederick Handel he would surely have composed something grand after encountering Sarah Struther's glorious breasts through her kitchen window. As his name was Morgan Groat, however, he had gone on home and filleted his trout. Now, though, his mind was filled with a glorious picture of Sarah, breasts swinging freely, opening the village fête and wearing nothing but a pair of waders and an oilskin hat.

'I think Miss Struther would do very well,' he said hopefully, shifting a little in his seat.

'I think we should still consider the young Lady Ormondroyd,' ploughed on the rector, dipping a digestive biscuit into his tea and losing it. 'It is her first year here, and we should be forging links, making friends, thinking of future fêtes—'

'Don't preach, Oliver dear,' said Rose, relieved that Sarah's name had been dropped. For a moment there had seemed to be a risk of the committee agreeing on something.

'Well,' said Mrs Groat, 'I don't think that she deserves to be asked. Young George would never have refused to host the fête if she hadn't made him.'

'Odd, really,' mused Harriet, 'George is quite an old

traditionalist. I'm surprised she had her way with him over this.'

Carol Sheldon tittered into her tea. Little did she know that Harriet's unfortunate turn of phrase was actually quite appropriate.

Rose frowned at her. 'Let's put it in the list for Action,' she said firmly, as if that decided everything, 'and then get on with things.' She wrote, laboriously on her agenda:

1. Site of fête. Yew Tree Cottage.
   Barking Hall?

2. To open fête.
   Lady Sybil.
   Angela Ormondroyd.
   Sarah Struther.
   Mrs Potter (her house).

3. Jobs . . .

The usual allocations were made. The same people generally did the same things each year. These people formed the self-selected Fête Committee. They arranged the fête and they manned it, which tended to result in everyone else feeling that their help was not needed or wanted, either at the meeting or at the fête. Even Caroline had only been asked onto the committee to replace the previous (deceased) occupant of her house. Mrs Groat would look after the cakes, and Jessie would look after the tea and refreshments. Harriet would, as always, run the tombola. Hetty would run the white elephant stall. The hoop-la would be Jacob's responsibility, Morgan would run the bran tub and Carol Sheldon would ask her husband to make the coconut shy. Carol took on the book stall, Rose would sell the plants, and Harriet would bring down her donkeys for rides. Caroline, as hostess, would not be allocated anything specific. That was all quite straightforward.

Rose, writing it all down, reflected that things were always so much simpler when they were done the way they had always been done. Unfortunately, her carefully compiled list was about to cause a major problem.

As she had begun to write the list of helpers down on her list, she had begun with the name of Mrs Groat. It was an unlined page, and she had written this to the right of and *above* the word 'jobs' so that to the hopeful eye it looked as though Mrs Groat's name was listed amongst those who might open the fête. There was no eye more hopeful than that of Mrs Groat, as she peered over Rose's shoulder and saw her name amongst the glorious few.

From that moment the question of who should open the fête took on the proportion, in the mind of Mrs Groat, of the search for Scarlett O'Hara. To be chosen, to be elected above the rest and granted the chance to gloriously declare the village fête 'open' seemed a pinnacle of greatness which even Vivienne Leigh was never able to achieve. Mrs Groat could feel herself glowing with pride.

'Oh Rose, Dear,' she said in dulcet tones, astonishing Rose so much that her spectacles fell into her tea, 'I am *so* flattered.'

Rose, looking at her page without the benefit of spectacles, had no idea what Mrs Groat was flattered about, and replied vaguely, 'Well, Greta, you always do a grand job with the teas.' This remark served only to reinforce in Mrs Groat's mind the belief that she was, at last, to be recognized for her years of uncomplaining service. So happy was she that she did not even notice that Rose had used her Christian name. Mrs Groat had always known that she was special. She had been a pillar of the church and moral guardian of Great Barking ever since she had come here as Morgan's bride in the mid fifties. Now, she felt, now at last a just reward was in sight. If only she were to be the Chosen One, the One to open the fête.

It had, in all, by the time they dispersed, been no more than useful, in that no-one knew much that they had not known before, and Jessie Bean was left with a great deal of washing up. Since the advent of dishwashers people seemed to have ceased to offer to help with washing up, but Jessie did not have a dishwasher. She squirted green liquid into the water, wondering idly if anyone really believed that putting their hands into it would make them softer. Some people would believe anything.

Mrs Groat had left with the rest in order to pick up any snippets of departing gossip on the subject of people opening fêtes, but she now returned, more to recruit an ally than to help. 'Oh, Jessie, dear, I think Rose plans for *me* to open the fête.'

Jessie frowned at her, wondering where on earth she had got such an idea from. She knew Rose's opinion of Mrs Groat, and she knew that Attila the Hun stood rather more chance than Mrs Groat of opening the fête, even though he was dead. She selected her words with some care. 'Did she say so?'

'No, but I saw that she had written me down with the other candidates.' Mrs Groat was acting as though she had just been nominated for an Academy Award. 'Oh Jessie, I could wear my pink suit.'

Jessie swallowed nervously. The pink suit was Mrs Groat's festive wear. She had bought it after reading in an article that the Queen favoured strong, bright colours in order to stand out in a crowd. She had no idea how much this particular pink made her stand out. In her suit Mrs Groat looked like a fluorescent pink stick insect. 'Don't you think,' she said tactfully, 'that it might be better to wear something a little less precious?'

'Not at all,' said Mrs Groat pompously, 'I must make sure that I look the part.'

Jessie was rather afraid that the part which Mrs Groat would look would not be the one which she had in mind.

Going home Rose and Oliver walked together up their garden path. 'I find these meetings so frustrating,' she told him. 'We talk for hours, but everyone goes off at tangents, and nothing gets decided.'

'I should imagine,' said Oliver, walking carefully on the gravel as though he might trip on his cassock (which he was not actually wearing), 'that in the world of business that happens all the time.'

'But what shall we do,' said Rose innocently, fumbling for her keys, 'about opening the fête? We really did not decide.'

'Well, I think you should simply sort it out yourself,' said Oliver, knowing that Rose would like to hear this. 'Personally I think we should have the young Lady Ormondroyd. We do rather rely upon the family's generosity, and not to ask her might be interpreted as a snub.'

Rose thought that she rather liked the idea of the snub. She was absolutely determined *not* to ask Angela to open the fête. She had succeeded in leaving Oliver with the impression that she would sort it out. Well, she *would* sort it out in the best possible way. She would ask no-one, and on the day she would pretend aloud that there had been a misunderstanding and imply quietly that Angela was the one who had misunderstood (she was, after all, American, and only a Lady by marriage). Then she, Rose, would open the fête herself. She would wear her pink suit. Rose smiled smugly.

# Chapter Four

The idea of pursuing Lucy Bellingham, the Ormondroyds' groom, occurred to Alistair early the following week. It was during the convivial atmosphere of lunchtime drinks in a Cambridge public house, where he was celebrating the completion of a particularly lucrative deal with his colleagues, that he actually found himself discussing sex with that pratt Andrew Smythe. They came from the same mould, Andrew and Alistair, they spoke with the same accent. They were both the kind of men who owned their own morning suits and always had their socks darned.

The pub was crowded, filled with the rise-and-fall hum of enthusiastic voices and the mingled smells of spilt ale, cigarettes and food. The clientele were a mixture of students and the people they were destined to become. The students wore jeans and earrings with sharp nasty bits and purple shiny bits all over them, like flotsam from Mars. The stockbrokers wore suits and did not loosen their ties. Alistair had been half watching the barmaid, who was stridently attractive in a blonde kind of way. She wore the kind of tight jumper that made him want to squeeze her breasts. The girls of Alistair's adolescence in the sixties had worn similar clothes; perhaps all men are habitually turned on by reminders of their early, frustrated sexual experiences. Mind you, he thought, if that were so then he ought to get an erection every time he saw a bus shelter.

Andrew was telling what he thought was a highly

59

amusing story of an occasion when his secretary returned unexpectedly during her lunch hour and caught him kissing his wife. The secretary had been furious. Alistair, although unsurprised by anything that Andrew might lay claim to – although it was perhaps somewhat surprising that he was on kissing terms with his wife – found himself listening.

'Does my marriage the world of good, having a bit of spice on the side,' Andrew insisted. 'Alison probably guesses, but she doesn't really want to know. Her sexual drive just isn't equal to mine, you see. Some men just need more. Surely you agree? After all, we all notice the available tarts in the office, don't we?'

'Yes,' said Alistair, not wishing to appear less of a man of the world than his peer, 'of course.' In his mind he attributed a few more inviting looks from Lucy Bellingham than she had ever actually given him. 'Local girl has been giving me the eye, as it happens. Horsewoman.'

'Go for it!' Smythe seemed impressed, and nudged Alistair so that he slopped his real ale wastefully on the bar. 'Horsey girls are the best. Take it from me. It's those strong inner thighs they develop. Wonderful balance – ride you like a jockey.'

Alistair downed his beer before he could be deprived of any more of it. 'I may give her a bell,' he said casually, wondering what it would be like to be ridden by Lucy Bellingham. Was he ever likely to find out? This pratt Smythe seemed to think that the world was full of pretty little things just desperate to be rogered by public school accents. Could that be true? Should he ask her out?

The barmaid leaned towards Andrew. 'Your plough-man's,' she said, licking her lips.

Andrew grinned lecherously. Alistair watched, fascinated, as she jiggled her breasts one at a time in Andrew's direction.

'Enjoy,' she said, a wealth of meaning in her eyes. Her nipples could be seen quite clearly through her jumper.

'Would you like one?' Andrew leered.

'I wouldn't say "no". Port and lemon, please,' she giggled, taking his money.

Alistair wondered if he could ever bear to be as blatant. The truth was that he actually despised men like Andrew, who acted with all the subtlety of a juggernaut, and somewhat less panache. In fact he was so embarrassed that he finished his drink and placed his glass on the counter, intending a swift exit. Unfortunately, though, he had to wait for his erection to reduce a little first.

Walking back along Free School Lane towards his office, he decided that he would give Lucy a call. Why not? He was a man in the prime of his years, his sexual prime, and a prime for which his wife did not really seem to have a great deal of enthusiasm. Everyone knew that women's sexual demands were on a downward spiral after twenty-five. Hetty had other interests. If she didn't want his semen, it wasn't as if he'd be taking anything from her that she needed. She would never know, and anyhow she would probably be relieved if he didn't pressure her for sex quite as much. He felt suddenly uncomfortable at that, as it had not previously occurred to him that he did pressure her – but he pushed thoughts of Hetty out of his mind. Now, where should he take the girl for dinner?

Back at his office, his hand was sweaty as he listened to the telephone ringing somewhere in the Ormondroyds' stables. He felt he had never done anything as wicked as this in his life. On the surface of it he was telephoning Lucy to ask her advice about riding lessons for Finn – but he knew that the riding lessons which were really on his mind did not involve horses at all.

'Hello?' The voice was a little muffled, but clearly female.

'Hello there,' said Alistair in his richest public school tones. 'Sorry to trouble you. Just after a piece of advice.'

'Who is this? Oh! George!' The phone went dead. That had been Angela, not Lucy. Alistair stared at the receiver in surprise. It had sounded almost as if – but no, Angela Ormondroyd was not the sort of woman who might be having it away in her own stables. Indeed, it was hard to imagine her having it away anywhere. Still, it was a good job he hadn't identified himself. *I'll wait until I see Lucy*, he decided, *bound to see her if I walk the bloody dog*. Hetty's dog was always 'the bloody dog' – had been ever since she deposited a large turd on the financial section of *The Sunday Times* before he had read it. Then they could chat and then perhaps . . . *perhaps I'd better just pop to the lavatory*, he thought.

In the event it was ridiculously easy. Alistair had spotted her on his way to Cambridge a few mornings afterwards, riding back a little late from her morning gallop on Sir George's hunter. A pause, a chat, we must have dinner. Tonight? A call home – a business dinner, he had told them – a room at a Cambridge hotel ('no-one knows me here') and here they were.

Lucy Bellingham wondered if any of those people who wrote for *Cosmopolitan* had ever truly had an orgasm just through straight bonking. She never had, and if this experience was anything to judge by, she never would. It was strange; after all, she was very widely read on the subject, having ploughed through everything she could find on the subject, from Mills and Boon to Jilly Cooper. It always sounded so inspiring: girls named Araminta and Persephone experienced electric currents and earthquakes, tumbled down through chasms and flew to the stars in mind-shattering experiences of sexual exhilaration, just because some arrogant bloke stuck his thing in. Perhaps you got that when you were in love – but then Lucy had fancied herself in love at sixteen, and the resulting fumble had been quite horrible.

Alistair, not sensing her detachment from the proceedings, and believing her unfocussed gaze to be a sign of intense enjoyment, paused and changed position. Lucy, slightly shocked, complied. After all, the whole point of having it off with an older man was to learn a bit. Assuming that what he did was pretty normal – how does one know without having hundreds of partners? – then she was acquiring a social skill. After all, having lost her virginity to Miles Wooton-Gormley at sixteen, there was little point in not having a good time now. She had not had a good time then: Miles had had all the finesse of a drunken prop forward, which of course was exactly what he had been. Ah, well, a chaste girl is rarely chased. That's what her friend Susie always said, and Susie had had ten different lovers. Lucy had only managed eight so far – well nine, now.

Now that felt interesting. Lucy let out a couple of 'ooh's for Alistair's benefit. It seemed to encourage him – he was becoming almost rough, but not quite. *He must have fancied me for ages*, she thought, *to have chatted me up this morning and got me into the sack the same day. I wonder if he's unfaithful a lot?*

*She must really have fancied me*, thought Alistair, thrusting as hard as he had hoped to. How easily she had capitulated. That pratt Smythe had been right. You just had to take advantage, seize the moment. She had not been a virgin, of course, but she was obviously not very experienced. He could mould her to his every whim. *She must* really *fancy me to let me do this. She's*

63

*not as good as Hetty*. The thought popped into his mind from somewhere outside.

Guilt shrank Alistair, and he wondered momentarily what he was doing there, rolling on a hotel duvet with George and Angela's groom. However, the build-up of pressure in his groin again brought his mind swiftly back to matters in hand, and he altered his rhythm in order to delay things a little. It sounded as though she was about to have an orgasm – she seemed to be moaning. Hetty sometimes had them, but she was always very quiet. Years of habit, with the children around. She wasn't always so. He suddenly remembered Fort William and the caravan, and it was fortunate that he had just reached Nirvana, because otherwise he would certainly not have got there at all.


Hetty wondered whether or not to save any dinner for Alistair. A meeting, he had said. That usually meant food, but occasionally he had arrived home, ravenous and cross, at half past ten. When they were first married he had hardly ever stayed late at the office, he had hurried home and told her all the fine details of his day. She had listened, too. *Did I stop listening before he stopped talking, or was it the other way round?* She stared glumly at his portion of cod pie.

'Is there any more, Mum?' asked Luke, eyeing it too.

'Here, finish this.' Hetty lumped it onto his plate.

'What about Dad?'

'He's eating out. Business.' Hetty was short. She felt as though she was making excuses for Alistair.

'Mum, I need new cricket trousers,' said Finn. 'Mine are too small, and Luke's have had it.'

'You'll have to ask your father.'

The boys retreated to their computer games and Hetty eyed the now-empty pie dish rather sadly. Alistair didn't like cod pie anyway. She put the dish to soak in the sink, and went to join Rory in the lounge.

It was much later when she heard Alistair come in, and she was glad that she hadn't saved the pie. It would have looked uninteresting and working class – at least, that's what he would have thought. Alistair was accustomed to restaurants, and he thought that anything with mashed potato on top was only for the consumption of people named Alf and Freda who lived in Grimsby and bred greyhounds. She was in bed by this time, wearing a thick nightie as there was a chill in the air, and reading P.G. Wodehouse in an effort to lighten her mood.

She heard him downstairs, pottering, fetching a drink, but he didn't come up. *I'll finish my chapter and then slip down and see how he is*, she thought. *I don't make enough effort these days*. Fate was against her, though, for she dozed off during the next paragraph. Alistair, creeping into bed an hour later, removed the book from her pillow and lay down with a feeling of relief. He had showered, thrown away the receipts; Hetty would never know. There had, of course, been that slight risk that she might make advances towards him tonight. He couldn't have managed it again; twice in a row had been quite an effort at his age, but he'd felt he had something to prove to Lucy. Actually, he felt a little sore. It was worth it, though, she had clearly been more than satisfied. He imagined himself rolling with her in the stables, remembered her firm, young breasts, her unmarked abdomen. Then, like a tidal wave, guilt overwhelmed him completely and he reached out to Hetty instinctively, meaning to stroke the Caesarean scar on her belly. He was foiled. She was wearing that awful winceyette nightdress. How could she?

\*   \*   \*

By the middle of May, the weather had actually become quite warm. Forests of daffodils and irises had given way to the first of the roses in both the carefully and the not-so-carefully tended gardens of Great Barking. Mrs Groat's and Rose Bush's roses never grew from year to year, so strictly were they pruned. Elsewhere they ranged from neat but loved (Jessie Bean's) through professionally managed (the Hall) to absolute thickets (Sarah's and Harriet's). The pest control man from the council was visiting almost every house on a weekly basis in an effort to get to the mice before the mice got to the electric wiring. Caroline Potter had been in tears several times at the discovery of dying mice which she had carried outside, twitching, by their tails. She and John had left it rather late to call the council – the mice were so pretty, and Henry and Josh so keen on Beatrix Potter.

The Stewarts' house, host to a rat some years previously – it had eaten Hetty's best coat – had been the first on the list. Hetty hated rats. She knew that the man from the council thought her neurotic, but she rang the council the moment she heard the patter of tiny paws.

Angela Ormondroyd, of course, had arranged for a private company to come and clear the rodents from the Hall. She would never have dreamed of using a firm without a royal warrant, and she certainly would never have rung the council. The irony was that the same firm, indeed the same man, visited Barking Hall as well as the other houses in the village, and the fact that Angela paid him did not alter the quality of the service he gave by one whit. He tried to chat her up, of course, but that was free, and in any case she just assumed the expression of a stuffed prune and left him to his lonely task.

The Beans and the Groats were rarely troubled by mice, as they did not have thatch. In any case it would have been a brave mouse who would dare enter Mrs

Groat's domain. Harriet kept a vast array of cats, so she was usually also clear. Sarah, who also kept cats, had once been a Buddhist, and would therefore not consider killing the mice. She resorted instead to soaking pieces of cotton wool in eucalyptus oil and leaving them in mouse-ish spots about the house. The mice left in disgust, and the aromas of Sarah's house grew ever more interesting. Oddly enough, the mice actually disliked her Chanel No 5 far more than the eucalyptus oil. She did not waste it on them, but when she felt like a treat she mixed a few drops of it with almond oil and rubbed it all over her body. Needless to say, she got through a lot of almond oil.

Caroline was in the garden with the children. India had taken to having occasional naps in her pram while they walked in the fields, and when they got home Caroline often left her sleeping for a time in order to weed the flower beds. She wished now that she hadn't buried quite so many mice just here: she hardly dared pull anything weedy up, lest something unpleasant should come out with it. Henry and Josh were arguing. Caroline, believing that they were discussing the ownership of a small plastic concrete mixer, took no notice. She would not have been so relaxed had she known that they were actually arguing over who should eat an upturned beetle. Her mind, however, was on other things. She had done a pregnancy test that morning, for no better reason than that she had found an almost-out-of-date one in the bathroom cabinet, and had not wanted to waste it. There was, it was true, almost always a pregnancy test in the bathroom cabinet, as Caroline did them so often when she was not pregnant that it was almost worth her buying them in bulk. Waiting for the result, she had held her breath. It was marvellous that these tests only took three minutes. It meant that she could do one in the bathroom without John finding out. He would only tell her off for using a test when she hadn't actually missed a period.

The plunger was meant to turn blue for a positive result. It had not turned blue. She had held it up to the light and squinted at it, put it against the white of the sink and squinted again . . . but no, by no stretch of the imagination had it been anything other than white. Only then had she realized just how much she had been hoping for blue. She had sat on the toilet, a mantle of flatness falling about her head, arguing with herself. *All through your last pregnancy you kept on saying how much you were looking forward to* not *being pregnant, wearing your nice clothes, not gasping for breath. Remember? Think of the chaos if you had another: you hardly have the energy for the ones you've got sometimes. And imagine if it were twins again – or even more!*

But she had not felt consoled. The truth was that she had been pregnant for so long that she had rather lost track of her non-pregnant identity. She had hardly been out of maternity clothes for the last three years. Her identity, her self image, was pregnant. It gave her confidence to be pregnant. It made her proud of her body, unashamed and bold. It gave her something fascinating to wonder about, and it made her incredibly sexy. So sexy, in fact, that at times she had surprised both herself and John with her enthusiasm. Sitting back on her heels, looking at the partially weeded flower bed, she wondered about Taking Action. Whatever the problems of another pregnancy, they would, after all, be far outweighed by the sheer pleasure of feeling so absolutely complete.

From the pristine whiteness of the gates, Sarah's voice disturbed her reverie. 'Caroline? It's me. I have a confession to make.'

'Come in.' Caroline dropped her trowel and got up. No bits of mice so far, thank goodness. Sarah was a vegetarian, wasn't she?

'I've come to apologize,' said Sarah. 'A couple of weeks ago I foolishly accused you of pregnancy, do you remember?' Caroline blushed painfully, giving herself away as she struggled for an appropriate response. 'Oh dear,' Sarah read her expression, 'I should have realized I might stir up a hornets' nest. I just came to tell you that I was wrong.'

'How do you know?' asked Caroline, feeling as if she had had another negative test. For someone whose hobby was choosing names for her future babies – and with the possibility of twins, or even triplets, with several names each, this could be quite time-consuming – this was another blow. One negative test, after all, had not seemed final when balanced against Sarah's coffee grounds. She had planned to buy another pack of two little plungers.

Sarah looked flustered. 'I miscalculated. I was setting out an astrological chart this morning and I realized that I have been making some incorrect assumptions. I have done it throughout the sun's time in Taurus.'

Caroline was mystified. 'But you read my coffee cup, not a chart.'

'Yes, dear, but the interpretation comes from many things. The planetary aspect, the age of Aquarius, the moon in Cancer—'

'I'm a Taurus,' said Caroline.

'You're not very Taurean,' said Sarah. 'Born on the cusp, I expect. May the twentieth?'

'Yes. How did you . . . ?' Caroline was so impressed that it did not occur to her to wonder why Sarah had come round now, worrying about a two-week-old mistake.

Mrs Barrington, who ran the post office, did not need

to wonder at all. When Sarah Struther came in for peanut butter, and bought a jar of pickled gherkins as an afterthought, she knew. She kept the pickled gherkins on their own special shelf, together with the anchovy paste and the peanut butter. Perming two out of three was proof of pregnancy. She had never been wrong, unless one counted the time when Morgan Groat was experimenting with trout bait and she had made the mistake of congratulating his wife. She was right this time, too. Sarah had intended to tell Caroline, but had changed her mind when she saw her expression, and had invented some astrological waffle instead. There would be time enough to tell people later, but for now she must consider telling the father.

He had been a very young journalist. Of course she had not planned it, but it only takes one of those four million little tadpoles to decide he is supersperm, the Indiana Jones of the seminal world, to do the trick. One alone has to look up and say, 'A diaphragm? There has to be a way past here,' and then wriggle round the side. It pleased her greatly to think that such a resourceful sperm had fathered her child.

Five months ago. It was not so strange that she had not realized – she was large enough to conceal full-term triplets with ease, and her periods were never regular anyway. No matter. She was wealthy, she was independent and oh, how she had longed for a child. What was his name? Tarquin, that's right, like the Roman emperor. She smiled at the memory of him – she had been celibate for so long beforehand that it had been marvellous to have her hinges oiled, so to speak.


'Tarquin d'Abo Smith? No. He's out of the office at the moment. No, for two weeks. No, he can't be reached, he's in the Seychelles. Yes, lucky him. He's on his honeymoon. Did you want to leave a message?'

So much for honesty. Now was clearly not the time to upset Tarquin's apple cart. She'd bet her life he'd married some scrawny blonde. Sarah genuinely found thin women ugly.

Meanwhile Rose was also gardening, but her mind was elsewhere. For Rose, the organization of the fête was the highlight of her working year. It had never really worried her before that the outward glory had all gone to Sir Hector and Lady Sybil Ormondroyd, because they had hosted and opened the fête. It had only been seemly, as they were proper gentry, and the people who really counted had known that Rose had done most of the work. The Ormondroyds had, to be fair, paid a price at times, for the annual invasion of their garden. There had been the time when the donkey, who was giving free rides, had eaten all of the prize dahlias, and the time when their Spanish cook had herself been discovered giving Sir Hector free rides in the kitchen. Their lawns had been trampled and their lavatories blocked, and it went without saying that their toilet paper had always been stolen. Nevertheless, they had always suffered these indignities with the graciousness born of long-standing wealth, good breeding, and having employees to do the clearing up. They had deserved their share of the glory.

Rose, though, had always had the comforting inner glow of one who knows that, without her, something great could never have come to pass, and of feeling sure that others were aware of it too. Now she looked forward to taking the credit publicly at last. She always tried hard to think of ideas for the fête. Ideas, that is, which were original, her own, and outside the auspices of the Fête Committee until she had thought them out and planned them completely. It was particularly important that she should come up with something special this year, as it would be *her* fête. Now, as she sprinkled slug pellets around the vegetable patch, she was visited by inspiration. Why, Great Barking boasted a woman so famous that she was featured in the national press, a woman whose work was collected avidly by people who had a taste for the – well – peculiar. Rose did not understand how pots could be art. In her view a vase was a vase and you put flowers in it. On the other hand, she was prepared to concede that there were some – probably Americans and actors – who perceived Sarah's work as such, and that for this reason it might actually have value. Either way, the woman was famous, so why not ask her to make a pot to be the centrepiece of the Great Barking raffle? They could display it at the fête, invite a reporter from the *Gazette*, sell hundreds of tickets . . .

Becoming quite excited, she flung slug pellets wildly across the path. Not only would the dry rot be consigned to history, but they could have the roof beams cleaned and polished. They must be caked in bat droppings. She, Rose, would receive all the credit for this, too. She could see herself now, resplendent in her pink suit, graciously receiving the vote of thanks. She began to feel quite pleased that the fête was to be in the Potters' garden rather than at the Hall. It would give her far more opportunity to shine in authority. Why, she might even be invited to tea at the Bishop's Palace!

Oliver was weeding slowly over by the house. He hated to weed, as he always felt so very sorry for the weeds which were, after all, only plants which were misunderstood. He spent a lot of time apologizing to them, which seemed to make them return in greater abundance within a very short time, giving credence to the idea that talking to plants encourages their growth. Oliver's weeds may have been weeded, but they were happy.

Rose rushed over to Oliver to explain her idea about Sarah and the pot, and he thought it was excellent. In fact, he had great admiration for Sarah's work. There were themes and ideas in Sarah's pottery which really was more fairly described as sculpture. Many of her pots were quite exotic, others feminist and others funny. It was quite remarkable how she expressed feelings and ideas through a piece of clay.

'Why don't you suggest an ecclesiastical theme?' he ventured cautiously to Rose. 'Something relevant to St Jude's, perhaps?'

'I know what ecclesiastical means!' snapped Rose, not wishing to reveal that she did not understand how a vase could have a theme anyway.

'Perhaps angels, or simply wings,' mused Oliver thoughtfully, 'or perhaps the organ pipes – they do rather dominate St Jude's.'

This was how Rose, who had not an artistic bone in her body, found herself suggesting to Sarah a theme for a pot. To Rose's delight, Sarah had proved quite willing to donate a pot, and quite interested in the organ idea, which she seemed to think had possibilities. Rose was triumphant. It was really all working out rather well. She looked forward to the next – and final – meeting of the Fête Committee. She must send out some notices now for white elephants and tombola prizes. Splendid. Thank goodness Angela Ormondroyd had turned out to be such an awful woman. It just went to show what happened when the gentry married Americans.

In fact Angela, although Rose did not know it, had been the saviour of the dwindling Ormondroyd fortunes. Her family's immense wealth was not old money, but they had aspirations, and understood how best to achieve them. They had wanted Angela to marry an English Title – any would do – and therefore she had had the Texan drawl almost beaten out of her when she had been sent to England to be 'finished'. Her school was one which felt it had failed if its charges did not acquire at least a Baronet's son, and it had charged accordingly. Angela had learned their lessons thoroughly. It was only when she was particularly stressed that the odd Americanism crept in.

Hers was a family who always got what they wanted. Angela had inherited the family determination. She was determinedly thorough. This was how she had won her way with George this time, too. What's more, it had not been unpleasant, especially in the stable block on Lucy's day off, when the straw and the sounds of the horses had allowed her to fantasize that she was Tess of the d'Urbervilles. Things must continue for a while at least, she told herself. Her family had taught her always to consolidate her victories.

George was delighted by her sudden attentions. Admittedly he had not had to work so hard since the chalet girl at St Moritz had introduced him to her friend – and he had been ten years younger then – but his self-esteem had been boosted to the extent that he now saw himself as a cross between James Bond and the Milk Tray man, rolled in libido and dusted with testosterone. The rather drained feeling was a price worth paying.

Although Angela had won on the subject of the hosting of the fête, she still felt that there was more for her to prove in Great Barking. The finishing school had never quite been able to inculcate in her the sense of having no need to prove anything, which is characteristic of the English upper classes. She did not understand that all one has to be is gracious; she was sure that being at the top of any social pile necessitates perpetually reminding others that they are further down the heap. She therefore planned to use the fête to make her mark upon the village. She did not need all of those dreadful little people with their gold-plated jewellery and chainstore coats running around her lawn in order to achieve this. No, her way was clear: she would open the fête. She would open it in style, for she was Lady of the Manor.

Angela was a clever woman. She had seen that both Rose and Mrs Groat had aspirations of greatness, and that Caroline did not. What's more, Caroline was not only hosting the fête, but she seemed to be of minor county stock. She recognized, therefore, that her position would be best strengthened through Caroline, and she resolved to go and see her. She would make sure that Caroline was left in no doubt that she, Angela, Lady Ormondroyd, was the only person who could properly open the fête. She was certainly the only person who could be relied upon to turn up in Burmese pearls and pink Hartnell.

George did not concern himself with his wife's aspirations; indeed very little – other than his horses and his haemorrhoids – concerned George most of the time. Right now, though, he did feel just a hint of another interest: his groom.

Modern hired help puzzled him. He had been brought up to believe that one of the advantages of belonging to the upper echelons of society was that one got to hump those less fortunate than oneself. These unfortunates, or staff, as they were often called, generally then said 'Thank you, m'lud,' and cleared off without further familiarity. There were said to be several Sir Hector look-alikes about these parts. George had not found his own staff to be nearly so accommodating. Lucy was the latest of a series of horsey girl grooms from distinguished families. Apart from her rather disconcerting tendency to speak with an accent similar to his own, her father had been at his school, and her brothers played polo. At least one had known where one stood in the old days, whereas now — well, the Bellinghams were a family so old that they outshone the Windsors, and so well bred that they could have run the two thousand guineas at Newmarket.

He eyed Lucy's behind rather hopefully as she picked out the hooves of his favourite hunter, and wondered what she would do if he offered her the proof of his manhood, as it were. 'Ahem.'

Lucy turned, just in time to spot the fleeting expression of lust on Sir George's face before he chased it away. It surprised her, but she definitely felt pleased. She was, after all, on her ninth lover. She was a woman of the world, and only one short of Susie's total. Mind you, Sir George was not exactly every girl's dream.

'How is Sir Hector now?'

'Absolutely fine, Sir George, it was only a flesh wound, and it has healed very well. The vet will be over later to take the stitches out.' Gruesome, she thought, naming your hunter after your dead father, but then Sir Hector, the person, had been alive when the horse was christened.

'Jolly good show,' said George, who had been at Eton. Lucy put Sir Hector's foot back onto the floor and peered at the little gash on his fetlock. It could have been a bit nasty there, he was lucky. He had caught it on something the last time Sir George had taken him out. This was particularly bad luck, because when Wilson and the gardener were sent out on their secret night-time forays with the oven-ready chickens, they checked the fences and hedges for anything sharp. One never knew if the hunt saboteurs might have been round, although it was unlikely that they would do anything which might endanger the horses.

Lucy grinned to herself. She wondered what Sir George would say if he knew that his daughter Zoë was an anti-hunting demonstrator. Lucy had seen her the last time she went home and rode with the Quorn. Meant to be at Butterton Ladies' College, too. Still, it was something of a joke these days. The Bumpstaple hunt rarely caught anything, and there were so many foxes on the estate that they were a genuine driving hazard at night. They dug huge holes in Mrs Groat's vegetable patch, and really it was probable that there were more foxes around Great Barking now, because of the hunt, than there would ever have been without it.

# Chapter Five

That Sunday was Caroline's birthday. It dawned sunny and fresh: a bright, Laura Ashley-coloured day. The church bell was ringing, announcing that this week's morning service was at Great Barking. They alternated, Great Barking, Little Barking and Bumpstaple. There were three services each Sunday: Early Communion, Morning Communion and Evensong. It was a source of constant irritation to Oliver Bush – although, of course, being a vicar he was only ever mildly annoyed – that the villagers were all so very villagey about it. No-one would up sticks and go to a service in the next village. Not even his wife. Rose was uncomfortable in the other villages, where different pecking orders applied. Her status as rector's wife in Great Barking was further enhanced by having been born there, but this counted for little in Bumpstable, where Marjorie Sythe was queen of the flower rota, nor in Little Barking, where Audrey Mainwaring ran the Women's Institute.

Caroline awoke to find that Henry and Josh were in bed with her. Normally this would have been rather sweet, especially as she could hear John downstairs making a cup of tea. Unfortunately, though, continence was not yet one of the twins' strong points and poor little India, who also shared the bed, had awoken to find something warm and wet seeping up through her babygrow by capillary action.

'Oh no!' Caroline had also realized that the warmth was not necessarily pleasant, and by the time John got back upstairs with her tea and presents, she had stripped the bed.

'I wanted you to open your presents before you got up,' he said, looking so crestfallen that she was filled with remorse for not having ignored the wee.

'Come on, let's sit on the carpet. Henry, Josh, if you wee on the Chinese rug I shall feed you to a monster.' She need not have worried; Henry and Josh were too busy adding pot pourri to her underwear drawer to waste time weeing on the carpet, Chinese or otherwise.

She opened her cards and presents: a Hermes scarf from her mother – she admired it and stroked it against her cheek, enjoying John's impatience as he waited for her to open the rest; novels from the boys, who were too involved with the drawer to come and be thanked properly; an Egyptian scent bottle from John's mother – it was rather beautiful, green and gold. It would match the bedroom, thought Caroline, who could not bear to have anything in a room which it did not match. It was fortunate that she planned to decorate rooms in almost every colour, it ensured that eventually there would be a place for everything. What was this? A book on training parrots from India. It took a moment for the significance to sink in. Then she realized what it must mean.

'Oh John, you mean I can have a parrot?' She had always wanted a parrot, ever since her childhood visits to Great Aunt Mathilda, who had kept one in Brighton. That unfortunate bird had been named Little Willie, and the stigma of it had affected him deeply. Despite all efforts to teach him to be polite, his conversation had remained limited to insults and lewd suggestions. He had nevertheless had charm, and he had known more names for the male organ than Caroline had ever heard anywhere else, before or since.

'I think you had better come downstairs now,' said

79

John, and she saw that it was true. There, resplendent on his perch in a shining cage, was a blue-and-gold macaw. He eyed Caroline suspiciously and said nothing. 'He's called Solomon,' said John. 'He's three.'

Caroline was overwhelmed. 'But he must have cost a fortune.'

'He was going cheap,' said John, grinning.

Caroline hugged him. 'Why did I marry a man with such an awful sense of humour?'

'Simple. You married me for my willy.'

'Willywillywilly,' said Josh. The twins had been amazed into silence by the presence of Solomon, who was, it should be said, a very large bird.

India started to wriggle, her attention span exhausted, and Henry was getting hungry. ''Enry want tiger Mummy. Tigertigertiger!'

'He wants the breakfast cereal with the tiger on the packet,' said Caroline. The trouble with twins was that they developed their own language. In some ways it was wonderful that they were sufficient unto themselves, but in some ways it wasn't.

'Wawk!' said Solomon, surprisingly loudly. Reaching down to his reservoir of mixed nuts, he selected a peanut, held it in one claw and then cracked it open with his great black beak. Once the nut was extracted, he stripped the parchment skin off with his peculiar black tongue. Then he ate it, thoughtfully. The twins watched, fascinated, cereal forgotten.

'He's wonderful,' said Caroline, kissing John. 'Thank you so much.'


By chance, a chance of which they were quite unaware, Hetty had the same birthday as Caroline. Alistair had placed a neat package beside her plate at breakfast. On opening it, Hetty found a string of pearls. They were beautiful, although for some reason the phrase 'pearls before swine' sprang into mind.

'Happy birthday,' said Alistair, and kissed her on the lips. It was not a tender kiss, nor a passionate kiss, nor even an unpleasant kiss. It was just a kiss.

'Thank you,' she said, 'they're lovely.' She put them on and Alistair did up the clasp. They felt cold and smooth against her neck. They were beautiful, but Hetty felt a little flat. Perhaps she was being unfair, after all, Alistair led a busy life, but you didn't have to think terribly hard, nor plan terribly carefully, to buy pearls. You just opened your wallet in the jeweller's shop, and if your wallet was as thick as Alistair's, that didn't hurt. Hetty liked gifts to be given with thought, planning and love in them, however little they cost. Once, when they were just starting out, Alistair had bought her a toilet flush on a chain from an antique shop and she had adored it. In fact, hadn't he waltzed around the bedroom with it, stark naked and singing 'True Love'?

The children did not disappoint her. Finn produced a wooden trinket box which was clearly the result of hours of labour in Design Technology, as woodwork was now called. Luke had bought her a pair of gardening gloves and a tin of slug pellets. She wondered, not for the first time, where he got his sense of humour from. Jonathan had bought her a little peach tree to plant in the garden, and Rory's gift, which he produced rather shyly, was a painting. It was a slightly abstract picture of a string quartet, which he had framed himself. Hetty loved it.

'Oh Rory, it's marvellous. Alistair, do look.' Couldn't he see how talented his son was?

No. One could see it in his face. He made things worse by joking, 'We've had you boys' pictures on these walls since you were at playgroup. I suppose one more won't hurt.'

Hetty glared at him, but Rory was used to his casual cruelty. It was so casual that it hardly seemed to be deliberate at times. He set his features a little and gave his mother a hug. It hurt her, he knew, far more than it hurt him. 'I'm glad you like it.' He had known that his father would say something derogatory, but then Alistair's opinions on art were about as valid as Attila the Hun's on fly fishing. Mind you, who knows what Attila did in his spare time? 'Do you suppose,' he asked Jonathan pointedly, ignoring Alistair, 'that Attila the Hun was actually christened as that?'

'Just Attila, I should think,' said Finn, taking the question at face value.

'Like Alexander the Great and Luke the Fabulous,' added Luke.

'Luke the dickbrain,' said Finn.

'Finn!' said Hetty and Alistair in chorus, and they all laughed, but Rory had not forgotten his father's mean-spiritedness, and after a while he slipped out of the house.

The sun was becoming quite hot. May could be truly splendid as exam time approached. Rory hardly noticed the blue sky, the fluffy cottonwool clouds drifting in idle contemplation of the slightly stirring tree-tops. The trees rustled, making a sound like rain, but there was no rain. The whir and hum, drone and throb of a variety of lawnmowers provided the backing which somehow seemed to define the scene as English.

The Ormondroyds, of course, had a gardener riding a sit-upon mower. John and Caroline had an ordinary petrol mower, and the Groats and the Beans had little electric ones. Alistair owned a sit-upon. *Just like Dad*, thought Rory bitterly. He would have bought it just for the pleasure of looking impressive, of showing himself to be one of those people whose land ownership requires the purchase of a sit-upon mower. He could imagine him in the garden centre saying, 'Well, we have a couple of acres of lawn. Of course it needs to be simple to use. It won't be me using it, you see, although I do so occasionally.' Foolish Father. Give him a bimbo sales assistant and then just sit back and watch. He couldn't manoeuvre the damned thing around the apple trees, and in fact it was Hetty who mowed the lawn most of the time, using a push-along mower. Alistair might enjoy implying that he employed various domestic staff, but in fact Hetty's only help was a lady who did some ironing for her once a week.

Rory kicked a non-existent stone, turning off the main road and heading down The Street and past the Hall. He could see Caroline Potter, through the hedge, playing in the garden with her children. Lucky old Henry and Josh, you would always have someone if you were a twin.

'Oh no!' he heard her cry. 'Josh, why didn't you use your potty?'

Rory wondered why people had children. He didn't know why on earth his father had had four. Perhaps, he speculated, his father had been a different man twenty years ago. He tried to imagine his father changing nappies, making love to his mother. He couldn't. Sarah Struther must be in her potting shed – he could hear the sound of *Gianni Schicchi* coming from her garden. Rory decided on impulse to go and see. He wouldn't talk to her about his father, that was too raw today, but he could talk to her about music and art, which would soothe his angry heart. He knew in any case that Sarah would dismiss Alistair as being trivial and of being the one with the problem. They had had such conversations before.

He let himself in through the gate. Sarah's potting shed was really a wooden studio with a glass roof. It was situated on the far side of her garden, up against the cypress hedge which separated her from the river. The studio door was slightly ajar, but he couldn't hear the electric wheel. He could hear Kiri te Kanawa singing, '*O mio babbino caro*'. It was Sarah's favourite aria. Not wishing to interrupt the music, for Rory had great reverence for music, he pushed the door gently a few inches and walked around it.

Sarah was completely naked. It was often her habit to do her work in the nude, temperature permitting. She felt far more in touch with the form and texture of her work, more at one with it. She felt that in shaping her clay she was allowing some external life-force to pour through her, to concentrate in her hands and sculpt the essence of her creations. She felt that she translated rather than created, and that anything could be her inspiration. Sometimes she worked in silence, translating birdsong, the murmurs of trees, the sound of wind and rain, the hum of bees, the buzz of an unwanted fly, the lowing of a cow – even the hunt bugles could alter a line or edge. Often, though, particularly when she was applying colour, she listened to opera. Puccini for light, bright, airy colours, Mozart for primaries, Wagner for richer, darker tones, Verdi for autumnals and Bizet for aquamarines. She often used her fingers and hands to apply the colour, and today her hands were green and turquoise. The rest of her was a smooth, unblemished olive-brown.

Rory noticed all and yet none of this. Her body filled his visual field like a revelation complete with heavenly trumpets. An entire millennium passed in a millisecond as it seemed that the history of mankind paled into insignificance next to what he could see. He had never seen anything, anyone so perfectly beautiful. She was woman, rounded and soft and, well, the word 'mammary' loomed large in his mind. She was light brown all over, and her skin was as smooth and unmarked as a baby's. Her long, dark hair hung down to her waist, and her breasts moved constantly as her hands applied paint to a smoothly rounded jug with a curved handle and a full lip. Then, to his intense alarm, he became aware of the growing and insistent pressure in his crotch. Oh God. He started to blush.

Sarah chose that moment to look up from her absorption in the pot. 'Why, Rory,' she said softly, 'I do believe you're pleased to see me.'


Nothing had prepared him for how wonderful he would feel, or how proud. Turquoise paint would never seem ordinary again. Rory lay on his back staring up at the cottonwool clouds through the studio roof. He felt beautifully drained. His thing actually *throbbed*.

'Aren't you going to say anything?' asked Sarah, lying on one elbow and watching him with amused affection. She had had some idea that Rory was something of an odd one out in his family – but what passion there was in him. How absolutely lovely he had been!

'That was wonderful,' Rory found his tongue at last – to speak with, that is – 'I mean I'd never before, you know, actually—'

'Made love,' said Sarah, 'or fucked. It's the same thing. Whichever you prefer.' She watched him flinch through narrowed eyes. 'They do refer to the same thing, you know.'

'It was lovely,' said Rory, then, 'you must think me an awful fool, really naïve.'

'Not at all,' said Sarah. 'It was truly lovely. I have had a number of lovers in my life, but an experience such as we have just shared goes in with the great.'

'Do you mean that? Or are you just trying to pep up my ego?'

Sarah grinned. 'I mean it, and there's more pepping

up than your ego, just now,' she slid a hand over his turquoise-striped body, and Rory could feel his interest rising.

Later they talked again. Rory, exquisitely tender, and delighted by the sensation, was playing with Sarah's amazingly thick hair, and wondering at the apparent total absence of moles and freckles from her body. 'Do you know, you are quite unblemished,' he said.

Sarah laughed her rather explosive laugh. 'Hah! That has to be the most inaccurate statement you've made so far.'

He kissed her shoulder, loving the feel and taste of her skin. She was so glorious, so unashamedly erotic.

'I've probably ruined you,' said Sarah, 'you'll be sexually fixed on huge fat women.'

'You're not fat,' said Rory, 'you're just voluptuous.'

'You make me sound like a strawberry blancmange,' said Sarah, stretching, and enjoying the gentle exchange. Through the ceiling she could see a fluffy cloud shaped just like a heart.

Rory rolled onto his stomach and rested on his elbows. 'I suppose you think this is just a one-off,' he said.

Sarah eyed him suspiciously. 'Rory, darling, you're not to declare undying love for me. I'm far too old for you.'

Rory, who had been planning to do just that, modified his approach with an instinctive wisdom which neither he nor Sarah had known he possessed. 'Don't write me off just yet,' he said slyly. 'I have a lot to learn, and the summer is only just beginning.'

Sarah stroked his cheek. 'What would your parents think?'

'Dad would say, "Thank God he's not gay," and Mum would say, "I'm just concerned about your happiness, dear." ' He didn't really much care what they said, not even Hetty. Right now he could imagine nothing more blissful than to bury himself in Sarah for the rest of the summer – quite literally, in fact, and beginning right now.

Sarah's lips twitched. The powers of an eighteen-year-old boy in the repeat performance stakes are, of course, legendary, but she had not actually experienced them before. How she had missed out at eighteen, when her lover had been thirty-six. Now fate had reversed the roles. If she were a man they would say she must be at That Time of Life. She wriggled a little to accommodate Rory. As she did so, she felt an answering wriggle, deep in her womb. It so surprised her that she said, 'Oooh,' aloud. Rory, delighted at such a response, continued that which he had begun, and the distant 'bong, bong,' of the church bell accompanied him perfectly.


Hetty could not sleep that night. She told herself that it was the heat, the owls, the first sign of the menopause, but avoided telling herself that it was anything to do with the unsatisfactory lovemaking or the rather flat birthday. In fact Alistair had thought the lovemaking perfectly satisfactory, but that was hardly any recommendation. After all, Hetty thought, if Cyrano de Bergerac had been only satisfactory as a lover, no-one would ever have fancied him at all. At least not after the first time. Satisfactory might be good enough for school dinners, ironing boards and motorway service stations, but it was not nearly good enough for sex. She slipped out of bed, not worrying about a dressing-gown as it was a warm night. The air felt gentle and soft on her bare arms as she walked downstairs. Jess, sleeping by the back door, looked up questioningly, then struggled to her feet resignedly as her mistress went outside.

Hetty's voluminous cotton nightdress blew against her, outlining her body like a half-sculpted statue, only shaped where the wind blew. The grass was cool and damp beneath her feet, blades tickling between her toes where Alistair had once used to tickle when they watched TV together in the evenings. She paced the garden slowly, Jess ambling behind, wondering in a doggy sort of way if this was going to be a regular thing.

Perhaps the progress of all marriages could be judged by the amount of tickling that the feet got. *I bet*, she thought, *that those old dears who have their fiftieth anniversary on* News East, *and claim that they're still sweethearts, have foot-tickling sessions. Only true love loves the gap between the toes, for one never knows what one may find there. I wonder if those old couples had crises in their forties? Perhaps that's all this is, my personal crisis.* Hetty stopped at the edge of the garden, where it met the far corner of the churchyard, and stared at the graves. This was her favourite thinking spot, hidden by its hollow from the road. 'Perhaps I just need to sort myself out,' she said to Jess. 'Perhaps I should wear beads and go to Nepal to smoke pot. That would certainly make a change.'

Jess whined slightly. She rather fancied going back to bed, but loyalty exerts a powerful pull if you are a dog.

'I need a bit of a lift,' said Hetty. 'I feel old and stale. Perhaps there's a new me trying to get out.' She remembered an advert which she had seen earlier in the evening, implying that all one required in order to change one's life was a new form of feminine protection. That made her think of another advert she had seen recently: for Carol Sheldon's beauty salon . . .

She stayed there for a little while, thinking. Jess dozed off and dreamed her doggy dreams, which usually featured Hetty, very slow rabbits, or both.

\*     \*     \*

Hetty had gone along to the salon the very next afternoon, whilst the impulse to act on her midnight idea was still strong.

'Do you like it?' asked Carol Sheldon, showing Hetty her reflection in the mirror.

Hetty wondered if anyone ever dared say no, I hate it, you've made me look like a Cindy doll. She said, 'Yes. Yes I do,' quickly, before she was tempted. She eyed the awful arrangement of her red curls on top of her head. At least it wasn't cut, just pinned and sprayed. She could taste the hair spray at the back of her throat. It tasted like fly killer.

'It's a new you,' said Carol smugly.

'Goodness,' said Hetty mildly, thinking *I wish*. Her face looked like porcelain, evened up and matte-finished. Her eyes looked, to her own mind, attractive only to another panda, and Carol's curling and spreading of her eyelashes gave her the startled appearance of an American Country and Western singer. Her lips shone with the delightfully named Faded Apricot lipstick; she had been tempted to point out that apricots did not fade, they shrivelled, but it had seemed like splitting hairs. They did not look like her lips – they had been outlined in 'peach tint' pencil to resemble Madonna's.

'See how the blusher gives shape to your face,' said Carol, who liked to feel that her clients walked in totally unaware of what make-up could do for them, and walked out feeling that because of it their lives had just begun.

'Alistair will be surprised,' said Hetty, thinking that Alistair would hate it. She had always believed that men liked all women to look like bimbos, apart from their wives, who must look like Madonnas. Well, at least I've got the lips for it. She paid Carol, thanked her effusively and skulked out of the salon, hoping against hope that she would see no-one she knew in Broomhill, or that if she did they would fail to recognize her. Stopping only in Woolworth's to buy some nail varnish remover, she abandoned all plans to do any more shopping, but fled for the sanctuary of her car. Once inside it she furkled in the glove compartment, found an old tissue and scrubbed at her lips.

Driving home, she wondered about all those before-and-after women in magazine make-overs. Do they scrub it all off before they get home? I bet they do.

The eyelashes were the worst. Carol had used several layers of waterproof gunk, and the liner had slid in between the lash roots. Having no teenage daughter, Hetty had no lotions and potions in the bathroom cabinet to come to her aid, so she had to scrub at her face for a good ten minutes with soap and a flannel until at last she managed to find herself again. Thank goodness. There had been that silly unreasonable fear that it would never come off, that she would be permanently changed.

She made herself a cup of coffee and sat down with a magazine, her feet on Jess, who was a willing footstool. She found the before and after page. Yes, those women's smiles were definitely insincere, and most of the 'before' pictures had clearly been taken in as bad a light as possible. She sighed. 'Well, Jess, I don't know what that was all for. I suppose I thought that perhaps there was someone different inside me, just waiting to come out.' What had she been thinking of? That she could surprise Alistair with a newer, more attractive Hetty? Surprise him into what, exactly? It just went to show that the person underneath could not be disguised. 'I suppose,' she said to Jess, 'that if he doesn't like me the way I am, then there isn't really a lot that we can do about it.' She remembered how once, and it seemed such a short time ago, Alistair had lavished praise on her every feature. He had said that he loved her wild red hair, had extolled the beauty of her scattering of freckles, her heart-shaped face, her wide-spaced green eyes. Now all these same features seemed to be faults which Carol Sheldon felt the need to disguise with the suitable placement of brown eye shadow, apricot-vomit blusher and hairpins. She could hear Carol's voice still, echoing in her head, 'If you put the blusher here it draws attention away from the point of your chin, makes your face look more oval.' Rats to that.

'You don't see men rushing off for makeovers,' she grumbled to Jess, then thought that perhaps, in a way, you did. They became weight-conscious, changed their aftershave, started exercising. Could Alistair perhaps be trying to change? He had certainly bought some new aftershave recently. Perhaps it was just the fear of middle age. That reminded her of something which she had read in the *Daily Mail* when she was at the dentist's. She searched her mind. Oh, yes, it had been 'How To Tell If Your Man Is Having An Affair'. No. That was too ridiculous to contemplate. She wandered over to the mirror, taking the coffee cup, and looked at herself again. It was, essentially, the same face that she had always had. The years had aged it, but the differences were subtle. It was difficult to define exactly what it was that made her look like a woman in her forties rather than one of twenty-five. A few more lines, of course, perhaps a little less plumpness in the cheeks.

'Stop it,' she told her reflection, 'you can't blame yourself.' After all, how many long-married couples *really* look at one another, facially? *We're just stale. We need to revamp our marriage, assuming, that is, that we really want to. Do I really want Alistair still, for Alistair, or is it more for stability and convenience? Do I really love him? How on earth do I tell?* Hetty fingered her pearls, noticing for the first time that she hadn't taken them off since Alistair fastened them the previous day. She sighed.

## Chapter Six

India Potter slumped in her baby seat, pulling a wizened-old-man face, and shut her mouth firmly against the puréed carrot. She had decided not to accept anything off a spoon today – it made life more interesting.

'She won't take it,' John said to Caroline.

'Keep trying,' she said, without sympathy. After all, she did this all the time; why shouldn't John help on his afternoon off?

India assumed an expression of intense concentration. It was quite clear what she was doing now, but in case further clues were needed, she emitted a series of gentle farting noises, fast and satisfied, like a revving moped.

'I don't blame you,' said John, giving up on the carrot, 'it does look like something someone ate earlier, doesn't it?' He hauled India out of her high chair, getting her legs caught in the process. She smiled and giggled. This was much more fun than mush on a spoon. Suddenly overcome with adoration for her, John hugged her, kissing her perfect cheek and receiving in return a wide-mouthed toothy slobbering on his own. The rancid but oddly pleasant smell of partially-weaned-baby poo filled his nostrils. She sank her two teeth into his face.

'Ow! She bloody bit me!' He held her away from him and she grinned in huge delight. Things were getting better by the minute.

Henry Potter, sitting at the table, realized that no-one

was paying any attention to him. He upturned his dinner plate.

'Mummy, look Enry!' shouted Josh.

'Oh, Henry, that was naughty.'

Silence from Henry.

'Yosh good, Mummy,' said Josh smugly, taking advantage of Henry's disgrace. 'Yosh eat dinner.' He showed his empty plate.

'Did you, Josh? Good boy.' Caroline mopped up the remains of Henry's tomato sauce.

'Yosh throw dinner,' said Henry in mutinous tones. Mummy did not respond to this, so he climbed down under the table and emerged with a handful of beans in order to demonstrate the whereabouts of Josh's dinner.

'Oh God.' Caroline felt the last of her energy drain away. 'John, take them into the lounge and put a video on.' John, wiping India's saliva off his face before it digested him, did not hear. How often, Caroline reflected, crawling under the table with kitchen towels and a dishcloth, had she promised herself that she would never resort to videos to occupy her children? Plans were one thing, reality another. There was a splatting noise.

'I wish that bird wouldn't crap on the floor,' said John, who only used bad language under stress.

'At least Solomon's doesn't smell,' said Caroline, 'which, I might add, is more than I can say for the other members of the household.'

John was still holding India, and she was playing the throwing-her-head-about game. 'Ow!' India's hard little head hit him, clunk, on the breastbone. She wondered whether to howl.

'God, I'm sick of mess.' Caroline sat on the floor and stared despondently at the messy table. The doorbell rang. 'Oh no. It's just bound to be someone who wants to come in,' she struggled to her feet. 'Someone who dislikes mess. John, will you clear it up?' It was Hetty at the door. Caroline supposed that she had seen her fair share of mess over the years.

'Can I come in? I'm on the scrounge.'

'What about the baby?' Caroline peered past her at the huge carriage pram out in the drive.

'That's no baby, that's my white-elephant collection,' said Hetty. 'I'm after things for the stall.'

'Come through!' called John from the kitchen. He sounded desperate. The twins had got under the table with the remains of Josh's dinner. It took a little while to clean them up. Caroline used vast quantities of kitchen roll and threw it all in the bin. It wasn't environmentally friendly, but sometimes she was past caring. Hetty put their discarded clothes into the washing machine.

'I got pink tinkler,' Henry announced confidingly.

'I gather that the fête is to be here, then,' said Hetty, helping Henry into clean trousers.

'Is it?' It was the first time poor John had heard about it.

Caroline looked helpless. 'Well, I offered, sort of half-heartedly really, you know. They were worried that there was nowhere to have it. But the vicar's wife didn't seem very keen.'

'I'm sure she wasn't,' said Hetty. 'You'll have stolen her thunder. She's a bit like that. Really, though, we're all terribly grateful. There just isn't anywhere else.'

'Oh well.' It wasn't that Caroline's offer had not been genuine – it had – but she was prone to making offers based on optimism and generosity, then being filled with pessimism and dread if they were accepted.

'Don't look so glum,' said John, who knew a *fait-accompli* when he saw one, 'be positive. It's arranged now, we'll get to know everyone, and we get to keep the left-over white elephants.'

'Lonts in ky,' said Josh, clearly troubled. 'Lonts turn off light.'

'What's that?' John had trouble understanding the twins at times.

'Elephants,' said Caroline, filling the kettle, 'in the sky. When we had the storm last week I told them that the thunder was elephants playing up there. Then the lights went out.'

'Say el-e-phant,' said John to Josh.

'Lont,' said Josh distinctly.

'Ellylont,' said Henry proudly.

'Enry say lont,' said Josh, 'lont in ky.'

Hetty sat on a pine chair and ignored the tomato sauce into which she had just put her elbow. 'No clothes,' she said, 'for the stall, but anything else. You will enjoy having it here, you know. Everyone will muck in.'

Caroline could not imagine Rose Bush or Mrs Groat doing any mucking. 'We're always so disorganized here,' she said.

'I think you do brilliantly,' said Hetty stoutly, 'with all these children.' She casually cleared the rest of the sauce with her elbow lest Caroline should see it. 'You know I'll help.'

'I'm on call that day,' said John. India began to complain, and he lifted her back out of her chair. India spent much of her life being lifted in and out of various chairs whilst people cleared up after her twin brothers. She squeaked in excitement, and dribbled generously on John.

'You'll have to swap your duty,' said Caroline.

'I'm only teasing,' said John. 'How about me doing some magic?' Caroline was doubtful but Hetty was fascinated. 'I didn't know that you were a magician,' she said, delighted. 'That would be wonderful. The children would love it.'

'Well, it would be easy enough to do a short routine if the fête were here in the garden,' said John, warming to the idea.

Caroline could see that the whole matter was out of her hands. She passed Hetty her tea. 'Well, I'm sure we can sort out some lonts for your stall,' she said, resignedly.

A little later, Jessie Bean inserted the huge iron key into the ancient oak church door furtively, and entered with stealth. This was quite an achievement as she was carrying a bucket of water, but in these days of dwindling congregations the church had to make all the savings it could, so the mains water had been cut off long ago. Jessie had a heart of gold, and it shone. She helped to clean the church in rotation with Mrs Groat. Together they formed a two-woman mini army of brass polisher, furniture polisher and floor cleaner. The rich, gentle gleam of the oak pews, the glowing ecclesiastical shine in the brasses, the freshly laundered altar cloths – all owed their state of grace to these two ladies. One could tell whose week it was by a sniff at the altar cloth. Lavender meant that Jessie had done it, vinegar meant Mrs Groat. It was oddly appropriate when you thought about it.

Jessie was not here to launder the altar cloth. It was Mrs Groat's week, and Mrs Groat would be in tomorrow to do her share. Therefore Jessie had, as always, waited until she knew Mrs Groat would be watching TV, so that she could sneak unnoticed past her house, in order to clear the bat droppings from the church in secret. Mrs Groat hated the bats. Many decades earlier, when hiding in a belfry in Sussex – for some complicated reasons which involved a goat, which she had genuinely believed to be rabid – a bat had become entangled in her hair. This unlikely event had so upset her that in her mind all bats were huge, hairy, evil creatures, repositories of ill-will and possibly

96

lurking vampires. She hated the bats in St Jude's with a vengeance, and would gladly have sprayed them with something very toxic had she dared. They were, in her view, the stuff of horror and darkness, the source of vast, putrefying, poisonous heaps of guano. They probably carried TB, anthrax and plague. She had been known to become quite enraged on the subject. Jessie, though, was fond of the bats. It always seemed to her that the oak roof and crossbeams high in the church were probably carved from the very same oak trees which had been the bats' original home in a woodier England. They had a right to them.

It was because of her strong feelings on the subject that she always came into the church a day before Mrs Groat, to clear the droppings. It helped keep the peace, particularly as the droppings always accumulated particularly badly around the back few pews on the right, which were, as fate would have it, Mrs Groat's particular territory. One would almost think the bats knew. For years, Jessie had de-batted the church on Thursdays, and Mrs Groat had never known. It was ironical that the very reason she always sat where she did was that she had always, upon cleaning, found it to be the most dropping-free area in the church. Did she not come in every Friday and find droppings everywhere but there? The bats surely knew and respected her. Jessie was no fool. She knew that Mrs Groat expected bat droppings, so once she had finished with her pan, brush and mop she would always scatter a few, arrange them for Mrs Groat to find. She often wondered if perhaps she was the only woman in the world who could claim arranging bat droppings as a regular hobby.

This particular Thursday, Jessie also planned to feed the mice who were nesting in two of the organ pipes. They lived in the top C-sharp pipe, and the bottom E flat. They had not been disturbed for years, as Jacob never used the relevant keys. They were too far away for him to see, and in any case he played all hymns in the key of C major, and did not believe in black notes, which accounted for his particular style. Jessie was fond of the mice. She brought them bread and bits of stale cheese, which she poked under the organ. It was, in fact, while she was crumbling cheese that Jessie was sprung. Fortunately she was not sprung by Mrs Groat, but by Hetty, with a jug of water and a bunch of chrysanthemums.

They greeted one another warmly. Hetty assumed that Jessie was taking her usual turn at the cleaning; she was not aware of the clues one could glean by sniffing the altar cloth. She explained that she had merely popped in to water and spruce up the flowers, this being her month to arrange them. Jessie, though, felt obliged to explain exactly what her nefarious purpose had been, just in case Hetty should think she had been planning to escape to Fiji with the silver candlesticks. Hetty was charmed to hear of Jessie's years of secret service to the bats of Great Barking. It seemed remarkable that she had managed to keep her activities secret from Mrs Groat, whom Hetty suspected of omniscience, although, of course, anyone else seeing Jessie unlocking the church would simply assume that she was going in to clean. It was, she thought, philosophically quite fascinating. Jessie's clearing up and then rearranging bat dung for Mrs Groat was an act of power, for Jessie was taking over Mrs Groat's role and then manufacturing for her a new one. She had also effectively chosen where Mrs Groat sat every Sunday morning. Hetty found it refreshing to think that Mrs Groat was being organized by Jessie, and all on account of a dozen or so pipistrelles. How wonderful!

The removal of a few wilting carnations did not take

long, and Hetty volunteered to help Jessie with her fascinating task. As they scraped at the poo, which Hetty planned to use on her dahlias, for who knew what might result, their conversation turned again to the Ormondroyds and the fête.

'I feel,' said Jessie, 'that Lady Angela should open the fête. Dear Lady Sybil is a little beyond us, but we should try to keep things in the family. Angela would do it very well. She is a most insincere woman, so the welcoming speech would come easily to her.'

Hetty giggled. It was quite a revelation to hear the mild and sweet Jessie speaking her mind. 'Perhaps we ought to ask Sir George directly why he isn't holding it at the Hall,' she said.

'Probably not worth trying,' said Jessie, scraping at the top of the remembrance plaque where the bats had created a little monument of their own. 'I doubt if you would hear the truth. I am quite sure that Angela has manipulated him.'

'Heaven knows how,' said Hetty, trying valiantly to suppress a very graphic image of Angela manipulating George, certainly not in the manner which Jessie had meant. It was a particularly unwelcome image, as it exposed to her imagination parts of George which she would have preferred to avoid, even in thought. 'They don't even seem to like one another most of the time.'

'They don't need to,' said Jessie, and Hetty suddenly wondered if perhaps they were on the same wavelength after all. 'They belong to the upper class, Angela and George. They live by different rules to the rest of us.'

They cleaned for a while in silence.

'Perhaps Rose should open the fête,' said Hetty after a while.

'No, I don't think she would want to,' said Jessie, 'although Greta hopes that *she* will be doing it. It seems that Rose may have asked her already.'

Hetty was surprised, but did not like to say so – Jessie and Greta were friends, after all. She resolved to keep well out of the whole dilemma of fête-opening. 'It doesn't seem to mark the wood,' she said, changing the subject.

'No,' said Jessie, 'we keep the wood well oiled. It's probably a bit stained high up in the rafters, but we can't get up there to clean.'

'You could always send Jacob up on a rope,' said Hetty, giggling.

'Don't laugh,' said Jessie. 'We did, in nineteen sixty-two. The fire brigade had to come and rescue him.'

Hetty gaped. 'Really?'

'Yes,' said Jessie, 'it caused quite a stir. You couldn't do it now, of course. It would disturb the bats. They're protected, you know.'

Hetty thought the bats must be pretty disturbed by the congregation's hymn-singing at times; after all, it would disturb a colony of deaf sarcophagi. 'Are they registered anywhere,' she asked, 'so that someone knows to protect them?'

'I'm not sure,' said Jessie, 'but there are some bat men in Cambridge, a preservation group of some sort. Perhaps we ought to give some of the profit from the fête to them.'

'I think that's a marvellous idea,' said Hetty, thinking how much Mrs Groat would hate the idea. 'Perhaps we ought to suggest it?' She wondered if the bat men would come to collect it, and if so whether they would wear their underpants over their trousers.

'Well, it usually all goes to church funds; I think the Fête Committee decides. It would be a nice gesture to give a little to the bats, though. It is their church too.' In her heart of hearts, Jessie knew that she would get a deep satisfaction from suggesting that the bats should benefit, a satisfaction born of more than just altruism. It would be her revenge against Greta Groat, for all the secret years of scraping guano. She had done the job willingly, of course, but not with pleasure, not really. It had been more from the certain conviction that if she had not done it then Mrs Groat would, by now, have found some way to harm the bats. She would have found a wood polish made from volatile warfarin, a window cleaner with paraquat, anything to slowly finish them off. In all these years, Jessie had never yet found a dead bat, but if she had, she would have suspected Mrs Groat as the agent of its demise. She believed that they went elsewhere to die. She was, as it happened, perfectly correct. They went to the belfry, which was sporadically swept by Jacob. He had never mentioned dead bats for fear of upsetting his wife, but he always interred them in their own little plot beside the entrance to the Ormondroyds' vault.

'Then we must be united at the next meeting of the Fête Committee,' said Hetty resolutely, 'and insist that the bats should benefit.'

Jessie felt that she had found a companion-in-arms. 'Here,' she said to Hetty, satisfied with their labours, 'help me scatter some droppings for Greta.' Then she added, throwing caution to the winds, 'This is the part I enjoy.'

Their chat was probably the cause of Hetty's rather odd dream that night, in which Jacob Bean, wearing only a loin cloth, hung by his ankles from a creeper in the church roof, polishing the rafters, while Jessie flung droppings wildly around the altar and Angela Ormondroyd and Greta Groat repeatedly declared the village fête open in glorious unison.

## Chapter Seven

'Hunting gives you piles,' said the sign.

Sir George glared, furious. Some person in a knitted bikini top was holding a placard next to his gates. Bloody hell! Sir George was of the opinion that if you gave these people an inch, there would be communists on the parish council. 'What the devil do you think you're doing?'

The figure emerged from behind her placard. It was Zoë. Bloody school *exeat* again, he supposed.

'Hello, Father. I'm prompting some original thought. After all, you hunt, you have piles, so it follows that—'

'I suppose this is some ridiculous reference to your wanting to leave Harpenden and go to some comprehensive.'

'Well, yes.' Zoë was George's daughter, and she always stood her ground. 'You do seem to suppose that because the newspaper boy goes to day school and he peed on the gravel that all day school pupils—'

'All right, I get the message.' He climbed out of the Range Rover and slammed the door. 'However, consider the subject dropped before it was ever raised.'

'Say!' shouted Zoe after him. 'What's all this about the fête? Mother says it's not going to be here. Can I ask my chums?'

'Chums?' Good God, wasn't that dog food?

'You know, friends.'

George thought that if her chums looked anything like Zoë, it was a blessing that he and Angela were not hosting the fête. They could have ended up with left-wing graffiti on the stable walls. Out of the corner of his eye he spotted two delightful rumps heading towards the stables. One was his horse, the other his groom. He felt a sudden urge to check up on his hunter.

'Pa?'

How could she call him that? It made him sound like a miner during the Great Depression. George expected a little more deference from his daughter. More than that, he expected gratitude. He had sired her, after all. If he had not chosen that exact moment to impregnate Angela, another second, a different sperm to the fore, then Zoë might have been Sebastian or Charles. She owed her life to him, not to mention her public school education. The fact that Zoë abhorred her school and hankered after Broomhill High struck him as irrelevant. She could not possibly be serious. Schools like that were for people who had to get jobs. No, Zoë was just interested in boys, and heaven help them all if she took up with any of the local louts. Why, she would be pregnant in a month. He knew Zoë.

George was wrong. He did not know his daughter at all, which was hardly surprising, as she had spent her life in the care of nannies and boarding schools. Zoë was one of the AIDS-aware New Generation. Her peers were interested in all-night parties, hunt protests, hairless pop stars, pyramids and celibacy. Even if he had tried, George could not possibly have understood, and George did not try.

Zoë was aware that her father's gaze was magnetically attracted to Lucy Bellingham's receding bottom. She personally considered it to be rather a horsey bum. It was a clever trick of nature, she thought, to give a certain class of Englishwoman bums like mares. This meant that the horse-minded men of their class could both fancy them and fantasize about bestiality at the same time, whilst they, once they had utilized their child-bearing hips, had a nice, stable seat on a horse. The disadvantage came, she supposed, when playing polo, for there was surely nothing worse than a polo player with a fat bum. Zoë regarded polo as the thinking woman's answer to hunting, and exercised her own bottom regularly to prevent it from ever looking like a mushroom.

'Father,' she persisted, 'the fête.'

'What? Ho hum. Yes indeed, your mother felt that we should not have the fête here this year. Your grandmother is ill, after all, and the village people have made rather a mess in the past.'

The trouble with weak excuses made by one who does not really believe in them, is that they sound exactly what they are. George was certainly not about to explain to his daughter that his own motives for going along with Angela's wishes had nothing to do with the fear of a few squashed dahlias. He was secretly rather daunted by Zoë, who seemed to him a creature from another world. Like most people in such circumstances, he became defensive and brusque.

'It really is time the fête was elsewhere,' he said. 'It really is too much work for Angela. She does so much.'

Zoë was well aware that by most people's standards her mother did nothing at all, but she couldn't be bothered to argue. Her parents were obviously in it together. 'I s'pose it is a bit feudal, lording it over them all,' she said. 'I guess the villagers are lucky that *droit-de-seigneur* isn't written into their freeholds.'

George, who had actually often fantasized about just such a situation, was lost for a reply. The child sounded not only sexually precocious, but almost like a liberal democrat. Liberal democrats were about as far left as George's imagination could comfortably go. Anything further meant communists, which he saw as another word for hardened criminals. It was lucky that he had not seen the nose stud: Zoë had not felt ready yet for the inevitable confrontation, and so had taken it out and powdered over the hole.

She had also sloped off before he could think of a suitably freezing response. To his annoyance, she was heading for the stables, foiling his own plan to get a better look at Lucy's rear. To add insult to injury, he discovered that he was holding the placard. He wondered briefly if hunting *had* caused his piles. After all, both the hunting and the piles had been with him for as long as he could remember. He stomped back into the Hall, where his wife was on the telephone, as usual.

Angela Ormondroyd had one thing in common with Mrs Groat: she was not the sort of woman to beat about the bush. Having decided that she must visit Caroline Potter, she set about arranging it. 'Hello, Angela Ormondroyd speaking. I hear that you will be hosting this year's fête, so I thought I might pop around to give you a few pointers.'

'Oh, I . . . er . . . well, thank you, yes, that would be very helpful,' said Caroline, fighting Henry off with her free hand. Henry loved telephones, and was prone to snatching them from her and saying, 'Yes, yes, I love you too,' into them repeatedly. He had not telephoned anyone by himself yet, but he had picked up the receiver and heard the lady telling him to please replace it. This had excited him immeasurably, and he lived in hope of repeating the experience.

'Would this afternoon suit?' asked Angela, purely rhetorically, for before Caroline could step in and stall her, she added, 'I have a lunch in Newmarket, but could be with you around four,' and poor Caroline found that she had agreed. Thank God Angela's idea of lunch kept her busy until four. That left five hours in which

Caroline could tidy up, bake a cake for her guest to refuse, press the twins' nice dungarees and clean the guano out of the bottom of Solomon's cage. She must be sure to hide all the beans and ketchup, too. What would Angela think were she to discover that the Potter children's diet was so, well, unrefined? Caroline's Nanny had taught her at an early age how to eat grilled sole and asparagus – English, always – without making a mess. She felt endlessly guilty for feeding her own children on tinned pasta shaped like daleks and pizzas whose toppings had been applied in a factory. Henry and Josh unfortunately both loved baked beans, and Josh's recent acquisition of the word 'farted' into their vocabulary meant that Caroline was often embarrassed in the supermarket.

Calling in while on his rounds later that day, John was surprised to find her scrubbing the kitchen floor. He had been hoping for a nice relaxed sandwich after a particularly irksome summons to examine Sir George Ormondroyd's bottom. Private patients really weren't worth the necessary kow-towing and cosseting that they expected, but his predecessor at the practice had looked after George, and this happy mantle had been passed to him. At least Angela insisted on going to Harley Street for her own medical needs. John doubted that he could have faced the next ten years in daily dread of the onset of Angela's menopause. He had a lot of time for Lady Sybil, though, and for that reason he put up with George's obsession with his nether regions. It was going to be the smallest pile they had ever removed at the private clinic in Cambridge, if indeed they could find it, but it would cost just as much to remove as a large one. The vicar of Broomhill had one the size of a golf ball, and had hardly liked to complain. Still, it was George's money, and the private patient is always right. John could quite understand why George might prefer to spend his money on his bottom rather than on his wife.

'You mustn't clean up for Lady Ormondroyd,' he told Caroline indignantly, 'she invited herself, she should take us as she finds us.' He took the cloth off his wife and helped her to her feet.

'I suppose you're right,' said Caroline reluctantly. 'I just hate the place to be a mess when anyone comes.'

'It's not a mess.' John filled the kettle and picked up India, who was rather lopsided in her chair. 'It's lived-in.'

Caroline sighed. She knew that he was right, but she was glad that she had hoovered behind the settee and made a cake. She put the beans out of sight. John stayed for a little while. A GP's lot is no longer a happy round of golf, with the occasional short surgery interrupting normally balmy days of rest. It was not often that he called at home during the day, and when he did he was telephoned endlessly by the practice. Sadly, the days of dragon receptionists whose sole aim was to make sure that patients and doctors never met were also long gone, and the afternoon was usually spent doing house calls on people who were not at all ill or immobile, but who considered that at their age a weekly visit from doctor, vicar and district nurse was the very least they were entitled to. They often waited in specially, before going to the supermarket or out to Bingo.

In fact, by the time John had gone, summoned back to the practice by an urgent wart, it was time to put the kettle on for Angela, and Caroline felt calmly resigned. Henry and Josh were having a nap. They had been playing with condoms earlier, sorting them out by packet colour. Caroline had bought them rather furtively in Cambridge as she had stopped taking her Pill. The problem was, they looked far too silly to use. It had been a huge relief to her when the twins began to look

107

tired. The thought of what Angela would think if she saw them fighting with the black ones had been too awful to contemplate.

Angela breezed in at ten past four, having changed out of this year's Chanel into last year's Harvey Nichols in the process. It was pointless to wear a ten thousand pound suit when expecting to drink PG Tips out of an earthenware mug. In fact, she was about to be very pleasantly surprised. Caroline had been brought up to believe that tea was not tea unless served in a china cup, and she always brewed it in a pot. Strict rules, she had been taught, governed tea. Darjeeling for breakfast, Earl Grey after lunch; cake should not be chunky until half past five, and tea bags were absolutely forbidden.

Angela had been taught to recognize a certain kind of upbringing, the kind which relies on nannies and the proper way of doing anything, from the unacceptability of paper napkins to the importance of eating cake with a fork. Now she recognized it in Caroline, and was very pleased. It would make her task so much easier. She accepted a thin slice of Madeira cake and set about discovering the Potters' income, accent, lineage and social connections, those things which, for some people, define absolutely one's position in society. She liked to be sure that she had everyone correctly pigeonholed. It kept her in control.

Caroline had been quizzed by her mother's friends throughout her childhood. She had always felt that they were criticizing her, and this felt no different. Generally she had been correct in her assumption, although they had been critical because they did not understand her, rather than because she was at fault. She had not fitted the mould of her peers, for whom Queen Charlotte's Ball was the highlight of the early years, and brains were something which Italians cooked on a leek-and-olive sauce.

'So you are originally from Dorset?' Angela angled carefully, approving of the china and of the fact that Henry and Josh were nowhere to be seen. India was sitting placidly in her baby seat, externally digesting rusk, so with any luck she would not be required to handle her.

'Yes, near Dorchester,' said Caroline, 'my mother's family farm there.'

'Really?' Angela's antennae twitched. 'You don't happen to know of the Smythe-Stevens?'

An image of a dreadful woman with three chins and more than a passing resemblance to a stuffed trout shot into Caroline's mind. 'Yes,' she said faintly, 'they are friends of my parents.'

'Really? What did you say your mother's maiden name was?'

Caroline hadn't, of course. 'Stella Ffoulkes,' she said.

'My goodness me, you are one of *the* Ffoulkes!' Angela was amazed to discover that this poor downtrodden doctor's wife was from a proper family. 'I believe I may have met your mother last year at Glyndebourne.'

'You may well have done,' said Caroline, watching in suspended horror as a gob of India's rusk hit the carpet, and hoping that Angela would not notice. 'Mother's membership came up last year.'

Angela was a good five years down the waiting list for Glyndebourne, but was certainly not going to let on. How fortunate, though, that Caroline should be associated with her by the ties of class. 'It is very brave of you to host the fête,' she said, now seeing Caroline as someone to whom she could speak frankly. 'I just couldn't bear the idea of all those awful people from Broomhill with their shell suits and double pushchairs stamping on our lawns and stealing our asparagus.'

'I didn't realize they were that bad,' said Caroline mildly, secretly appalled by Angela's change of attitude towards her. It said far more about what a snob she was than her choice of words alone. 'It is in a good cause,' Caroline added.

'Oh yes, but they will use your bathroom, dear.' It had not occurred to Angela that Caroline might not be wholly with her. 'You must borrow my housekeeper to disinfect it all afterwards.'

Caroline helped Angela to more tea, and wondered what 'it all' would be. It hardly bore contemplation. Nor did Angela's housekeeper, who sounded like a bottle of bleach. Still, that was probably how Angela thought of her. 'You were going to give me some pointers,' she said, wondering what she should call her guest. She could not bring herself to call her Angela, but Lady Ormondroyd sounded awkwardly humble, and the very act of saying it would make her spit cake.

'Oh, do please call me Angela,' said Angela, separating Caroline completely from everyone else in the village by that single phrase. 'Yes, indeed. The main thing, of course, is to make sure that the village people do all of the clearing up. You must not be saddled with folding up trestle tables or picking up litter.'

'Oh, I'm sure they will,' said Caroline, hearing a thump from upstairs which meant that someone was out of bed.

'Indeed they must,' said Angela, launching from this stepping stone in full sail. 'I suggest, my dear, that you have someone experienced to open the fête, and to close it, too. When they draw the raffle and announce the prizes, that is the time for a little practised encouragement, to remind people of their duty.'

'I see what you mean,' said Caroline realizing, with sinking heart, exactly what Angela was getting at, and wondering desperately how to handle it. She knew that

Rose Bush would be terribly cross if she took it upon herself to make any arrangements with Angela about opening the fête. 'I will mention it to Rose – I'm sure she will arrange things properly.'

'I knew you would understand, dear.' Angela was in fact more confident than Caroline had realized. She felt no need to press the point further. She had said enough. Caroline was the right sort, and to Angela, Caroline's reference to arranging things 'properly' had clearly indicated that she would make sure that Angela was asked to open the fête. Of course, Angela fully intended to open it whether or not she was actually asked to do so, but it would be pleasing to receive a deferential committee asking for her help. Whatever happened, she would take her rightful place on the rostrum, and if that pretentious Mrs Bush or the awful Groat woman thought otherwise, they would not dare to say so. Her only concern, really, had been that Caroline herself might expect to do the honours, but she was clearly far too much of a mouse.

Caroline had gone to fetch the twins, who seemed to be having a riot upstairs, and Angela eyed India rather nervously. The baby waved her half-eaten rusk, wondering whether to offer Angela a suck, but deciding against it on the grounds that she looked far too much like that parrot.

Josh appeared first in the lounge and rushed up to Angela, who decided that it was clearly time that she was elsewhere. 'Mummy,' he said, as Caroline appeared in the doorway, 'lady farted.'

It was the clearest statement he had ever made, but Caroline was obliged, to her sorrow, to pretend she had not heard.

Angela took her leave a few minutes later. Tea had been pleasant, the Madeira cake pleasant, and she had been able to make clear to Caroline her expectations.

Caroline had turned out to be the Right Sort, even if she had rather fallen from grace by marrying a doctor and, though it hardly bore thinking about, breastfeeding his children. Still, the younger generation did that kind of thing these days, and since the recession there were plenty of perfectly acceptable people who had no domestic help whatsoever. She felt confident. She was aware, of course, that many of the older people in the village felt great loyalty to Lady Sybil, but they would soon transfer it to her. It was only natural. George's mother was hardly an object for admiration now. She might look like a sweet old lady, but underneath she was sharper than she appeared, an old harridan.

Angela detested her mother-in-law, but knew that she must not let it show. English society demanded that she must appear to look after her simple and aged relatives with patience and affection, and must never mention the unpleasantness of incontinence to anyone. It was fortunate, she thought, that she would be able to pay for the very best sort of nursing home. How on earth did the masses manage? Angela did not know, and did not much care.

Caroline, left behind, was busy with Henry and Josh, who had found a pot of red finger paint and used it to alarming effect in their bedroom. She was trying to wash it all off and keep them out of further mischief, while an awful worry buzzed in her head. It stemmed from the knowledge that Angela had somehow left *her* responsible for the village fête and, worse, for ensuring that Angela was firmly instated as Top Dog. Should she mention it to Rose? No, Rose would surely think that she was checking up on her or, worse still, trying to muscle in on the whole organization of the fête. She decided that she could do nothing except fervently hope that things would sort themselves out, that Rose would ask Angela to open the fête anyway, and she, Caroline, would not have to dabble in village politics. She had not yet realized that, merely by living in the village, she was already hopelessly entangled in village politics. That is the nature of the English village. The politics of trying not to have any politics is, in fact, considered particularly anarchic and undesirable. Like it or not, Caroline was involved, and she feared that if anything went wrong, it would be Her Fault.

Angela walked home. She could have asked Wilson to fetch her, but had decided that, on balance, she was unlikely to meet any common people between Yew Tree Cottage and the gates of the Hall, the distance being only forty yards. She was not planning to attend the final meeting of the Fête Committee, for she felt quite sure of her victory. She was, in any case, too great a snob to imagine that anyone in the village would dare to try to usurp her rightful place as speech-maker and prize-giver, now that she had made her wishes clear. There was, after all, a natural order in the village, and she was unquestionably on top. This thought reminded her of another, rather less public, aspect of her life. Sex with George had become a rather frequent event. You could even say it was often and regular, and it meant that Angela had been very glad that she had read about pelvic floor exercises in one of those awful weekly magazines. It had been awkward the first time, as the article had suggested that she should practise these unusual manoeuvres when washing dishes or waiting for the bus. Since she never did either of these things, she had wondered where to start. Finally she had surprised Cook by appearing at the kitchen sink armed with a teaspoon. Fortunately it had quickly become apparent that the muscles involved in actually washing the teaspoon were not the ones in which the magazine was interested, and she had retreated, relieved, to practise in the library.

The problem with the sex was that it was upsetting her routine. Poor Angela was having to go to bed twice, once after her bath with just a dab of moisturiser on her face, then again after IT, when she washed off the moisturiser and went through her normal ritual of creams and potions. The trouble was that Angela's night cream was a thick substance which would have found many applications in a piston engine, and if she had worn it during sex, then George might well have slid off her and onto the floor, always assuming that he had recognized her in the first place. She used it on her face, her throat, her neck and her chest. Then there was the anti-cellulite gel on her bottom and the rejuvenating gel around her eyes. It was terribly important, the lady in Harrods had explained, to apply these products last thing at night, after a bath, when the pores were open. Angela, who knew very little about pores, assumed that sexual activity might well close them, and it stood to reason that physical contact with George would disturb the lotions and potions so that – heaven forbid – a wrinkle or old-age freckle might creep in. What the anti-cellulite gel might do on contact with George's thing did not bear thinking about.

Therefore Angela needed two baths each night, one to prepare for George, and the second to prepare for the creams. Occasionally, when George was feeling particularly excitable, a third bath had been necessary. The other problem generated by the sex was still more awkward – it was that Angela had no-one to discuss it with. Her lunching friends in Knightsbridge spoke about sex a great deal, but not in relation to their husbands. Husbands were for credit cards and charity balls – definitely not for any other balls, except under duress on their birthdays. The public admission of regular and enjoyable copulation with George could mean social death.

Despite the pores and even despite Knightsbridge, Angela decided that there were plenty of reasons for the sex to continue, for she was developing a plan of even greater importance than the fête. She planned to get rid of Lady Sybil – not, of course, in any murderous sense, although that did have its appeal – but merely into a home. In any case, although she had not admitted it to herself, she was enjoying the sex far too much to give it up.

The day on which George had first brought her to Barking Hall, Lady Sybil had made it clear that she found Angela pretentious, brainless and a bore, and that had never changed. It was intolerable, having to put up with such a disparaging mother-in-law. Angela hated her. She hated her memory loss, her flashes of lucidity and her wicked old cackle. She hated her occasional incontinence, her denture glue and her long-line knickers. Most of all, she hated the constant feeling that Lady Sybil was laughing at her.

An episode the previous night had epitomized the problem for her. Angela was sorting through her underwear when Lady Sybil wandered into her bedroom. Whereas most women crumple their undergarments into a drawer beside the bed, Angela kept most of hers on special hangers in the wardrobe. The hangers were wooden, and had been made by a mystified local carpenter who had been sworn to secrecy. The reason behind this was the designer labels. Angela could almost have been said to have a fetish for designer underwear. She did keep a small drawer of underwear from the usual chainstore, for occasions when it did not matter. In fact, given Angela's previous apathy in the bedroom department, it was hard to imagine any occasion when it had mattered, but in fact she had a few simple rules. Designer knickers were for London, good hotels, weekends with friends and trips to gynaecologists. Chainstore covered the rest. Like most genuinely extravagant people, Angela was mean with her extravagance. She did not wish to waste her knickers. Furthermore, some of the designer wear bore such fancy lace – one pair was even pearl-encrusted – that it was actually quite uncomfortable to wear, so she also needed the other sort for occasional relief.

She had been highly annoyed at Lady Sybil's intrusion into her underwear-sorting. Since Angela's very first stay at the Hall, the old lady had always had a lot to say about spending large sums of money on one's underclothes. Angela had, unfortunately, deliberately slipped a mention of her collection into one of their early conversations in order to let her hostess know just how wealthy a family she came from. This misfired when Lady Sybil had hooted with laughter and shouted, 'The only sort of breeding that starts with your underwear, my girl, is the sort that finishes in the maternity ward!' Angela had never forgiven her.

Lady Sybil was wearing her habitual vacant expression, the one which Angela always felt was a screen behind which a mean, sharp old lady still lurked. 'Who are you?' she had asked, predictably.

'I am Angela, you silly old bat.' Angela actually had no manners at all when no-one else was listening, despite all her breeding. 'I live here.'

Lady Sybil wandered into the dressing-room where the knickers hung in a neat row. 'Are you a Turkish tart?' she asked.

'You ridiculous creature!' Angela retorted. 'Come out of my wardrobe.'

Lady Sybil came out. 'The last time I looked, this was *my* house,' she remarked haughtily. Sitting on the bed, her eyes had looked clear and sharp.

116

'As you well know,' Angela replied, 'Sir Hector put it in trust for George in his will, so it's not yours.'

'I am to live here,' Lady Sybil said with satisfaction, 'for ever.' This, of course, was Angela's great fear: that her mother-in-law might linger in Barking Hall for decades, embarrassing her at dinner parties and ruining the linen sheets. Cook simply could not just boil them, as though she were an Irish navvy, so Angela insisted that she threw them away when they were soiled. This explained the unusual number of homes in Broomhill with pure linen sheets on their beds. Their occupants were all related to Fred Perks, who worked the Barking and Bumpstaple round of the County Council Refuse Collection. There was a waiting list of thirty men for his round.

'You,' she said spitefully, 'will live here for just as long as I am prepared to put up with you and your rattling marbles.'

'Oh. Oh dear.' Lady Sybil had begun to laugh.

'What now? What is it?'

'I have wet the bed.' Lady Sybil spoke with difficulty, as she was laughing so hard.

'Oh Jesus.' Angela would have made an even worse nurse than she would a topless go-go dancer, and that was saying something. 'If I'm ever as disgusting as you, I hope someone will finish me off.' The slightest hint of a transatlantic drawl had crept into her voice.

'I've thought it was that time for ages,' Lady Sybil responded, getting off the bed and wandering to the doorway, where George had appeared suddenly, just in time to see his mother's face crumple. 'Oh dear,' she said. 'Who are you, young man?'

'I'm George, Mother,' he replied patiently. 'Angela, have you been upsetting her?'

'Oh for heaven's sake,' Angela said guiltily, 'I haven't said anything, and our bed needs changing. I have

117

better things to do than engage in slanging matches with your mother.' She stalked out of the bedroom and headed for the kitchen, telling herself that she needed to go and instruct Cook on the menus. It almost completely squashed the niggling feeling that her mother-in-law had just won a round. Somehow she always did, which was why Angela was convinced that she was not quite as disordered in the head as people seemed to think.

It just exemplified, thought Angela now, as she walked in through the gates, how impossible and manipulative the woman was. Only last week she had overheard Angela booking seats at Covent Garden for *Tosca*. Angela had been demanding the best seats, and her mother-in-law had called her a social climber with the musical appreciation of a tone-deaf guinea-pig. It proved that she must know what she was saying, for it was absolutely true.

Angela was not a cruel woman. She was not planning to put Lady Sybil into just any tacky old rest home. It would be somewhere suitable, full of the Right Sort of People. That ridiculous companion of hers, Hawthorn, could go with her – that would get rid of both old cabbages in one go. The idea of her and Lady Sybil hanging around Barking Hall for the next twenty years, wetting the beds and losing their teeth over dinner, was quite intolerable.

John Potter had been over that morning, and she had overheard him talking to George about the old lady. They had also talked about George's piles, a subject which Angela found gruesome in the extreme, and which proved that if eavesdroppers do not hear ill of themselves, then they hear something which makes them feel ill. John had been theorizing to George about how important familiar surroundings were to those with early dementia, explaining that this could help preserve the lucid periods. They had both agreed that

Lady Sybil was better off at home, and worse, John had also been of the opinion that, apart from her dementia, she was actually fairly fit. He had even suggested a brain scan, but George was dubious. John's predecessor, Charles Partridge, had been sure it wasn't necessary. Dementia, he had said, just one of those things. Angela privately thought that the old cabbage had brought it on herself by her habit of drinking brown ale before breakfast, and stout every night before bed. It might, as she had always claimed, have kept the doctor away for eighty years, but he was certainly here with a vengeance now, wasn't he?

## Chapter Eight

On the evening of the final Fête Committee meeting, Alistair was late again. Hetty had begun, quite seriously, to wonder what he was up to. The idea that he might be seeing someone filled her with a kind of aching feeling of betrayal, like a diffuse and deeply unpleasant pain, and yet, on a different level, she felt curious but detached. Did this mean that she did not love him, or that she did? The more you thought about love, the more confusing it became. When they were young she had never had to think about it; she had known, with the great, certain knowingness of youth, that she loved him. It had been easy, for she had also adored, desired and admired him. Now that she no longer found anything adorable, desirable or admirable in him, she was down to the bare bones beneath, and she was rather afraid to examine them. They were, after all, those crumbling old bones, the foundation upon which her life was built.

There was a small but ominous rumble of thunder from somewhere over towards Broomhill. She listened for more – it was easy to mistake the RAF jets for thunder – but the noise came again. She switched on the local TV news. A perfectly groomed woman was interviewing a local vicar who had made a remark about women priests and witches, in which he had implied that there was little difference, and both should be burned at the stake. The combined mass of the press had now descended upon his small church in the hope of persuading him to say something even more inflammatory. Just at that point, there was a flash of lightning and the power went off.

Hetty sighed. Power cuts were a regular event in the life of the village, and she kept a supply of candles. She fished out a couple, although it was not yet quite dark. Looking for matches, she went out into the hall where Alistair's spare overcoat hung on the hat stand. He had a habit of pocketing matchbooks in restaurants, and sure enough she found one in there. As she got them out, something fell onto the floor. It looked at first glance like another matchbook, but when she picked it up she realized that it was a packet of condoms. She and Alistair had not used them since they were married. It took her a few moments to realize that it was not Alistair's coat but Jonathan's, and it shocked her to discover how prepared she had been to believe the worst of Alistair. What on earth had happened to trust?


Henry and Josh had heard the thunder too, and they were screaming. Caroline was ruing the day she had told them that there were elephants playing in the sky. Instead of giving them a rational attitude to thunder, it seemed to have given them an irrational fear of elephants. Balancing India, who was too young to worry about either elephants or thunder, on her hip, she plodded upstairs to sort them out. She was halfway up when the lights went out, and the mood in the twins' bedroom moved up a notch from panic to hysteria.

'It's all right Henry, Josh!' she called out desperately, cautiously mounting the gloomy stairs. 'Mummy's coming.'

'Mummy, lonts turn out light,' sobbed Henry, enraged and terrified.

'Oh, bloody hell!' shouted Caroline, stubbing her toe

121

on the oak beam which formed part of the door frame to the twins' room. With their curtains drawn, the dusk was quite dark. The twins were not silenced by her outbreak, as they understood neither that she had blasphemed, nor that she did not usually do so. She felt her tiredness growing inside her head. Where was John? She felt for the light switch, then realized her mistake.

'Come on, boys, calm down.' The trouble with the twins was that they always tried to outdo one another for volume. 'Would you like to get out of bed?' She felt something damp underfoot, and hoped that it was nothing to do with either Mr Blue Potty or Mr Green Potty.

'Yeah, yeah, yeah,' chanted the twins, sounding for all the world like American football supporters, and she fished them out of their cots, one at a time. They both wanted to be held, clamouring and hanging onto her clothes like lost lambs. That was the trouble with having three children – they all wanted to be picked up at once, and when you tried to oblige, you gave yourself a bad back.

The lights came back on suddenly, without a flicker. Caroline settled down on the floor beneath a heap of small children. 'Now then,' she said, 'I'm going to tell you a nice story about some elephants . . .' The twins, mesmerized by the word 'story' prepared to be entertained.

Letting himself in downstairs, John was surprised, in view of the thunder downstairs, to find the house quiet. He had expected screaming and wild accusations directed against all elephants. He was terribly late, having been delayed by a protracted conversation with Mrs Rosemary Stebbings, who believed that the Health Service existed purely for her convenience. She had rung at the end of surgery to demand that her verruca be seen at once, and, since the doctor would be coming anyway and she had no transport, could he call in at the all-night garage on his way and bring her a bottle of white wine? Anything would do, he could choose.

John, who had spent his first few months at the practice giving in to his patients' every demand for fear of their complaining about him, had refused to choose Mrs Stebbings's wine. Furthermore, he had refused to visit her verruca, which he did not regard as a medical emergency. He was feeling a mixture of outraged righteousness and concern. The argument he subsequently had with Mrs Stebbings had taken far longer than visiting her verruca would have done, and although he knew he was right, he did so hate an argument. General Practice these days seemed to be full of patients who argued. They argued, then they lodged formal complaints, then service committees assembled to investigate them. It all took months . . . He wandered into the lounge. A woman deacon on TV was saying, 'Let him come at me with the matches.' John wondered what Oliver Bush had thought about the ordination of women. He was not the kind of man one could imagine wishing to burn anyone at the stake, but then one could never tell what hidden depths there might be in a rural vicar.

By the time the Fête Committee members set out for their meeting, rain was falling in huge, fat, cold drops. Caroline left John and India together on the sofa, and waterproofed herself with John's Barbour, a waterproof hat and a huge black umbrella. She hoped that the twins would remain asleep, and was glad that 'Edward the Elephant's Day At The Zoo' seemed to have soothed their fears somewhat.

Hetty, on the other hand, left home late and flustered. Alistair had finally got home in a terrible mood because, he said, of a traffic jam coming out of Cambridge. It was actually because of an afternoon off spent in a rather unsatisfactory effort with Lucy. He had asked her if she ever faked 'IT' and she had laughed and said of course, everybody did. This had had the doubly disheartening effect of shrinking his assets and making him wonder whether Hetty had been faking, too. Then, when he did get in, wanting to be friendly and close to assuage his guilt, Hetty was waiting to go out, and he was crosser than ever, accepting his dinner from the oven with poor grace.

Hetty forgot her umbrella. She pulled the hood of her walking coat up as the rain hit her, then, testing the drops on her face, she changed her mind and threw the hood back again. As she plodded down the lane in the darkness, her way was occasionally illuminated by the eerie diamond-white of lightning. She wished, suddenly, that she were miles away, a million miles from the pettiness of the fête, the unattractiveness of her relationship with Alistair, the sameness of home. *Where would I go, if I could go anywhere?* she wondered. When she was young, she had always believed that if things ever got too much for her she would take a slow boat to China. Now, well, things were no longer that simple. In any case, there probably weren't any slow boats any more, everything went by overnight Jumbo Jet. The world had shrunk, and was now unsuitable for escaping into.

The rectory loomed too soon out of the stormy night, looking oddly like the Hammer House of Horrors. Suddenly feeling that the day had already been too long, Hetty almost turned tail and fled home. She was prevented from doing so only by the thought that an evening with Alistair, in her present frame of mind, had no more appeal than an evening with the Fête Committee. A section of her ginger fringe hung down over her forehead like a wet corkscrew and dripped a fast pitter-patter of rain onto her nose. She had better pretend that her hood had blown off, otherwise they would think her odd and be rendered uneasy. This way the wet hair would upset no-one and she could borrow one of Rose's pink, ironed towels. Hetty had never understood why anyone ironed towels. Ironing towels was on her long list of things which she intended never to do, along with boning chickens, turning smoked salmon into mousse, and pot-holing.

Rose enjoyed hosting the meeting. She had never really excelled at anything except hosting things. It was a useful skill in a village and it quite made up, in most people's minds, for the appalling quality of her short-crust pastry. Tonight she had prepared coffee and ginger biscuits. It was good coffee. Rose had always resented the fact that, as a vicar's wife with only a small inheritance of her own, she could never really afford to buy the best of anything. The coffee was her small defiance, her rebellion against a life of sensible economy. She always bought the most expensive, no matter which it was, and with no regard to its taste, for expensive must surely mean best.

Harriet was a little nervous. She had seen the tray, and she had reason to fear Rose's ginger biscuits. Two years earlier, at a coffee morning, a particularly toffee-ish biscuit had stuck to her upper denture and caused her excruciating embarrassment. She had tried to offer Rose the loan of her sugar thermometer on a subsequent occasion, but Rose had clearly not understood the hint, and Harriet, as usual, had not persisted for fear of causing offence.

'My dear Harriet,' said Rose now, 'do come through. No, you are not late. Oliver will join us shortly, he is working on a sermon.' She could not bear to tell the truth, which was that he was actually in the sitting-room watching the end of the broadcast about the would-be woman-priest-burning Rural Dean of Frimmingham.

Harriet sat at Rose's old oak dining table, inherited from a great aunt with good taste and no children, a combination which Rose had at times felt to be inseparable. She eyed the ginger biscuits nervously – it would not do to offend by refusing. Dear Hetty was in Rose's kitchen being dried off, and she was alone with the biscuits. Perhaps she should take one now, and hide it in her pocket? Rose would certainly have counted them, so when offered she could decline, claiming truthfully to have had one already. Would that cause more offence than simply not having one at all?

Oliver wandered in and Harriet blushed. Many years ago she, Rose and Oliver had been at school together in Great Barking. Oliver had been a tall boy with a lanky lock of brown hair which fell across his eyes; he was studious, kind, and a little older than herself. She had adored him from the moment he had stopped Jimmy Roberts from pulling her hair, and she adored him still in the same schoolgirlish way.

Harriet had never married – she had never even had a serious sweetheart. She had made her way in the world as a music teacher and now lived a comfortable, spinsterish life with her cats and a bookcase full of girls' public school novels and sexless romances with which to enlarge her view of the world. She would never have wished to steal Oliver from Rose. She had never even fantasized that she might be able to, but she always blushed when she saw him.

By the time everyone was assembled, several of Rose's biscuits had been eaten, so Harriet did not have to worry that Rose would know that she had put hers back. You could tell, with a little knowledge of Rose's biscuits, who had and who had not partaken. All the ones who had, wore the facial expressions of angry hamsters. It was, as always, very adhesive ginger biscuit.

They were a little distracted by the storm, but they managed to work their way through most of Rose's agenda. On the first point, 'Venue', they confirmed that the venue would indeed be the garden of Yew Tree Cottage. The second point was the official opening. Rose's plan was to gloss over this quickly, so that everyone would think it was in hand. Unfortunately, anything which is glossed over is liable to be misunderstood, especially by those who are filled with dreams and aspirations. Mrs Groat was one such. Mrs Groat had wondered what she should do in order to convince Rose that she was the ideal candidate. She had even considered wearing her best suit tonight, despite the weather. Now, when Rose said that she would make arrangements, Mrs Groat seized the chance of prompting her.

'I do hope,' she said rather smugly, 'that you have someone smart in mind, a good suit makes such a difference to appearances.'

Rose thought at once that Greta was making fun of her own, rather impoverished wardrobe. 'Perhaps,' she said icily, 'we should even specify the colour of the suit. Pink, do you think?'

Sarcasm was entirely lost on Mrs Groat, who was far too acidic in her own speech to appreciate that others used such tones only in irony. She took Rose's comment as all the confirmation she required.

'Oh I do,' she said conspiratorially. 'Pink would be marvellous.'

Rose regretted her comment. Her own secret new suit was, after all, pink. She hoped that none of the committee would put two and two together and guess that she planned to take the glory for herself. It certainly did not occur to her that Mrs Groat could possibly consider

127

herself and her awful pink outfit candidates for the honour.

Jessie smiled across at Mrs Groat rather anxiously, sensing grounds for misunderstanding. Interpreting the smile as one of congratulation – after all, all of Jessie's smiles had an anxious quality, it was just the way that her face was arranged – Mrs Groat settled back in her seat, secure in her victory. Caroline felt less secure. She had no idea what Rose and Mrs Groat were talking about, indeed, excepting Jessie no-one else had either, but it did not sound as though Rose had spoken to Angela Ormondroyd yet, and Caroline felt thoroughly responsible for the fact that Angela already assumed the role would be hers. She resolved to speak to Oliver after the meeting – he was far less daunting than Rose.

The others all assumed that Rose had the opening of the fête under control, and as they all hoped to avoid another argument on the subject, or on the presence, or not, of Lady Sybil's mental marbles, they then moved swiftly on to the raffle.

It was, generally, a successful meeting. All the gritty details of who would do what, when and where and with whom were ironed out and recorded, laboriously, by Rose. She wrote in a neat, tiny script which allowed for no flowing tails or roughly dashed t's, and her writing was perfectly legible. In fact, if writing could be described as irritating, it was.

Caroline delighted the assembled group by suggesting a magic show by John. Even Rose's fear of being upstaged evaporated completely at the thought of the gnashing of teeth and beating of chests which would go on in Bumpstaple and Little Barking when this became known.

'Don't you think,' she asked Caroline privately, malice completely concealed in sugar-pink coating, 'that it would be most appropriate for young Lady

Ormondroyd to be asked to assist Dr Potter with a trick?'

Caroline, assailed by a sudden horrible vision of Angela wearing a G-string and two gold tassels being cut in half by a chain saw, swallowed and nodded weakly. She wondered if Rose could possibly have meant the comment maliciously. Surely not, she was smiling too nicely.

Carol Sheldon, who was mother to two thoroughly badly behaved girls, decided that she must get to know Caroline better, even though she looked a bit stuck-up. A magician's wife could be a useful acquaintance. She thought about possible ways of opening a conversation with Caroline. Her usual means of engineering a social get together, a sex-aid party, didn't seem likely to be Caroline's thing. Mind you, someone had told her that the battery-powered humming object with the rather odd pump action was awfully popular in Knightsbridge. She made a mental note to test the waters. Caroline had conceived twins, after all. Carol had a vague notion that it must take a particularly erotic type of sexual encounter to produce twins. She had read it somewhere, she was sure. In fact she had read it in a journal on pig husbandry which she had browsed through in the dentist's waiting room, but that had skipped her mind.

When they had finished with the fine detail of the fête – everything from who would string up the bunting to who would carry the tables – they lapsed into gentle conversation. At least, it would have been gentle had not the subject turned as irrevocably as the tide to women priests. The neighbouring village of Bumpstaple was currently without its own vicar, and it had been suggested that a lady might be available. As one would expect, opinions round the table were divided into those for, those against, and those who agreed with everyone. Carol Sheldon, who had not darkened a church door between baptism and marriage, and had no plans to do so again until burial, believed firmly that women priests would be more approachable. Rose, instinctively conservative in all things, was against the whole idea whilst Harriet, who was innately fair minded, thought a woman would be fine as long as no-one was upset. The Beans and the Groats did not want to express an opinion before they had heard what Oliver Bush thought, so poor Oliver was put on the spot.

He had already fortified himself a little against the trials of the fête meeting with a small glass of sherry, and as a result he failed to agree with Rose. 'I feel,' he said happily, 'that the history of the church is one of movement and progress. It is not a case of moving with the times, for the church is above political correctness. I feel that change and growth are essential to a living, breathing, growing church, and I would go so far as to suggest that my colleague, the Rural Dean of Frimmingham, should himself be tied to an appropriate stake and barbecued. He always was a most ungodly man, as was demonstrated by the occasion when he was nearly expelled from theological college for smoking banned substances. Indeed, one could draw parallels with Satan himself – he was, after all, a fallen angel, cast out of heaven for his sins.' As he finished speaking, an immense peal of thunder shattered the night, making them jump, and all the lights went out again. There was an eerie silence, which stretched for a few seconds, then Carol Sheldon whispered, 'God.' Rose, who disliked blasphemy, replied, 'Quite possibly,' and Morgan Groat's mouth fell open and stayed there.

Mrs Groat maintained afterwards that it had been a Sign in response to the rector's likening the Rural Dean of Frimmingham to the Devil, and some, having seen the twisted and partially melted state of the weather-cock on the tower of St Jude's after the lightning strike, were inclined to agree. No-one, however, could say whether the sign was in agreement or in disagreement with Oliver Bush's stated opinion. Signs could be like that.

The power did not return that evening. A tree had come down at Broomhill Poultry. The factory was surrounded by large trees which had been intended to screen it from animal rights activists, but which instead seemed to provide them with a foothold over the fence. The fallen tree had dragged electricity cables serving the village down with it. The Electricity Company, inundated with calls about fallen cables arcing and flashing across Suffolk, gave the Great Barking tree fairly low priority.

Rose, delighted at the chance to be both benevolent and capable, offered large quantities of candles around before they all left. 'Ecclesiastical candles,' she told them proudly. 'I always buy plenty.'

They dispersed, a little tired, but mainly full of good intentions, as one generally is after such meetings. Caroline hung back for a quiet word with Oliver, who reassured her that, as far as he knew, Rose planned to ask Angela Ormondroyd to open the fête. He was fairly sure that was how things had been left, and was far too devoted a husband ever to imagine his wife to be capable of plotting or subversion.

Everyone else left fairly quickly. For some reason Rose, despite her apparent benevolence and her perfectly placed laughter lines, was not the kind of hostess whose guests all tried to linger and be the last to depart. They betrayed, by their actions, an opinion of Rose that they did not consciously hold. When Rose hinted that it was time to go, you went – particularly if not all of the biscuits were eaten. There was an insubstantial quality to Rose's hospitality rather like that of a lemon soufflé lifted too quickly from the oven.

When Hetty got home from the meeting, Alistair was sitting in front of the blank TV, glaring at it by candlelight, swishing a twelve-year-old single malt between his teeth and feeling neglected. He was not quite sure what difference Hetty's presence would have made to his mood, but she would at least have been someone to complain to when the lights went out, and the series which he had been watching was cut off in its prime. It was not particularly good, nor was it particularly exciting, but in Alistair's experience those were the ones which niggled for the longest if you missed the end.

Hetty felt a sudden urge to heal things, to bring back at least the illusion of a happy marriage. 'Hello, you look fed up.' She dropped a light kiss on the top of his head. 'Did you have your supper?'

'Yes, thanks.' Alistair was not prepared to be cosy. If he could muster up a good-going sense of grievance against Hetty for having left him alone with a kept-warm dinner, then he would feel less guilty. If he had to have a miserable evening, she might at least have had the decency to share it with him.

Hetty sighed inwardly. 'Where are the boys?'

'All in their rooms. Finn's in bed, Luke's just in from Youth Club. I don't know what Rory's doing.'

Sadly, Hetty knew that Rory would be doing anything which did not involve him being incarcerated in the same room as his father all evening. 'I do wish that you and Rory had a better relationship,' she said, sitting beside him on the sofa. The unmistakable scent of her rain-damp hair filled his nostrils, evoking memories of their happier past, and Lucy seemed suddenly irrelevant.

'I know you do,' he said, 'but somehow we don't seem to have anything in common at the moment.'

Hetty's temper sharpened, despite her wish for peace. 'Oh, for heaven's sake, Alistair, he's your son, not your blind date. No-one says you have to have anything in common, but if you push him away, you will lose him.' And me, she nearly said, but only nearly.

'I do try,' said Alistair, 'but when I do he's always so—' he stopped, not wanting to say 'soft', knowing that Hetty would see it as a reference to what boys call 'girliness'. He avoided looking at Hetty, concentrating instead on the flickering candle shadows on the green speckled Axminster. His fear that Rory might be gay, and her disgust with him for fearing it, hung between them like an extra shadow. Hetty took a breath, then let it out again. They must talk about it, she knew, but not now. Not whilst she was feeling so annoyed and distant with Alistair. Why did she feel that way now, when she had arrived home feeling conciliatory? *Is it me* she wondered, *am I pushing him away?*

She asked herself the same question again later, in their bed, when she had expected Alistair to reach for her, and he had not done so. She had dreaded his touch on her breast, wanting to rebuff it yet not wanting to make the distance between them even greater. The fact that Alistair seemed not to have his usual urges tonight – indeed had not had them a lot recently, either – only added to her frustration.

'Alistair,' she said softly into the darkness.

*Oh God*, he thought, *I can't with Hetty, not after this afternoon. Even if I could physically, and I'm not sure about that, it'd be the pits.* 'What?' he asked, in what he hoped was an exhausted tone. The thought of being inside Hetty only hours after being inside Lucy tempted him suddenly, simultaneously revolting and fascinating him.

133

'Have you gone off me?' She moved back a little, against him, so that they nestled like spoons.

Alistair tensed as things began to move on the hormone front. 'No, of course not,' he said. His conscience and his libido were shaking one another by the throat, and he hardly dared breathe. 'I'm just tired. Things are rather difficult at work at the moment.'

At least he was talking.

'Anything you want to talk about?'

'No,' said Alistair then, remembering earlier, 'except . . .'

'What?'

'Someone was talking at work,' said Alistair, suddenly overwhelmed by the need to know how much of what he had always believed was a sham, 'and they made me wonder, do you ever, you know, fake it? Sex, I mean.'

There was a short silence as Hetty reflected upon the sheer oddness of the question from someone who, if he was honest, had not recently spent a great deal of time concentrating on her sexual pleasure. Then she said, 'No, I don't. I thought you would realize, since when I don't have an orgasm I don't pretend to, so why would I need to fake?'

Alistair, both literally and metaphorically deflated by her honesty, was silent. After she had fallen asleep, though, he lay awake for quite some time. He had intended to reflect upon the difference between Hetty and Lucy, but instead found himself wrestling with his conscience. There was no doubt in his mind that Lucy was merely his bit on the side, but considering the risk, her being in the village, was it worth it? He certainly had no strong feelings for her. The truth was, she was a convenient bit of fun at a time when his wife and his marriage were both a little stale. OK, Hetty was worth ten – a hundred – of Lucy, but Lucy was spicing him up.

Goodness, it was actually improving him for Hetty. By the time he finished with Lucy, which was likely to be fairly soon, he would have worked the whole bimbo thing out of his system. In addition, he would have given Hetty a little rest from what seemed at the moment to be rather unwanted attentions.

By the time he fell asleep, Alistair had more or less convinced himself that he was actually doing Hetty quite a favour by sleeping with Lucy, and that if Hetty had known what he was doing, she would have encouraged him to continue. He really was, he felt, a rather good husband, both desirable and considerate.

Alistair slept the sleep of the truly smug.

## Chapter Nine

If you were going to see a specialist in Harley Street, then it was imperative to arrive early. You never knew who might be in the waiting room. On this occasion, arriving early paid off more dividends than usual, for in addition to Lady Helena Smythe (good pearls, awful spots) Angela had the good fortune to run into Marsha Millington.

Marsha Millington was a society columnist for *Tatler*, and she had realized long ago that if she reserved her vitriol for those cast out by the Cartier-and-San-Lorenzo set, and was very pleasant about the rest, she could make many useful friends. Society columnists make a contribution to society which is essential in some social circles. Those people fortunate enough, or deranged enough, depending on your point of view, to consider themselves only a step away from the Royals, appreciate that in order to retain this position, and in order to feel that it matters, they need to be seen regularly in the places, and with the people, that count. For maximum effect, this needs to be recorded for the less socially successful to see and envy. Marsha's column was ideal for this purpose. Anyone who was anyone appeared in it, and those condemned by it were universally regarded as social outcasts. This made her a highly desirable friend, ally and party guest, and the perks of her job were, not surprisingly, considerable.

Marsha had no intention of keeping her 'allergy' secret. A minor rash was quite socially acceptable. She had come openly to Professor Quincey for treatment which she could have obtained free on the NHS, and with far more confidentiality. However, like Angela, she was not paying for the treatment. She was paying for the privilege of joining the starred ranks of Professor Quincey's patients.

Once poor Lady Helena and her dreadful teenage affliction had been escorted through, Marsha and Angela were able to chat. Angela was delighted to reveal that she, too, appeared to have an allergy, and Professor Q, as only the in-crowd could call him, had seen her a few times in an effort to determine its cause. She hoped today would bring her an answer. They compared rashes, laying their arms side by side in the light from the huge sash window. Angela was pleased to note that Marsha's arm was not as thin as her own. Marsha was also pleased, particularly as she had no freckles and poor Angela was positively afflicted. The rashes were only vaguely similar. Angela's was red and raised, Marsha's more coppery in colour, but the women were united by the bond of shared adversity, and Angela felt that she had found a potential ally.

This was wonderful! The Ormondroyds of Great Barking were sure to get a mention in Marsha's column. Angela told Marsha all about the village ('You *must* visit') and its famous potter ('Dear Sarah, such a charming girl but, my goodness, so *fat*!') and had even got onto the subject of the Great Barking Foxhounds ('Not that I begrudge the money, of course') when Marsha was called through. Angela, glowing in anticipation of next month's *Tatler*, settled down to read *Horse and Hound*.

She was blissfully unaware that through the polished double doors Marsha's happy mood was being cruelly destroyed. Sadly, her rash was not the innocent allergy she had supposed, but an affliction so totally

137

unacceptable in San Lorenzo's as to make lunch an impossibility until it was completely gone. It certainly made anyone who had actually seen the rash a possible threat to her position.

Marsha left the consulting rooms without speaking to Angela again, plotting feverishly how best to contain the situation. What if Angela talked? Even in these enlightened times, the quality press were unlikely to employ a gossip columnist who had been exposed as being afflicted by an intimately transmitted disease.

Professor Quincey, a handsome American who could charm the suspenders off a countess — and often did — considered the patch tests on Angela's back carefully, making copious notes on thick, headed vellum. Angela, who always felt rather awkward with doctors, particularly when her flesh was exposed, decided to say nothing, and concentrated on the photograph of the President of the United States on the opposite wall. It hung next to a picture of the Queen. Was it her imagination, or was the President's picture just slightly higher? She frowned. Her own allegiance was quite clear, of course. Particularly now that the President was not a Republican.

'Well, Lady Ormondroyd—'

'Oh, please call me Angela,' she said.

'Well, Angela, we certainly have a result. If you'd like to dress and come through to my office, we can discuss it.'

'Of course.'

He left the room and Angela slipped on her clothes over the designer underwear bought expressly for the occasion. It would not do to be seen wearing last year's designs in Harley Street. She adjusted her Chanel suit in the mirror which Professor Quincey provided for just that purpose, and applied a little pressed powder to her nose. She redid her lipstick, patted her hair, then went through to the beautiful panelled room which added so much weight to the professor's diagnoses.

'Now, Angela, the news is really quite interesting,' he said. Angela was not quite sure whether having an interesting skin disease was necessarily a good thing. Dermatology, in her mind, was a rather odd speciality, rather akin to witchcraft. She did not want to be too interesting. She waited.

'You show a few minor reactions to common allergens,' he said, resting his handsomely cleft chin on the back of one hand as he fixed her with his blue eyes. 'You have mild reactions to horse hair, one or two pollens and the house dust mite.' Angela made no comment, sensing that the best was to come. 'However,' he leaned back in his chair, 'none of these would explain the intermittent nature of the rash, the itching of the eyes and, um, extremities, and the occasional tightness of the chest.'

Angela flushed. Why had she told him that she always got an itchy undercarriage in church? She had hoped it might help the diagnosis, but on reflection one should never tell a handsome man that one's bottom itches.

Professor Quincey barely noticed her discomfiture. He had, after all, seen far worse things which itched than bottoms. He sailed on down the breeze of his discovery. 'As you know, I pride myself on the range of my allergen testing – I cover many agents which are unusual, and it is for this reason that I have been able to determine the cause of your problem so quickly.'

'Oh yes?'

'You are allergic to bats. More specifically, you are allergic to the faeces of bats.'

'Son of a . . . oh God!' Was he implying that she had been eating them? Could Cook have been trying to poison her with bat dung? She stared at him in horror.

'Don't look so alarmed, my dear. It's very simple. The bats live in the roof of your church. The droppings fall, dry and become powdered. Even though the church is cleaned, traces remain and are stirred up by the presence of the congregation as dust. You are allergic to that dust. In your case the mucous membranes are irritated in addition to the skin, hence the rather embarrassing itch. You also appear to have a mild asthmatic component to your allergy. I will give you an inhaler.'

Angela left Harley Street spitting mad. That she, a member of the British nobility both by marriage and wealth should be forced from her church by bats! The fact that Angela attended church only when she wished to be seen was suddenly irrelevant. Something must be done about the bats. Surely it would not cost very much to spray them with something disgusting? George, Angela resolved, would pay.

'You know, I think Alistair might be seeing someone,' said Hetty on the telephone to her mother that evening, surprising herself. 'I was reading an article in the *Daily Mail* about—'

'I didn't know you read the *Mail*,' said her mother in delight. Ever since she had met Alistair, Hetty had read *The Times*, and bought only white toilet paper. Perhaps there was hope for her yet.

'I don't usually,' said Hetty, who genuinely preferred *The Times*, 'it was my act of rebellion. I wanted to play the Bingo game. The prize was a sports car.' *No, in truth the real prize was another me, the chance to become a woman in a red dream-mobile.*

'Hmph,' said her mother, thinking, *we may be working class but we don't go to Bingo. Our toilet rolls match our bathroom. Blue.*

140

'Oh, don't be like that, Mum. It's just a card that's free with the paper, like a lottery.'

'Oh. Now, what about Alistair?'

'Well, there was this article on infidelity, how to spot it. It talked about the signs. Working late, becoming health conscious, new after shave—'

'Sounds like fear of redundancy,' said her mother. It wasn't that she couldn't believe the worst of Alistair – in fact, she usually did. It was just that she was unable to credit him with sufficient brains or sufficient charm to have an affair with anyone.

Hetty seized on the explanation thankfully. 'Of course, I should have thought, although he is a partner. He did say he was under pressure at work. I suppose we're just that age: younger men coming up at the office, and so forth.'

Finn wandered past her and helped himself to a huge bowl of cornflakes, dumping his schoolbag casually on the floor and laying his cricket bat precisely on the kitchen table. 'Who's what age?' he asked, between mouthfuls.

Hetty ignored the question. 'Take that off there, Finn, it smells of linseed oil. I don't want it on my table.'

'What's that?' asked her mother.

'Nothing, Mum, I must go. The boys are just getting home.'

From wanting to talk to her mother, she was now relieved to get rid of her. At least her boys were wonderfully uncomplicated compared to Alistair. Even Rory, with his dreaminess and his recent secrecy, was easy compared to a distant husband. *I'm beginning to feel he just doesn't want me, not in any sense*, she thought. Last night Alistair had woken her in the early hours. He had been a little rough, but somehow detached, and Hetty had been left feeling that, far from patching up small cracks in their relationship, sex was

141

now widening a yawning gulf. She had lain in the darkness afterwards watching the occasional shadow on the ceiling as a car drove by, feeling quite the opposite of cherished.

'The cornflakes are all gone, Mum,' said Finn, noticing that Hetty looked unhappy, and needing to say something.

'Oh, Finny,' she said, and hugged his head, and Finn managed not to tell her off for calling him by his baby nickname.

'Have you and Gran had a row?' he asked, with the deep sagacity common to all twelve-year-old boys.

'No, love, I'm just a bit tired. Would you cycle up to the post office for cornflakes?' Doubtless Luke would want a bowlful when he got in. Luke always got home later than Finn. He was probably chatting to some girl. Hetty lost track of Luke's girls. Rory, of course, would be staying late at school doing music practice.

She wondered about Rory. He did seem happier, lately. Could there be a girl? Hetty couldn't remember if Jonathan had had anyone serious at this stage. If it was a girl, he was being very secretive. *Oh, Rory, I hope you're not gay. Alistair would never forgive you, and I could never forgive him for that.*

The telephone rang.

'It's me,' said Alistair.

Hetty frowned at the phone. 'Hello.'

'Meeting cancelled. I'll be home for supper. Just leaving.' Brrrr, the dialling tone. Hetty decided to walk Jess before he got back; it was rather misty and damp, and it would be nice not to have to go after dark.


As she set out Alistair, thinking in the car about his bit on the side, wondered if he was being played for a fool. The girl had been so keen — all that humping in odd places, odd positions. Then, tonight, when he had rung her to cancel, feeling like a quiet evening at home, she had not seemed bothered at all. Perhaps she had another man. Would he feel jealous if she did? He tried to imagine her with Sir George, but someone hooted behind him as the lights turned green. No, he wouldn't be jealous, just put-out. He would not like to think that she might be laughing at him. Over the last few weeks he and Lucy had coupled in the car, joined in the hay, rolled on the carpet and humped against the wall. In fact, most of Alistair's basic fantasies had been played out, together with one or two which he had never had, but which turned out to be quite interesting. These largely involved items of saddlery and a riding crop, and had been Lucy's idea. It had somehow always left him wanting more. At first that had been grand: he had felt insatiable, youthful, and she had been pliant and saucy. Gradually, though, almost without his noticing, it had taken on the quality of a Chinese takeaway, the sort which fills you up till you can manage no more, yet is oddly unsatisfying, so that you look in the cupboards for something else half an hour later. What on earth was he missing?

He pulled onto the big roundabout. *Bloody cars cutting in! Hetty was never into my fantasies. Not even at first. She let me tie her up once, but only gently and not for long, and I felt guilty because I knew she didn't really like it.* He hooted hard at the green Range Rover and blocked it successfully. Blast! It was Sir George Ormondroyd. Alistair tried to cover the sign he had started to make by turning it into a hair-flicking gesture. He wondered momentarily whether George might really have tried it on with Lucy. No, he wouldn't – *she* wouldn't. The idea was preposterous. George was a pompous old fart, and he was running to fat. If it weren't for the rumoured port and the handmade shoes, Alistair would have envied George nothing. Nothing.

Sadly he did not comprehend that people still live their lives in a series of tiers, social strata determined primarily by family, accent, schooling and money. Most of those lower down look up, aspiring, envying and, at times, crawling. Some of those at the very bottom attempt to defy gravity by spitting on those at the very top. They do not realize that the spit will always drop back onto them, together with the spit of those at whom it was aimed. Those in the middle layers, and such was Alistair, do not spit. They cannot escape from their place. They watch the spit fly by. They admire and yet despise those above them, they despise and yet admire those below them. Foolishly they do not see that they are considered nothing by those below them, and are less than nothing to those above. So in his folly, Alistair envied George, whom he also despised, and despised Lucy, whom he desired. It did not occur to him that Lucy, coming as she did from the Right Sort of family, might actually be up there with George, spitting on him.

Something had been digging in the churchyard. There were little mounds of scraped-up earth around the base of the ancient yew, and also here and there amongst the graves. Hetty supposed it had been done by foxes, and Jess strained at her leash to investigate the fresh, damp earth. She was unaware that the mysterious digging creatures had already been spotted by Jessie Bean, who had been in her little garden hanging out her washing – all except her smalls, which she always dried on a rack over the cooker. It would not do to hang her smalls in view of the church. Jessie belonged to the generation who were taught that God, although omnipotent, omniscient and omnipresent, is easily offended by smalls.

Poor Jessie had retreated indoors in terror, and had telephoned Rose Bush to inform her in whispered tones that there were monsters in the churchyard. 'Oh, Rose, they were huge! You won't believe it, but they were black and ugly and hairy. I couldn't be sure, but I think that they were wild boar.'

Now, quite by chance, Rose had been reading an article in *Rural Living* about the farming of rare breeds in Britain. It had happened to mention that wild boar were being farmed on a commercial basis in Suffolk, and she was thus well primed to take Jessie very seriously. 'I must come and see at once,' she said, wondering what a vicar's wife was meant to do when confronting wild boar in a churchyard. Such etiquette had never been discussed at the deanery parties.

'Oh, no, Rose, dear, they can be dangerous,' warned Jessie, and Rose dithered for a while.

By the time she actually got to the churchyard, armed with her garden fork, there was nothing to be seen. The small mounds of earth could have been dug by anything, and Rose felt sure that Jessie had merely seen a couple of dogs. She felt rather foolish. Wild boar indeed!

Oblivious to the possible presence of ancient wild beasts in Great Barking, Hetty plodded dismally on through a light drizzle of cold rain. She felt rather drizzly herself. She felt that her life was, in some respects, a sham. There she goes, they would say, jolly, capable Hetty, always a little untidy but very dependable. She was not quite sure who would say it – not Rose Bush, that was for sure. Beneath the surface, though, she was beginning to feel cracks opening up. She let herself out of the churchyard gate, walked down the main road a little way, past the Hall, and turned into The

Street. Jess, now unleashed, rushed forward to investigate a still-steaming heap of horse deposit. Hetty was suddenly reminded of Lucy Bellingham, and of an occasion when Alistair had almost seemed to be chatting her up when they had met her on their way home from church. They had conversed showily whilst she, Hetty, had shovelled manure dropped by Lucy's horse. She had felt excluded and ignored. That little incident had opened up one of the cracks.

The rain became a little heavier, but she liked rain, and Jess liked absolutely everything, she was that kind of dog. It fell onto Hetty's upturned face, the multiple little prickles reminding her of those odd electrical facials that people paid Carol Sheldon to do. The rain smelt fresh and clean, even though it was probably full of dissolved environmental pollution from further up. Didn't most of London's smog drift over East Anglia? There were probably special fans blowing it north, away from the Houses of Parliament. Hetty's corkscrew curl dripped onto her nose. She tried to remember when Alistair had last walked in the rain with her, but could not.

The river was high. Sometimes Hetty and Jess waded through the ford on their walks, but today the water was swirling, deep and muddy, and there were branches and debris caught against the railing which divided the ford from the sudden drop in the river bed below it. They stood on the bridge, gazing at the eddies and whirls in the water. There was a low, damp mist descending, and they could not see far, but in the distance, at the edge of the river, Hetty could just make out a dark shape sniffing at the ground. It was far too large to be a cat or fox, and it didn't look like a dog – more like a pig, in fact. How odd. She squinted to try to see more clearly, *Now, why do people do that?* she wondered, but the creature was lost amongst the trees.

She shrugged. 'It probably was a dog,' she told Jess. 'Come on.'

They took the path beside the river, as Hetty did not feel like saying 'Hello, awful weather' to anyone who might drive past. Even Morgan Groat would not be out fishing, with the river like this. As she walked and Jess scampered, chasing phantom birds, she thought about Alistair again. How did you know if you still loved someone? When they had both been joyfully and youthfully in love, they had been joyful, youthful people. Could it now follow that as old, sensible, stale people they could still be in love in an old, sensible, stale kind of way? There was an old park bench by the river and she sat down, hoping that her mac would protect her from piles, which she still believed were a certain consequence of sitting on anything cold and damp. Jess, ever hopeful, brought her a wet, mossy stick, and Hetty threw it for her. *If only I could just throw my cares away in the same way*, she thought. *Think of all the positive things in my life.*

She thought of her sons. She loved them passionately, and had always resented those little comments from people who assumed that she would have liked a daughter. It had been worst when she had Finn. Everything from 'You must be running out of boys' names' to 'Never mind, dear'. Hetty had adored her sons with a passion which was at times physically painful. She loved having four boys. They made her feel female, motherly and protected all at the same time. She had loved their little willies when they were babies; having led a fairly sheltered and brotherless life, the only other willy she had had any close contact with was Alistair's, and the difference had amazed her. Sometimes she had worried that she would lack the instincts to deal with the awful afflictions of teenage boys, but they had muddled through together. Alistair had been a

147

part of all that, and that counted for something. They had been through so much together. She could surely not have slipped out of love, without even noticing, with the man who had shared her life for twenty-five years?

There was a long, low growl of thunder, and Jess whined softly. Being a dog, she was not keen on these long, introspective sessions stuck in one place, particularly not when it thundered.

'Sorry, Jess.' Hetty collected herself and turned back for home. As they crossed the bridge again, she resolved not to dwell on something which she clearly could not resolve just by thinking about it. It might be that there had been a sea-change in her relationship with Alistair, but it could just be a little menopausal eddy. The thought of a little menopausal eddy made her giggle, and Jess brightened at the sound. Hetty's step lightened. If she were this concerned and worked up about it, then it at least proved that she was not indifferent. That was something.

A hint of a puff of breeze caught Hetty's scent as she and Jess walked on. It carried a mixed dog-and-perfume smell along the riverbank to where the two Vietnamese pot-bellied pigs, who had escaped from Rope Hall Prep School and Farm, half a mile away, were foraging for food. They were not much interested in the smell, humans and dogs being as familiar to them as other pigs. Besides, they had just found some lovely mushrooms.

'Good Lord!' said George Ormondroyd into the telephone. 'You can't be serious!'

'I am, I'm certain,' came back Lucy's panicked tones on the internal line from the stable. 'Please call the police, and bring your gun!'

'Now, calm down, my dear,' said George, thinking

148

furiously. 'Angela will call Constable Huxley, and I shall be with you in a moment.' George sounded braver than he felt. Whilst he did not want his hysterical groom calling in the local constabulary to say that there were wild rhino in the yard if there were not, he was not at all sure that he wanted to go out and confront the beasts with nothing more than a twelve-bore. George's last experience of a rhino had been on safari with the Egbert-Shaws. Ruth Egbert-Shaw had insisted that the native guide took them on foot to watch a small group of jackals. While they were out of their Landrover, a rhino had taken offence at the car, and had made several attempts on its life. The petrol tank had been holed, and they had crouched, terrified, in the grass for nearly half an hour whilst their guide went to fetch help. Angela never mentioned safaris again. Remembering this, he hesitated. A rhino could well gore him to death by its sheer momentum, even after he had shot it, and if there were two . . .

'Oh, for Christ's sake,' said Angela, 'we haven't got bloody rhino in the yard. It's probably an escaped Doberman sniffing around.'

That did it. George telephoned the police.


The two pigs never really understood what all the fuss was about. Since eating those rather unusual mushrooms down by the river, life had taken on a rather curious quality, and when several uniformed police arrived with two vets and a tranquillizer gun, they were, for them, unusually unco-operative. It really was rather a shame that it was so dark, for the spectacle of policemen, vets and George pursuing a pair of drugged pot-bellied pigs around the stable yard would have made a wonderful photograph.

It was Zoë who, having been a pupil at Rope Hall Prep

School, guessed where the pigs had come from, and telephoned the headmistress, Mrs Pennington-Jones. This dragon of a woman arrived in a blaze of fury, just as the vets had decided that they might have to use the tranquillizer gun after all.

'Troilus! Cressida!' she boomed at the pigs who, through their LSD-induced haze of pig-type hallucinations, recognized at once the ruby-rich tones of the woman they loved. They stopped careering round the yard and trotted obediently to their beloved mother, who bundled them one at a time into the back of her pristine Range Rover and drove away, humphing and snorting her opinions of pig-persecuting policemen as she went.

The gathered forces of the law were left standing around in the dark, smelling of pig and feeling rather foolish. Angela, fortunately, rallied round with offers of coffee and brandy. It was, after all, a chance to play Lady of the Manor, and she had popped upstairs during the excitement to change into Chanel.

Not included in the invitation, Lucy returned to her staff cottage on the other side of the yard. She felt small and ridiculous for having thought that a pair of pet pigs were rhino. They had sounded so awfully loud, and had seemed such huge, dark shapes through the crack in the stable door. They could have been small rhino, she told herself – there was, after all, a small zoo only a few miles away.

Sir George had been brave. Lucy did not realize that he had called the police without venturing out, nor that the shouts and threats which she had heard from him had been issued inside the Hall and not, as she imagined, from the middle of the yard. He had not actually come out until the vet arrived and the animals were identified for what they were.

George was not a sensitive man, but he did notice the

glances of grateful admiration which Lucy had cast his way. He was not about to miss an opportunity such as this. 'Let me walk back with you, my dear, you have had rather a fright, and I did promise your father that I would look after you.'

Lucy, capitulating to George's amorous attentions as soon as they got into her cottage, could not help feeling that this was not what her father had had in mind. She also found, to her surprise, that she was quite enjoying it. George, who had previously seemed ignoble and pompous, now seemed strong, brave and sexually appealing, and the smells of stable and pig rather enhanced the experience. Her moaning was, for once, quite genuine.

# Chapter Ten

A terrible thought had occurred to Rose. It was the kind
of thought which, in younger days, would have caused
her nanny to mutter warnings about coming to a bad
end, and nasty black things coming down the chimney.
It had popped into her head like a little squashed loofah,
a tiny dried piece of loofah which no-one had bothered
to hydrate. It had been sitting in the corner of her mind,
undeveloped, between the bats and the white elephant
stall and then, alas, something had watered it. Now it
filled her whole brain. It had been watered by something Oliver had said the previous evening, during
dinner with the Vicar of Broomhill.

'Vicars,' he said, 'are at a great disadvantage,
compared to rectors. Rector is a far better word, for it
rhymes with no item of ladies' underwear. The word
"vicar" is mocked by society, the butt of every joke. We
have "tarts and vicars" parties at every turn, and the
number of jokes I have heard on the subject of vicars'
organs would keep a night-club open for a year!'

As they had all laughed and discussed and joked and
been convivial, Rose's subconscious had taken the
word 'organ' and made a swift, surreptitious, hitherto
unsuspected connection with Sarah Struther. Had not
Sarah Struther suggested, with Rose's collusion and
encouragement, that she would provide a pot and a
picture based on an organ? Rose's feverish brain
conjured up a dreadful picture of a giant pot, centrepiece of her village fête, depicting a huge and

unmistakable penis – with a picture to back it up, in case anyone should have any doubt as to what it was meant to be. Poor Rose. One might have expected, having grown up in the countryside at a time when cattle were not artificially inseminated and dogs were not always on leads, that the male organ in all its glory would hold no fear or shame for her. A rector's wife should not be floored by a willy. Alas, Rose was not made of such stern stuff. She had only seen one of Those Things on one occasion. She had never looked again.

She would have to check up on Sarah. How, though, was she to broach the subject? She could hardly explain her fears which were, after all, most unworthy for a rector's wife, and she would appear so foolish if she were wrong. On the other hand, if her worst fears were confirmed, and there was indeed a huge clay Thing in the making, there might yet be time to request a different pot. She decided to go and see Sarah. She could express friendly interest in the progress of the pot, and Sarah would have to show her. She would go at once and set her mind at rest.

Thus resolved, Rose headed at once for Sarah's cottage, proving that impulse is, without a doubt, the enemy of common sense. It is never wise to catch anyone unawares, for you never know what they might be doing. It had not been Rose's intention to catch Sarah unawares, but as it happened to be a day for love rather than a day for potting, Sarah was only aware of a few things, and Rose was not one of them.

In knocking on the door of the potting shed, having heard music from inside, Rose inadvertently pushed it ajar. Thus she was faced with a sight which reminded her of some of the more alarming illustrations in a copy of *Paradise Lost*, which she had viewed illictly in her youth. Sarah and Rory, fortunately, remained oblivious of her presence. They were engaged in enjoying one another as only the truly uninhibited can, as Sarah had, some time ago, taken up Rory's offer of teaching her all he knew. They were using quite a lot of enthusiasm today, working out what they thought he knew. Poor Rose. Not only had she failed to see The Pot – if indeed Sarah had even got around to beginning it – she had also failed to identify the man in the shed, owing to the rather alarming relative positions of the bodies of the lovers. To make things worse, she fled with such undignified haste that she tripped over a potted cactus on Sarah's patio and twisted her ankle rather painfully.

She hobbled round to the Potters' house, where she explained to Caroline that she had turned her foot whilst walking. Caroline led her, limping, into the kitchen and sat her down.

'Oh dear, Mrs Bush,' she never knew what to call Rose, 'sit down. Here, let me raise your ankle. We need to put something cold on it to limit the bruising. John will be home shortly – he's just popped out on a call.'

'I don't wish to be any trouble,' said Rose faintly, her mind too full of images of a sexual nature to worry about the loss of face involved in having to be grateful to Caroline.

Caroline ran the tap; Solomon shuffled on his perch and ruffled his feathers. Rose eyed him nervously, and tried to edge her chair away.

'He won't hurt,' said Caroline, 'he's just a little nervous.'

Rose sniffed. She had had a Godfather with a parrot named Charlotte, whose awful habit of saying 'Bugger Off' to nice old ladies had rendered both her and her owner relatively unwelcome as Christmas guests at the vicarage, when she was a child. As a result, she had missed out on quite a few promised Christmas gifts, and had never quite got over her dislike of parrots. 'Does it speak?' she asked, mainly out of politeness, but also in

154

order to be prepared for any possible foul language. It seemed certain to her that parrots who did speak were extremely vulgar birds.

Caroline prayed silently that Solomon would not fart. 'He just squawks,' she said. 'We don't think he'll ever speak.'

'Birds,' said Rose, 'were never meant to speak. It is undignified.'

Solomon raised his tail feathers in what Caroline thought was a threatening manner.

'Shall I help you through to the sitting room?' she asked hastily. 'You would be far more comfortable.'

Rose, who was not enjoying Solomon, agreed readily. Caroline's sitting-room looked, depending on your point of view, either reasonably tidy, considering that the children were in it, or like Dante's vision of hell. There were, depending again on your point of view, a few toys and a plate of upturned sandwiches, or hundreds of scattered toys and a half-eaten meal, all over the carpet.

Caroline, for once, did not feel guilty, for Rose had arrived unannounced. She produced a support bandage for Rose's ankle, together with an old bamboo walking stick which John used when he was pretending to be Fred Astaire. 'Would you like a cup of tea?' she asked.

Rose hesitated for a nanosecond, just enough time for Caroline to realize that the quality of her tea was being questioned, then accepted. *I'll show you*, thought Caroline, and left Rose with the children.

Rose sat, very still, on the sofa. Henry and Josh were watching a video of a plasticine penguin. The penguin, she felt, was exceptionally rude. India was sitting in her bouncing chair, waving a rattle. Rose hoped that none of them would notice her, and prayed that no parts of them would emit anything unpleasant before Caroline

155

returned. She had no idea of the correct etiquette in the event of such a thing. Fortunately for her no-one was snotty, pooey or sick. The penguin continued to be a juvenile delinquent. Rose wondered if it was the inspiration behind all those rude children one saw out shopping.

Caroline made tea with a vengeance, the best tea of her life. It was China tea, of course, in a china pot, and not even Rose could possibly complain. When she returned to the sitting-room, everyone seemed mesmerized by the penguin. 'Isn't it marvellous?' she asked Rose. 'So clever.'

Rose, impressed by the china, swallowed and agreed.

Unaware of Rose's shock, Sarah had discovered that she liked having Rory around while she worked. It was nice, companionable. She was, in fact, working on the pot for the fête. She knew that Rose had no artistic imagination, and that, despite muttering about angels and organs, she would expect just a vase with a few odd colours in the glaze, and perhaps more than one handle. Nothing that Sarah ever did was conservative – except perhaps the missionary position, but she certainly did not limit herself to that – and she planned to make The Fête Pot as much a work of art as anything she ever did. She put her mind to the task, and felt the clay with her hands.

Rory, messing in the corner of the studio with easel and oil paints, put down his pallet and came over to her, marvelling as he always did at her perfect womanliness. She was his Venus, and he could not look at her enough. 'Can I paint you?' he asked, putting his arms around her from behind.

'Mmmm,' Sarah opened her eyes. 'Oh. Don't you dare!' She was too late. Anticipating her assent, he slowly and gently smeared yellow paint across her breasts. 'Rory, you devil!'

'You,' said Rory, turning her around, 'bring out the devil in me.' He made his way firmly into her affections whilst the wet clay slab idled in the sunlight.

'Why don't you paint the picture to go with my pot?' Sarah suggested later, idly scratching with one finger at the dried paint and clay on Rory.

'Are you serious?' He could think of nothing better – well, one thing, perhaps, but they had just done that.

'Yes, perfectly. I like your work. I think it's worth a try.'

'I don't know what to paint; you haven't done the pot yet,' he said.

'No, well I shan't tell you what to do,' said Sarah, 'but we'll be listening to the same music, experiencing the same sunlight. You must paint what that makes you feel.'

Rory felt randy. He always did.

He watched her afterwards as she put on her kaftan. 'Where are you going?' he asked.

'To switch on the kiln,' she said. 'I've nearly finished the pot. It wouldn't do to go messing with the kiln in the nude.'

Sarah's kiln was in a separate shed over by the hedge.

'I dare you to go in naked,' said Rory.

'Bog off,' said Sarah. 'If Morgan Groat is around, I could give him a heart attack. He passes here when he goes fishing.'

'I love it when you talk dirty,' said Rory. 'Say "bog off" again.'

'Bogoff, bogoff, bogoff,' said Sarah.

'Cor,' said Rory, 'come 'ere, little girl.'

They rolled, giggling, on the futon, the pot forgotten, the picture too. 'It's amazing,' said Sarah later, 'how this is working out.'

'Don't see why, stud like me,' said Rory, airily casual.

'Yes you do,' said Sarah, 'you know just what I mean. You've never been in a real relationship before, and I planned never to be, ever. Our expectations are completely different, yet it works.'

Rory smiled. 'It's because we enjoy one another,' he said idly, hoping that Sarah would not realize how passionately he felt, and fearing she might cast him aside.

'Perhaps,' she said, 'or perhaps we're made for one another.'

'Do you think so?' He held his breath, hoping he sounded casual.

'Rory, you are as transparent as thin air,' said Sarah. 'Stop trying to hide the needing part. It's just as important as the rest.'

Rory thought of his parents. They needed one another, too. Perhaps that explained why they were still together after twenty-five years. After all, they didn't seem wildly in love these days. He frowned.

Sarah had become suddenly serious. The moment seemed to have come, quite unexpectedly, as such moments do. 'I have to tell you something important,' she said, seizing it baldly. 'I'm pregnant.'

'Good Lord,' said Rory when it sank in. *Am I some sort of virility God?* 'That was quick.'

'No, you don't understand. I'm five months pregnant.'

Rory's bubble burst and he sat up as rage and jealousy surged through him in a tidal bore. 'Whose baby is it, then?'

Sarah disliked feeling guilty. She had successfully avoided it for most of her life, but now she desperately wanted to say the right thing to Rory. He was important. Sarah had always avoided the word 'love'. Love was for girls named Liz who married men called Colin, and lived in a really nice starter home in Rickmansworth. Surely it hadn't finally caught her? 'Look, Rory, I didn't know that I was going to meet you. I had a one-night stand, the sort of encounter I'd always preferred before now. No ties, no promises. He was just a journalist, passing through.'

'Oh Christ,' said Rory, 'not Tarquin d'Abo Smith?'

'You know him?'

'He just married Jonathan's ex-girlfriend,' said Rory miserably. 'She's got a face like a fried egg and a body like a praying mantis.'

'He doesn't know,' she said, 'about the baby. Not yet, anyway, but you see, it must have been meant to happen. Everything is fate. This is my time for a baby, and I have no regrets.'

Rory couldn't think straight. To think that Tarquin's . . . thing had been . . . oh, God, it was horrible.

'Rory, you've nothing to be jealous of,' said Sarah.

'But you're pregnant,' said Rory, unnecessarily.

'Yes, and it's what I've always wanted,' said Sarah, gently.

'Why didn't you wait? It could have been my baby. I want it to be my baby.' Rory knew that he was being unfair. He put his palm on her stomach, as if little fists might suddenly shake his hand.

Sarah found the sexual jealousy oddly good. 'You are free to walk away,' she said, 'but I don't want that. I have never said this to anyone before, Rory, but . . . I love you.'

There was a brief yet interminable silence, as joy filled Rory at the realization that his dreams, which he had feared would always be dreams, were fulfilled. Then his words tumbled out. 'I love you too!' he cried passionately. 'I know that it's absurd, that you're old enough to be my mother, and that I was almost a virgin when we met—'

159

'Hey, less of the mother, thank you, and what do you mean, almost?'

Rory decided that now was not the time to explain about Emma 'Lollipop' Carter behind the bike sheds. Besides, it would have been more fun using a doughnut. 'Well, I was really,' he glossed. 'But look, you need me around now that you're pregnant. I'm moving in.'

'What will your parents say?' Sarah was surprised into using one of those clichés she had always hoped to avoid.

'It doesn't matter what they say,' said Rory. 'This is my life. I may be young but, hell, things may never be this good again.'

'What about college? Your plans?'

'It'll work out – especially if I get into Cambridge. It's only twenty miles away, after all.'

'OK,' said Sarah, amazing even herself. After all, if you let the problems put you off before you began, you would never do anything.

'Why on earth are you moving in with Sarah?' Hetty was mystified. 'What's wrong with living here? Is it because of your father?'

'Of course not.' Rory straddled the kitchen chair the wrong way round, seeing her concentration desert the onions, and the onions turn black. 'You don't understand, Mum. I'm moving in *with* her. I love her. We're lovers.'

Hetty sat down with a bump, staring at her son. *How can this have happened without my knowing it?* she asked herself frantically. *What sort of a mother am I?* 'Oh Rory,' she said aloud, 'I didn't realize. I didn't know you were . . . Why didn't you tell me before?'

'Because it was private at first,' he said earnestly. 'I was falling in love. It was wonderful, exhilarating, but it was just for us, for Sarah and me.'

Hetty took it in slowly, a word at a time. 'And now it's not?'

'Now I want everyone to know. I want to grab hold of life and start living it!' Hetty swallowed, remembering that feeling, wanting it back.

'Mum, don't cry.'

'I'm not,' said Hetty. 'It's the onions.' She tipped them into the sink. Hopefully Alistair would have to undo the U-bend the next time he poured coffee grounds down there. With any luck it should be really disgusting. She sat at the table, facing Rory. For once they had the kitchen to themselves. Finn and Luke were out cycling, and Jonathan was deep in some vet school project which prevented him from popping home at weekends. She was called Emily.

'What am I supposed to say?' she asked. How did you respond when your son confronted you with his sexuality and his independence? It was supposedly harder the first time, but with Jonathan it had not been sudden like this. Jonathan had gone through the standard adolescent progression from computers to acne to antibiotics to thinking that no-one knew he kept his condoms under his mattress. Each stage had seemed predicted by the last. Rory had done none of those things, and, oh, she loved him so much. She gazed at his thick, sandy hair, remembering how angry he had looked at his moment of birth. Her only red-haired boy. 'You're the one I'm closest to,' she said. 'I can't bear for you to get hurt.'

He took one of her hands. 'We all get hurt, you know that. Sarah is worth the risk. She makes me feel wonderful. She's also pregnant. It isn't mine, but she needs me.'

Hetty didn't feel able to take it all in. At least, she assumed that to be the explanation for her apparently meek acceptance of this latest revelation. She wondered

161

what a soap-opera star would have said. It had often struck her that many people were beginning to base the whole way they responded to life on soap opera stars. They laughed where a soap-opera star would laugh, cried where they would cry, and pretended that lavatories did not exist and all headaches were brain tumours. Of course, the difference was that soap-opera stars always had their troubles one at a time, in order for the scriptwriters to extract the maximum mileage from each. The central character might give birth in a shopping centre, but her house was never repossessed at the same time. They certainly never had a son move in with a woman twice his age whilst his parents' marriage was in crisis. That was worth more than one episode.

'Tell me all about it,' she said resignedly. Forget the dinner. No-one seemed to be around to appreciate it anyway.

## Chapter Eleven

The following morning Mrs Groat was in the post office, attempting to buy a birthday card for her nephew. She was finding this difficult, as they all had such awful endearments on them. What she really required was a card saying, 'Happy Birthday, don't expect a present – the stamp is more than you deserve', but instead she had picked up 'Nephew – to a darling little boy, may your birthday bring you joy'. It was particularly inappropriate as her nephew was thirty-two. Angela Ormondroyd had just been in to send a package of copies of *Tatler* home to Texas, and Mrs Barrington, the postmistress, was feeling put-out at being left to stick on Angela's stamps.

'Do you know,' she said to Mrs Groat, 'that is the rudest woman I have ever met.'

'Well, what do you expect from an American?' said Mrs Groat, dismissing two hundred million people in a single phrase.

Mrs Barrington stuck the air mail stickers onto Angela's parcel. 'You'd think she would stick on her own stamps,' she said, thinking, *My spit is not free.* She was something of a socialist and hated feeling that there was a kind of allegory between what she was doing and the act of licking the Ormondroyds' boots.

'Well,' said Mrs Groat smugly, 'if she thinks we will treat her like a queen, she's in for a shock.'

'What do you mean?' Mrs Barrington was intrigued.

'Well,' Mrs Groat leaned over the counter

conspiratorially, although there was no-one else present, 'just between ourselves, she thinks she will be asked to open the fête, but she's wrong.'

'Really? You mean she isn't to do it?'

'No,' said Mrs Groat. 'Rose is intending to ask me.'

'My,' Mrs Barrington was impressed. 'That should put her nose out of joint. Have you prepared a speech?'

'I am working on it,' said Mrs Groat, 'but don't tell a soul.'

'My lips,' said Mrs Barrington, 'are sealed.'

The lips of ladies who run post offices are not often sealed very tightly, and by closing time Mrs Barrington had told Harriet, Sarah and the postman that Mrs Groat was to open the fête. Harriet was surprised, the postman did not listen – he spent a lot of time not listening to postmistresses, and had therefore missed a lot of fascinating gossip in his time – and Sarah could not have cared less. It would perhaps not have mattered, but Harriet ran into Mrs Groat that afternoon when she was on her way to Broomhill on her bicycle.

'I gather that congratulations are in order,' she said. 'I hear that you are to open the fête.'

Mrs Groat was trimming her grass verge with a pair of scissors; she did not like untidy edges.

'Oh! Thank you.' Mrs Groat was delighted. She had been confirmed in office! She assumed automatically that Harriet had heard it from Rose, her best friend. It did not occur to her that Harriet might have simply withdrawn it from the post office, where she herself had deposited it so recently.


The realization that he had been rather a fool hit Alistair the same day. It was a nasty moment. A touch of self doubt, a slight shrinking of confidence, the thought that perhaps you have been used – none of these things are pleasant but, when compounded by the feeling that you have not actually enjoyed any of it particularly, they are quite ghastly.

It began when he was driving home from work. It was four o'clock on the Friday evening (some would say that is hardly evening, but then he was a partner), and Tammy Wynette materialized over the radio, singing 'Stand By Your Man'. The song made him think of Hetty and Lucy, and how he could only imagine one of them singing it about him. The chance to knead breasts that a soft porn editor would pay money for was no use if there weren't any real feelings there. What on earth was he playing at? He was, even now, on his way to an assignation with Lucy. As he drove, his mind and his groin fought a brief but desperate battle. If he hadn't just been approaching the Bumpstaple turn-off, his mind might have won. Unfortunately, his willy was able to use the knowledge that Lucy was already primed and ready for him only a hundred yards away. It therefore doubled its vote on account of growth.

It was sadly ironic for Alistair that he had almost, but not quite, abandoned that last meeting, and yet that was when he was spotted, and lost his chance to brush the whole affair under the carpet. It was chance, of course. Harriet Harbour cycled by just as Alistair and Lucy kissed their hello. It was too much of a kiss to mean anything less than it actually did, and Harriet wobbled so much in shock that she fell off her bicycle into the ditch behind the car, and thus was not observed by the lovers. She might have said nothing, but she had a complete inability to keep secret anything which seriously worried her. It was just, as in some gruesome fairy tale, a matter of whom she would see first.

Poor Harriet. She did not wish to draw attention to herself so, being trapped in a ditch beneath her bicycle, a proper old-fashioned one, and very heavy indeed, she was forced to remain there until she was sure that the coast was clear and she had heard Alistair and Lucy leave.

They had gone, in fact, for a quick drink at the 'Stanley Arms', up at Castle Stanley. It was a pleasant pub, not too fashionable, and not likely to attract anyone that Alistair knew so early on a Friday. If the brewery who now owned the pub had had their way and, against local opinion, renamed the establishment 'The Frog and Bullet', then it might have become very trendy and served Japanese rice-crackers and teriyaki. As it was, however, there was a choice of lasagne, chilli and baked potatoes, and no-one trendy was present.

The drink was quick, as Alistair was quite anxious to head for the nearby cottage, belonging to one of Lucy's friends, where they did most of their meeting. He had a PCC meeting later, so time was of the essence. Every minute lost meant a few thrusts fewer. Lucy was still rather enjoying Alistair's pursuit. She had fast discovered that after the initial heady excitement of what she called the Night of the Pigs, sex with George was less fun than sex with Alistair. In fact, with George it often felt rather cumbersome, like spaceships docking.

They were well in the thick of things when it all went rather wrong. Lucy slipped up and called Alistair 'George', and when he jokingly said, 'You're not sleeping with him, are you?' she turned red and shifty-eyed, and it was all over in one withering – embarrassingly withering – moment.

He drove her back to Broomhill in a cool but adult silence. Lucy was peeved at being treated as though she had done something wrong. After all, he was the one with the wife. She snorted her upper class derisory snort.

Alistair was glad it was over. It had started to become something of a chore, really, and now that his willy had less than half a vote, he could see that he did not wish to continue with bonking that had no real soul to it. He hated the guilt he now felt with Hetty, hated himself for being weak and chasing an easy little tart just because she had ancestors who knew William the Conqueror, and breasts which had never breastfed. What had he been doing, bonking a girl who possessed a derisory snort? It was all so sordid. God, what if Hetty should find out? Alistair very much did not want Hetty to find out.

Harriet, meanwhile, had been found by Oliver Bush, dusted off and loaded into his old Volvo. Her bicycle, remarkably undamaged, was loaded into the back, and Oliver did up her seatbelt himself. Harriet was all a-twitter, and when Oliver asked kindly, 'How did you come to fall?' she poured out the whole story in her confusion and dismay.

Oliver, being a vicar, had seen much of human nature. He was not altogether surprised by Alistair's apparent faithlessness – he had always felt that there was a streak of something rather selfish in him. However he felt terrible for Hetty, whom he much admired. She was the only woman he had ever seen who could unblock her own drains, and look as pretty as a picture in the process. She must be in her forties by now, but she had a special quality, a sort of blitheness of spirit, which made her seem younger. What might her husband's betrayal do to that? He had no doubt that Hetty would find out. Villages are like pressure cookers: little bits of gossip, which no-one ever meant to pass on, all bubbling away together until they burst out of the top all at once, in a vast shriek of steam. (Oliver knew a lot about villages but was not well-versed in pressure-cooker technology.)

He drove poor Harriet home, then returned to Rose deep in contemplation. Rose, who had hoped to discuss with him a rumour which she had heard about a rhino, was annoyed by the mood. She had seen it before. When you married a man of the cloth you became accustomed to all of these moods – introspective moods, self-doubting moods, thoughtful moods, meditative moods – to Rose they were all the same, they were silent moods.

She muttered and peeled potatoes, balancing on her good foot and wearing her most martyred expression. 'I wonder where Harriet is?' she remarked. 'She was going to stop by on her way home, before the PCC.'

Oliver said nothing, and sloped off to work on his sermon at the earliest available opportunity. Abandoning the one he had planned on deceit as too near the mark, he decided that love would make a far better subject.


Later that evening, Sir George Ormondroyd made his way stoically to the Parochial Church Council meeting. Being a country landowner through and through, it was one of the things which he regarded as his duty. Normally such evenings were brief and rather uninteresting affairs, set as they were in the rectory, with nothing stronger to drink than tea and, like as not, biscuits with cherries on the top. Tonight, however, proved to be a little more diverting than usual, for the meeting was enlivened by the unfolding story of the dry rot, and the problem of the bats.

The PCC consisted of Oliver Bush in the Chair, Morgan and Mrs Groat, Jacob and Jessie, Alistair, Harriet and George. Despite Oliver's position, they normally deferred to George. Rose was not formally on the Council, as she felt that this was somehow not quite proper, but she normally stayed at the meetings as a kind of hovering, tea-pouring presence. Tonight, however, she was resting her ankle, which had apparently been sprained as she walked along The Street earlier in the week. Now it was in plaster. All present agreed that The Street was really rather uneven.

Normally, George was about as easily embarrassed as a rhinoceros, but he thought it would be deeply awkward to have to explain Angela's allergy to the assembled group. He had seen the rash, and, inasmuch as it bore no resemblance to his piles, he could not see what made it such a problem.

The best way, he felt, was to omit all reference to Angela from the discussion, and concentrate on the general unpleasantness of bat droppings. That way he could gauge the climate of opinion. 'I was wondering,' he said, a little stiffly, 'if there were any plans to do anything about the bat-fouling in the church. Have we looked into eradicating the creatures?'

Oliver Bush sighed. Like Jessie, he liked the bats, always had done, and although he knew them to be quite safe, it always troubled him when parishioners got up a sweat about them. 'I'm afraid that the bats are protected in Law,' he said. 'They are an endangered species.'

'Good Lord!' said George, genuinely surprised, as he had been brought up to believe that animals were only put on this earth to be ridden on or shot at. 'Protected, heh?'

Mrs Groat would happily have torn the bats limb from limb, pickled them, and fed them to her niece's children, which said a fair amount about her opinion of the children, as well as that of bats, but she did not wish to argue with George.

It was left to Alistair, who did not particularly care whether or not he was seen to be Christian, but who still entertained hopes of tasting George's stocks of port, to stand up for the right of the common, or not so common, man to worship without being defecated upon. 'It seems to me,' he said, 'that something could be done on grounds of hygiene. After all, I believe that they can carry rabies.'

'Oh my!' Rose could not contain her comment. What if Oliver had rabies? She had read that it could take years to develop. Perhaps that explained why he was sometimes so odd after Communion.

Oliver Bush, wanting to move the meeting on, said, 'I really don't think much can be done, but perhaps we could defer this and I will check our position.'

'I,' said Harriet, 'shall contact the Bat Group.'

The others looked at her in surprise. She looked quite angry, an impression somehow enhanced by the Elastoplast on her forehead. She had apparently had some sort of a tumble from her bicycle.

Alistair felt uncomfortably certain that Hetty would support her, so he felt obliged to placate her. 'That's an excellent idea,' he said, hoping that she was not about to have the vapours, whatever they were.

'I believe,' said Harriet, ignoring him, 'that we should be supporting the local Bat Group with some of the proceeds of the fête. We should show our gratitude because our church is *blessed* with bats.'

Oliver Bush beamed at her, which silenced her far more effectively than anything Alistair could have said. George choked on his tea. Whatever would Angela say? He had the dawning conviction that he was not going to win this one. He cleared his throat and produced his trump card. 'I'm afraid that my wife has developed a serious allergy to bats,' he said, 'which may eventually render her unable to attend St Jude's for reasons of health.'

Oliver, who would not stoop to pointing out that up until now Angela seemed to have had a fairly serious allergy to church, expressed his sympathy and his willingness to deliver Communion in her home should she be too ill to travel to a neighbouring, uninfested church such as St Julian's in Bumpstaple.

Harriet, though, had no such misgivings. Her blushes forgotten, she rounded on Sir George. 'What nonsense!' she told him. 'Angela hardly ventures into St Jude's for long enough to be allergic to anything, but the point is that the Law protects the bats and that's the end of it.'

'Then the Law's an ass,' said George, thinking of his Godfather, a peer, who was about as sharp as a sponge and had a similar capacity for absorbing port. With people like Archibald passing the Law, it was really not surprising to find it to be an ass.

'I'm so sorry, Sir George,' interrupted Oliver. 'Perhaps you would like to plan a private Communion for your wife next Sunday? I have my diary.'

George swallowed, imagining Angela's likely response. Such a service could end up as his last rites. 'Very good of you, Rector. I'll get back to you,' he muttered, recognizing an immovable obstacle, and deciding to give up. Angela was being ridiculous anyway, fussing over a little rash. She should have his piles.

'And I,' reaffirmed Harriet, 'will speak to the Bat Group.'

Mrs Groat glared at her. Silly woman, sticking her oar in. She didn't have to clean the beastly stuff.

Jessie, however, was full of admiration. Harriet had stuck to her guns in the face of all of those men *and* Mrs Groat. 'Good for you, Harriet,' she ventured, startling everyone, as it was the first time anyone could recall hearing her speak at a PCC meeting.

'We should,' said Oliver Bush, deciding that it was time to change the subject, 'discuss the melted weather-cock.'

'Wrath of God, it was,' said Mrs Groat in hushed tones.

George let his attention wander, wondering how on earth he was to tell Angela that the great wealth of the Ormondroyds had been defeated. Then he wondered what his mother would think, if indeed she possessed any capacity for rational thought. That young Potter had been mumbling on about brain scans again, talking about clots in a persuasive doctorish way. He, George, had dismissed the idea. Charles had never suggested it, and Charles had been at Eton. Mind you, he had been a bit of a drinker, old Charles. Perhaps he hadn't known his onions – after all, he hadn't treated George's piles. The fact that they had been undetectable was no excuse, not for a paying patient.

He resolved to discuss it with Angela. 'Indeed I will,' he said aloud, and was astonished to discover that he had just agreed to pay for a new weathercock for St Jude's.

Back at the Hall the following day, Angela could hardly wait to leaf through the society pages of *Tatler*. She had rung Marsha Millington on the day after her appointment with Professor Quincey, wishing to let her know of the amazing diagnosis which the Professor had made. She was still unaware that Marsha had had rather bad news from the Professor. News so bad, in fact, that Angela's call rubbed salt in her wound in a major way. Angela had seen Marsha's rash, so it was imperative to remain cautiously friendly, at least for a week or two, until the cure was effected and the rash was gone. As long as Angela did not seem to be malicious on the subject of rashes, she must be retained as a friend.

For this reason, Marsha had dealt kindly with Angela in this month's *Tatler*. There was an airbrushed photograph, and a fawning paragraph explaining how Lady Ormondroyd, pillar of the local community, was engaged in a one-woman crusade against bat-fouling in our beloved churches. The text portrayed Angela as a cross between the Princess of Wales and Joan of Arc, and Angela was over the moon. All day friends had been telephoning, ostensibly to arrange to meet for lunch ('It's been so long, dear,') to ask advice ('I just thought of you at *once*, dear,') and to strengthen recently shaky friendships ('My dear, I was so afraid that you might have taken my comments about your plastic surgeon *personally*,'), but in fact wishing to confirm and renew their relationship with this issue's Lady of the Month. A whole page for the photograph! Who else had had that, apart from Sophie Montfort-Bryce when she was a deb, and look what had become of her! She had run off with a driving instructor from Dagenham and gone to live on an estate in Walton-on-the-Naze. It had been the worst case of social death anyone could ever recall.

In between calls, Angela telephoned the newsagent at home to reserve another two dozen copies of *Tatler*. She must make sure that there were plenty to spare for friends who might not have seen it. She positively glowed with the inner light of one who has just won a place on the honours list, or who has been consulted for fashion advice by the Queen.

Those who rise the highest, it is said, have the furthest to fall. Months later there were those who said that perhaps Angela should not have sung quite so loudly from her perch on top of the castle. However, glory comes so seldom that perhaps it should be enjoyed while you have it. As in most walks of life, there is no course to follow which guarantees that no-one will ever laugh at you. However, unaware now that the future might not go entirely her way, Angela had been having further thoughts on the possibility of institutionalized care for her mother-in-law. She had thought up a little more ammunition. She was sure that a malicious old harridan burned brightly behind the screen of vagueness, and felt that this made her a danger to herself. Yes. Wasn't that when you put people away – if they were a danger to themselves? Angela wondered if there might be a way of transporting Lady Sybil out of Barking Hall on the grounds of concern about her health. She would speak, very carefully, to John Potter. Meanwhile, it was an excellent reason for continuing her seduction of George; she must keep him sweet.

George himself was still delighted by the turn which his sex life had taken. He was aware that, for men of his age and class, sex which was not clandestine was often rare, and rarely enjoyable. He had, however, taken to checking the length of his willy with a tape measure, remembering the awful predictions of Smythe Junior at Eton, who had said that if you used it more than three times a day it eroded away. He was, it's true, not quite up to the thrice daily mark, but he was averaging almost twice and was beginning to notice a constant heat down there. If this was a friction burn then he might get a blister, and if so, would it then be smaller than before the blister? Size was very important to George. It had, after all, been the longest in the dormitory by a sixteenth of an inch. Fortunately there had not, so far, been any measurable reduction in the size of his endowment, so he was more than happy to continue to partake of what was on offer, both in the stable and in the bedroom.

# Chapter Twelve

Alistair had spent a rather fruitless day at the office. He had not slept well the previous night, and profoundly regretted the selfish way in which he had leaped upon Hetty in the middle of it. He had somehow hoped that a little more activity on the physical front might erase his infidelity, and that he could speedily put the affair with Lucy away into the past and be happy again with his wife. He loved her, didn't he? He wanted her, he respected her – so why wasn't it working? Somehow, some basic lines of communication seemed to be missing. It didn't feel as though they were friends any more.

Driving home, he reflected, as Hetty had done so often recently, on the changes in them since Fort William. He remembered the caravan, laughing and hugging, her crying on his shoulder over something long-forgotten. Nostalgia filled him, a longing for how it had been. Surely things could be that way again? They could be. They *must* be! The boys were growing up, they soon would not need him – apart from his bank account. He must find a way of rediscovering the marriage they once had.

By the time he turned into the Old Forge, he had made a brave decision. He was going to tell Hetty everything. He was going to confess his shame and guilt, wipe the slate clean, beg her forgiveness and – pray, perhaps? Despite being a regular churchgoer, Alistair had not prayed for years. It did not occur to him that his reasons for confessing all were not entirely altruistic, but resulted from his need to purge himself of his guilt. He was not a reader of agony aunt pages, where such analysis of motive may often be found. He truly believed that he was about to do an honest and noble thing. Unfortunately he was to be, as once before, just too late. Hetty was not at home. There was a note on the table: 'Doing church flowers with Harriet. Open some wine.' Alistair looked for the corkscrew, and could not hear the great bell of doom beginning to toll.

Hetty and Harriet were, by unhappy chance, rostered together on the flower rota. They had almost finished, and were clearing up the leaves and cut stems, when Harriet found a discarded pink carnation. 'Oh look, it's one of yours from last week, but it's still perfect,' she said. 'Let me add it in.'

To think that fate, and all its permutations, can hang on one pink carnation, on a wobbling stool, on a slip of the tongue. Harriet tottered and fell, landing smack on her knees between the pews. 'Goodness me,' she said, a little winded. Fortunately the scattered kneelers took the impact from her. 'That's two falls in two days.'

'Are you hurt?' asked Hetty anxiously.

'No, dear, only my pride,' said Harriet. 'Not nearly as bad as the other night. I came off my bicycle almost underneath Alistair's car.'

Hetty was surprised. Dusting dust, and presumably guano, off Harriet she said, 'I didn't realize that Alistair had caused your downfall. Rose said that it was Lucy Bellingham smooching with a man.'

Harriet, who had indeed told that story to Rose in a confused attempt to explain turning up late at the rectory on the evening of the PCC meeting all covered in Elastoplast, was caught. She turned a painful shade of

176

ripe tomato, and her complete inability to improvise or lie told Hetty all that she had never wanted to hear. Alistair and Lucy. Of course. How clear it all was. Poor Harriet realized that her stuttering attempts to soothe things were hopeless. Hetty had already left.

She saw Alistair through the kitchen window before he saw her. He was sitting at the table with two glasses and a bottle of Australian red from that beastly pretentious bloody wine club. Hetty's nearly boiling blood heated up a little further as she opened the kitchen door with the immense delicacy of one who knows that she might otherwise smash it into a thousand pieces.

Alistair took a deep breath when she came in, and as she pushed the door shut with her back, he began the speech which he had not dared rehearse. 'Hetty, there's something I have to tell you, something terrible. Please, sit down.'

Hetty swallowed, but her tight throat would not complete the sequence, so the ball of effort stuck halfway down her neck, rendering speech impossible. Slowly, and still with infinite care, she walked to the table and sat down, facing Alistair. He pushed a glass of wine towards her and she took it, took a large mouthful, and swallowed. The lump went, but she was not sure that she had a voice. He was going to tell her, she knew that for certain. Was he going to leave? She felt afraid, full of cold dread, then the wine hit her empty stomach and turned her pale cheeks raspberry pink.

'I've had an affair,' said Alistair quickly, wanting to get it said. 'It was stupid, juvenile and pathetic. I've been a ridiculous, greedy fool.'

'I know.' How could she sound so steady, so controlled?

Alistair's mouth fell open. He was shaken to the core. She knew. She clearly knew. How long had she known? His whole speech had centred on the fact that he was confessing something that she did not already know, might never have known. He had somehow hoped that this was what would vindicate him, bring him her forgiveness.

'I just heard,' said Hetty coldly, 'from Harriet.' She waited.

Alistair swallowed. 'It's over, I promise you. I'm sorry. I can't believe I was so crass, so stupid. I've been the classic middle-aged fool, flattered by a pretty girl.'

The bungled apology puffed oxygen at the smouldering wick of Hetty's resentment. She glowed dangerously. 'She's young enough to be your daughter,' she said, feeling the pot of rage and fury and hatred and jealousy stirring and seething with the wine in her stomach. Soon, she knew, it would erupt. Perhaps she would murder him. Could she? *If I were a uranium rod*, she thought, *they would be evacuating Suffolk.*

Alistair shook his head. 'There's nothing I can say to defend myself. I've betrayed you.'

'Why?'

'I don't know why. Somehow the life had gone out of our relationship, our sex life was—'

'You bastard,' screamed Hetty, flinging the rest of her wine at him, and knocking her chair over as she stood. 'You crass, fat, despicable, grotesque, greedy, lying, cheating, deceiving bloody MAN! How *dare* you blame us, blame me for your sordid willy dipping? You're not even trying to say that you loved her, are you? *Are you?*'

'No, I'm not. I didn't bloody well love her. For God's sake, calm down!' Alistair had wanted her to shout, but now he didn't like it.

'Oh, you'd like that, wouldn't you?' raged Hetty. 'You just hate histrionics. Well, histrionics you're going to get!' She snatched Alistair's glass from him and hurled it across the kitchen. It hit a cupboard and sprayed shards of recycled glass across the floor. 'You betrayed *our marriage* with that stupid, fat, horsey *slut*, and you think I should calm down? You disgust me.'

'I know. I'm sorry. What else can I say?'

Hetty paced across the glass which crunched satisfyingly beneath her shoes. 'You can say sorry, sorry, sorry for *ever*! Damn you, Alistair, you've thrown away twenty-five years of marriage for a few rolls in the hay. How could you?' Her voice had risen to a scream. Finn, Luke and Rory, filtering cautiously down the stairs, paused at the doorway.

'You didn't seem to want me,' said Alistair miserably, 'not really. I'm just a man. I was weak, a fool.'

Tears were streaming unchecked down Hetty's face. 'That's crap!' she shouted. 'You were a nasty, greedy bastard. Why are you telling me about it? Why don't you go and tell Lucy-bloody-Strumpet how hard-done-by you are? Then see how sexy she is after twenty-five years with a man who has forgotten that she has a brain. Not that *she* has, of course.'

'I—'

But Hetty was on a roll. 'Did she dump you? I bet she did, you stupid, pathetic, middle-aged idiot. How dare you do this to us? I hate you, do you hear me? Get out. *Get out!*'

Alistair stood up, tried to put his hands on her shoulders, but put his foot on the glass. He was not wearing shoes. 'Bloody hell!' The sharp pain started tears to his eyes.

Hetty did not notice. 'Get your dirty cheating hands off me!'

'I can't,' said Alistair, gasping. 'I've cut my foot.'

They both looked down at the spreading red pool on the floor. 'Oh God,' said Hetty as Alistair sagged against her. He never could stand the sight of blood, particularly not his own. 'Rory, help!' she shouted.

The boys rushed to the kitchen, then stopped, appalled. 'She's killed him,' said Finn, loudly.

'Don't be stupid,' said Hetty, 'he's fainted. Rory, help me. We need to lie him down, but there's glass everywhere. Luke, get a brush quickly and clear the glass.'

They coped swiftly, but in stunned silence. Alistair was laid on the floor and Finn fetched a cold wet cloth and a glass of water. He was coming round already. Hetty took off his blood-soaked sock. It was a nasty, deep gash, and blood was pumping out in a rather alarming manner. She pressed on it hard with her hankie. Serve him right if it wasn't a clean one.

'Rory, could you telephone John Potter?'

By the time John Potter arrived, the bleeding had stopped, and Alistair was looking a touch less green. The boys were still silent and shocked, and Hetty knew that they must have heard at least part of the row. She busied herself making tea, pushing everything else away while John stitched up Alistair's foot. Alistair was normally the most appalling patient, particularly in the presence of a needle, but he said not a word.

John didn't stay for long; he didn't even finish his tea. The atmosphere in the Stewarts' house was of the knife-cutting variety. They obviously had things to talk about and he was, in any case, having a rotten evening on call, having been summoned to the police cells to see a hopelessly inebriated traffic warden, who had called him a police collaborator, taken his name and promised him an endless stream of parking tickets from wardens everywhere.

After he had left, silence remained. The boys hovered rather uncertainly, as if, by staying, they could prevent their parents from tumbling back into their awful fight. Hetty sat at the kitchen table, emotionally and physically exhausted. Alistair looked strained and pale, and Hetty guessed that he felt sick. The foot drama seemed to have defused the situation, somehow. She had felt afraid for him, and that had conflicted so much with the other things which she had been feeling that they all seemed to have fizzled into nothing, like damp squibs.

'Would you go upstairs, please,' she said quietly, 'your father and I have to talk.'

Luke and Finn, eyes like saucers, retreated in relief, but Rory remained, staunchly loyal. 'I'm not going,' he said. 'I think you need a bit of moral support.' He came over to stand beside her, his hand on her shoulder.

'It's OK, Rory, really,' she said, squeezing his hand. 'We'll discuss it later.'

'All right,' he said doubtfully, 'I'll hang around. I was just packing some things.' He retreated.

'What does he mean?' asked Alistair, dully. 'What things is he packing?'

'He's moving in with Sarah Struther,' said Hetty. 'You know, as her lover.'

Alistair gaped, still too dazed for any greater expression of shock or bewilderment. 'I didn't know they—'

'No,' said Hetty, 'you were too busy.' Then her conscience pricked her and she added, 'I didn't know either, at least, not that it was Sarah, nor that it was serious.'

'I thought he might be gay,' said Alistair sadly.

'Would it have mattered so much?' asked Hetty.

'I'm afraid so,' said Alistair, 'to me. It's just the way I am. Mind you, the way I am doesn't seem to have much to recommend it.'

Hetty sighed. 'I think I'll take Jess for a walk.' She rooted in the kitchen drawer for a lead.

'What do you want me to do?'

'I don't know,' said Hetty, 'I have to think.'

'Do you want me to move out?'

She looked over at him, and felt a wave of unwanted pity. He looked defeated and ill. A few minutes ago, before the foot, she would have said *Go, go and never come back*. Now, though, the wind had been taken out of the sails of her anger by one of life's more ordinary crises, the kind of small crises which had formed an occasional part of their lives throughout the years. In the midst of her shouting and fury, life itself had demonstrated its ability just to carry on regardless. If she had truly hated Alistair, she would not have dealt with his foot and his fainting. She didn't know what she wanted from him now, but she did know that they needed to talk, when she was ready.

'No,' she said, 'I don't. I just want to be alone for a while. Then we have to talk.'

'I love you,' said Alistair, rather sadly.

Fastening the lead on the dog, she glanced back at him. 'It doesn't mean much if you only say it when you want something.' She let herself out of the door, quietly.

Alistair looked at the door for a moment, then let his head drop into his hands.

Hetty towed Jess through the churchyard, her salty face stiff and sore from earlier tears. It was no use telling herself endlessly that Alistair was the worst kind of scum, that she would be well rid of such a philandering heap of slime. Part of her still wanted to shout and scream, to throw the food processor – his gift to her last Christmas, and heartily resented – at his head, to smash his glasses, if he had any, to emasculate him. The rest of her wanted to curl up quietly, discover exactly what her wounds were, and clean them.

The church was still open. Workmen were in looking at the dry rot, estimating the repairs. Although the money was not yet raised, there was not a day to lose as the fungus spread its dreaded red tendrils through the fabric of the ancient building. She could hear them on the staircase; doubtless they would not be long. Jacob or Morgan would be over soon to lock up. The church, alas, could not be left unlocked any more. The insurers would not allow it, even though the silver was kept in a bank vault and only brought out when the archdeacon came to preach.

Hetty sat down in the pew which she habitually occupied, then, noticing a draught from the tower stairs, moved up to the choir stalls. Jess sighed loudly and sat at her feet with a grunt. A faint scent of disinfectant lingered, reminding her that someone had Done the Droppings. She leaned on the seat in front, laying her chin on her forearms and looking up at the stained-glass windows depicting events in the life of Christ. Birth, death, resurrection. Hetty had always liked that window, which seemed at times to glow with a light made up of more than just the light behind it.

Jacob Bean did not see her when he let himself into the church, and Hetty did not come down to reveal herself. She was in a turmoil, her mind a mess of unclear choices in the presence of which doing nothing at all looked horribly tempting. Should she leave Alistair? Should she give this strange, abject Alistair a chance? She examined her pain. The betrayal, the sexual betrayal might be the most obvious, but there were greater hurts than that. The mental rejection was worse, and that seemed to have set seed long ago. *Did I reject him?* she wondered, *or did we just lose one another somewhere along the way, rather as you can leave your purse somewhere, and not notice until you actually need it for something? Was it my fault too? Surely it must take two to make, or break, a marriage.* She tried to think of times when she and Alistair had been lovers, in the true romantic sense of the word. She remembered odd occasions, like snapshots in an album, but they seemed to be years ago, in that sunnier life which we all

183

store in our past. There was the time when they broke the kitchen table in a rented villa in Corfu, because the boys were asleep in the bedroom. She could still see the expression on Alistair's face when she had told the rep that she had bonked the table accidentally, in passing. Then there had been that time in the back of the Morris Minor, on their own drive, just because she had said that she wondered if she had missed out by never making love in a car.

She sat, silent, for what seemed an age. She could hear Jacob talking to the men on the stair, then she heard him at the end of the aisle, switching on the organ bellows. He climbed onto the stool, hitting an array of pedals as he did so. From the tower a voice called, 'Gawd! Thought you were the Phantom of the Opera.' Jacob spread his fingers on the keys, and Mendelssohn's triumphant Wedding March burst out of the pipes. He knew it so well that it sounded not only correct, but triumphantly correct. It startled Hetty, engrossed as she was in the state of her marriage. Perhaps it was an omen. She was a believer in omens as statements of intent by God and the fates. She tried to think of Alistair, just Alistair, but could not picture him in isolation. Always she saw him with herself, being mean to Rory, holding forth to someone, somewhere, never alone. Did that mean that she didn't want to think of him alone?

The workmen were preparing to leave, and were discussing their respective requirements of woman-kind.

'She's someone I can talk to, someone to share things with,' said one.

'Nah, a good pair of knockers and goes like a train, that's my Shirl,' said the other.

Hetty could hear them more clearly as they came out of the vestry and into the main part of the church, where

184

Jacob was seated at the organ. She must leave too, before Jacob locked her in. She stood and walked down the aisle, Jess trailing behind, totally bored. Jacob, whose peripheral vision was limited, due in part to his spectacles having slipped down his nose, was not startled because he did not notice her at all. He was still playing wedding music, but now it was the March from *Lohengrin*, quietly. Hetty remembered singing 'Here comes the bride, all fat and wide', long ago at someone's wedding, and being sent outside. She felt like that now, sent outside, outside her marriage, alone. The workmen had gone and she left too, heading for home. Alistair would doubtless be ready with a speech. She didn't like him being cowed, even though he deserved to be. The worst of it was, he had clearly intended to tell her, even if she hadn't found out from Harriet. More than that, he had actually told her.

She blew her nose as she walked between the topiary bird and the topiary phallic thing to the lych-gate. She tried not to feel that she would rather not have found out, for it wouldn't have changed the facts. In any case, Alistair's confession and Harriet's fateful slip had come together. The veil had been lifted from her eyes and the awful knowledge had been hers, but the suspicion had already been there. It had been only a matter of time. All those late evenings, the aftershave. The *Daily* bloody *Mail* made this happen.

A bat flitted overhead, then another. Their lives were hanging on the church and on the likes of Rose and Mrs Groat. How good, though, just to be a bat. No affairs, no betrayals, just high, sweet singing and dropping guano whenever you felt like it. She thought of Jessie, cleaning for all those years, and smiled.

She was home in minutes. The dahlias were coming out, a storm of colour. They reminded her of Alistair's flirting with Lucy on their way home from church, aeons ago. She remembered spreading the dahlias with manure that day. It had been late April. They could only have been flirting then: wouldn't dare have done so if their affair had already begun, so it must have been since then. Only a matter of a month or so. Hardly a grand passion. Not even time for a dahlia to grow and flower, let alone a passion. From the drive, she could see Rose pottering around in the rectory vegetable patch. Hetty did not try to catch her eye. She avoided the kitchen door, letting Jess off her lead into the garden and following her slowly.

Her life was changed now, she was at a watershed. Rory was leaving, Alistair had betrayed her, but she had a choice, at least. Did she want to reject Alistair now, for ever, and go on without him, or was twenty-five years of marriage worth trying for? The fact that her mind could phrase the question in that way seemed to be an answer in itself. *Of course it's worth trying for, if you think you can.* She tried to imagine herself going on without him, running the house, looking after the boys, maybe finding a job. It looked bright, sunny and unreal, like an episode on children's TV, or a washing powder advertisement. The characters in her mind appeared wooden, puppet-like.

Then she thought of the future with him, trying to be together again. Now the scene in her mind had real quality. She could put herself into it and was conscious of a feeling of hope. If only it worked, it could be very good. Would she know if it had failed, though? Would she know before he betrayed her again, if indeed he did?

Alistair came out of the kitchen limping slightly. It was growing dark, and the night smelt of early summer: soft, and scented with cut grass. She noticed that he wasn't looking quite so cowed.

'If you want me to go for a while,' he said, 'I will.'

'No,' said Hetty, not looking at him, looking at Jess, 'I don't want you to go, not unless you want to.'

He touched her shoulder. 'I don't want to. I made a mistake.'

'That's a bit easy, don't you think?' She turned to look at him. 'Just a mistake?'

'I know,' he said, 'I won't insult you by trying to suggest it doesn't matter.' Hetty flinched. 'It was unforgivable.'

'Were things so bad between us?' she asked.

Alistair was silent for a moment as Jess wandered back towards them. 'I'm not trying to blame you,' he said, after a moment.

'You mean they were,' she said. 'We were miles apart.'

'It doesn't excuse anything,' he said, turning away. 'I do know how stupid it was. I'm not just saying it for effect.'

'I know.' She was silent. Alistair waited. Jess tried to lie on all of their feet, but couldn't quite manage it. 'Hold me.'

Cautiously he put his arms around her, held her. Hetty relaxed against him, felt his chin in her hair. Jess shoved at their legs.

'I want to forgive you,' she said. 'If we're not worth trying for now, it makes a nonsense of almost my whole life. I can't bear that.'

He took a deep breath, kissed her forehead. 'I don't deserve you.'

Hetty smiled weakly. 'I'm not used to you being abject,' she said. 'Let's go and find some coffee.'

They walked together into the house and Jess followed, content.

\*　　\*　　\*

Although it was by now quite late, Angela had decided to telephone John Potter, to make an appointment to discuss her mother-in-law. It did not occur to her that she might be telephoning at an inconvenient time. She dialled. Great Barking still possessed an old, three-figure exchange, with a reassuring purr for a dialling tone. It was still possible to choose your own telephone number, on payment of a small sum, and provided no-one else was in possession of the number which you desired. She dialled the Potters on treble three.

It had been Caroline's idea, changing to treble three – it meant that her mother could remember it easily. John always felt slightly uncomfortable with it, as it had been the code one dialled for a cardiac arrest alert in his last hospital job. For long, long hours he had toiled on the wards, occasionally rushing in a surge of adrenalin to someone's bedside crying, 'Three three three!' It was so ingrained in him that whenever he telephoned home he was slightly nervous, as though a hoard of sweaty doctors might come running through the door and start pummelling his chest. Those nights were still so vivid: the times when the crash call had come when he was in the lavatory, in the bath, in his wife. It was his own fervent wish that, should he ever arrest on a hospital ward, it would be on a night when the Indian take-away was closed and the crash team had all had pizza. He could imagine nothing worse than being dragged back to life and then blasted with prawn vindaloo.

When Angela rang, the Potters were thoroughly occupied, John being on top. He was, however, psychologically incapable of ignoring a ringing telephone. 'Hello. John Potter.'

'Angela Ormondroyd speaking,' said shrill upper-class tones, so loudly that Caroline could hear her too. She pulled a cross-eyed face at John.

'Did you want to speak to Caroline?' John tried hard to keep his voice steady.

'No, no, it was you that I wanted,' said Angela, an unfortunate remark, considering Caroline's current position.

'How can I help?' John asked, trying valiantly to ignore his wife's inner muscular activity. He had once told her what girls in Thailand could reputedly do and she had been exercising ever since. She might not be able to smoke a pipe down there but she wasn't at all bad.

'I want you to come over and discuss my mother-in-law,' said Angela, trying to sound concerned. 'I feel she is becoming a danger to herself.'

John was a very good GP; he had an eye for the hidden agenda, and he guessed at once what Angela was planning, but he trod carefully. 'Of course, Lady Ormondroyd, I would be delighted to come and see you, and you can tell me of your concerns. You must realize, though, that I am not at liberty to discuss Lady Ormondroyd's health with you.'

Angela had expected this and was not deterred. She did not need to hear about Lady Sybil, she just wanted to plant a few seeds in the minds of John Potter and, more especially, George.

John, who was hoping to get back to planting some seeds of his own, allowed her to make an appointment the following Monday, just to get her off his back. 'Bloody woman,' he said to Caroline after she had gone, 'awful bloody woman. If George weren't such a pompous twit I'd feel sorry for him.'

'I feel sorry for Lady Sybil,' said Caroline. 'Dementia is so undignified.'

'Well yes,' said John, 'assuming that's what she has.'

'Might it not be?'

'Well, it is the most likely thing, I suppose,' he adjusted his pelvis, distracted, 'there's just something not quite right about it.'

'Right?' Caroline was only half listening. She was getting quite good at the squeezes, and it felt very nice. She was so glad that he had agreed to forget both the Pill and the condoms.

'Well, she went downhill virtually overnight when Sir Hector died, according to George. I've been trying to persuade him to get another opinion, a scan, but he had a lot of faith in old Charles, and Charles said nothing could be done.'

'Can't you do anything?'

'Maybe. I'll see what Lady Snoot has to say on Monday. She certainly doesn't mean to help Lady Sybil, other than out of the Hall, but she might end up doing so.'

'Ooh,' said his wife. He had just found his rhythm again.

# Chapter Thirteen

Hetty had agonized for quite some time over whether she, or Alistair, or neither of them should sleep in the spare room. She really wasn't sure what she wanted. On the one hand, he deserved to sleep in the garden, on the other, she did not like sleeping alone. On the one hand, what he had been doing was stomach-churningly revolting, on the other, she still wanted to be held.

Alistair limped into the bedroom where she was sitting on the edge of the bed, thinking about it while he had his bath. 'I'll use the spare room,' he said. 'I just came to say "good night".'

Hetty felt awkward. Now that everything had changed, she didn't know the rules any more – perhaps there weren't any. Perhaps Alistair did not want to sleep with her. 'Good night,' she said, not looking at him.

Alistair hovered in the doorway, but when she continued to ignore him, he left the room. She could hear him rooting in the airing cupboard for the spare duvet, and resisted the urge to help. After a while she heard him head for the spare room, which was downstairs at the back of the house. His sounds were lost to her. She turned out the light and got into bed, curled into foetal position as the sheets were cold. Rejection sat like an iceberg in the pit of her stomach, and she wanted to cry, but the tears balled up into her throat instead, and threatened her with earache. Horrible, unwelcome thoughts flapped around in her head like huge black moths. Perhaps Lucy had made him realize that she,

Hetty, was now old and used. Perhaps he didn't desire her any more. He might want their marriage to go on, but might only love her as a companion, a friend, a mother. Would there be no passion from now on? Was he actually relieved to be in a separate bed? Who could desire me, when they can have a firm, young, unused body? Mine has had four children. I'm past my sell-by date. Self-pity and insecurity, friends of darkness and loneliness, piled upon Hetty in her empty bed.

There was a knock at the door.

'Alistair?'

'It's me, Mum.' Rory.

'Come in, Rory.' She sat up, put on the light.

'I thought you might need company,' he said.

'I thought you'd gone to Sarah's,' she said, and burst into tears. When she had first had sons, Hetty had imagined a day when, big and strong, they would comfort her. There was an odd sense of *déjà-vu* about it all. 'I used to imagine you boys looking after me in my dotage, when I was all alone,' she said, sniffing.

'You're hardly there yet,' said Rory. 'I couldn't leave tonight, though, with you and Dad rowing, and Luke and Finn so gob-smacked.'

'Oh dear,' said Hetty, realizing that Luke and Finn had skulked off to bed without a word. 'I should have spoken to them. The trouble is, I haven't finished talking to myself.'

'Don't worry about them,' said Rory, 'they're not as daft as they seem. You'll be all right, too.'

She sighed. 'I don't know. I want things to be all right, but it's hard when trust has been broken so – bitterly.'

'Get some sleep,' said Rory. 'I'll tuck you in.'

Downstairs Alistair tossed and turned uneasily on the spare bed. There was nothing wrong with the bed, of course. The unease was all on the inside. He felt lonely and stupid. Having to contemplate a life cast adrift from

192

Hetty and the boys, he suddenly saw how pointless that would make him. When he pictured them all in his mind, he saw Hetty surrounded by a kind of warm glow, the centre of everything, the source of all the comfort and love. They – himself and the boys – were dependent upon her for all the important, human things in their lives. How could he ever have thought that the physical act of sex with someone who meant nothing to him was worth risking even an ounce of Hetty's happiness for?

Having seen himself as the worst sort of fool, Alistair now lay in the dark, grinding salt into the wounds of his folly. What would he not give for her forgiveness?

It was about three in the morning, when he had almost dozed off, that he was awoken by Hetty getting into the spare bed with him. Wisely he said nothing, kept very still. She snuggled up against him, insinuated her curly head into the crook of his shoulder, draped a leg and an arm across him.

He thought at first that she was not going to say anything then, just as he was finally falling asleep, she said, 'Alistair?'

'Yes?'

'I don't like sleeping alone.'

He lay awake for quite a lot longer afterwards as Hetty slept, feeling extremely lucky.


Alistair guessed that Rory had told Jonathan. There could be no other reason why his secretary should give him a message saying that his son had rung, arranging to meet for lunch. She had taken the liberty, she told Alistair, of booking a table at 'Pepe's'. Was that all right?

He sighed. His secretary was called Philippa and, like most secretaries at the firm, had come straight from the Sloane College, and was waiting for the Honourable

Giles Fortescue to propose. She always booked him into expensive restaurants because she did not trust establishments which provided ladies with menus on which the prices were listed. Then she always made him feel that only cheapskates made a fuss.

There is a kind of restaurant in which salt is never placed on the table, where a request for salt is likely to bring an enraged and incoherent chef spitting garlic and waving a meat cleaver to the table, to enquire where one would like the salt to be put. In fact, the likelihood of finding salt on the table is inversely related to the prices charged by the establishment. 'Pepe's', suffice to say, did not have salt on the table, and the very act of crossing the threshold was liable to make non-gold credit cards melt in terror.

Because he was nervous, Alistair arrived early. He explained to the waiter that he was meeting his son and would like a gin and tonic. The waiter curled his lip ever so slightly, which Alistair took to mean that he knew all about men like him. Jonathan arrived on time and joined his father, requesting another gin of the waiter, whose upper lip was now halfway to his nostril. In fact, Alistair had misunderstood the snarl. The waiter, who was named Jeremy, did not waste time despising customers who were, after all, a valuable source of tips. In truth he believed he resembled the young Marlon Brando, and the sneer was a manifestation of this.

The atmosphere at the table was somewhat cooler than the gin and tonics. Alistair did not like gin and tonic, but then he did not like himself much either, so it hardly seemed to matter. He found himself wishing that Jonathan, whose personality, he had always liked to think, was rather like his own, was a little more like Rory instead. Jeremy returned, looking haughty, to take their order. Alistair felt his appetite slip under the table and crawl out of the door.

'I'll have the free-range chicken breast stuffed with mousseline of leek and glazed with the orange and mango *coulis* with a truffle fan,' said Jonathan, whose appetite stopped for no man.

Jeremy looked interesting as he tried to speak without straightening his lip. 'Of course. And for you, sir?'

'Could I just have the chicken breast plain, with salad?' Alistair asked faintly. He wondered if the chef would collapse, screaming.

They waited for their first course in silence. Jonathan was obviously going to have this conversation on his terms and Alistair knew there was therefore very little point in trying to get in first. Their first courses arrived and left. Alistair regretted accepting a table by the window. He felt like a goldfish, as a party of Japanese tourists doing the Cambridge College circuit peered at them, waving cameras and smiling.

It wasn't until dessert that Jonathan spoke properly. 'I take it it's true, then,' he said, so quietly that Alistair nearly didn't hear him through the sound of crunching cheese biscuit in his own mouth.

He swallowed. 'I suppose Rory told you.'

'Yes. How could you do it, Dad? Why did you?'

'Jonathan, I can't explain it just like that. What do you expect me to say? All the reasons sound like clichés. The truth is, I don't know.'

Jonathan sniffed. 'I hope you haven't given Mum anything.'

It took a while for Alistair to pick up the meaning. Then he said, 'Oh God, of course not,' realizing as he did so that he didn't honestly know that to be true. What if Lucy had had something? What if Sir George did? If rumour were to be believed then George's late father, Sir Hector, had been on intimate terms with his horse, not to mention every groom he had ever employed, of either sex. Was George cast in the same mould? He

195

swallowed hard, imagining a sexual contact tree which linked him to the entire population of East Anglia, both human and equine.

Jonathan, watching the flitting expressions on his father's face, was glad to see him suffering. 'The clinic, then,' he said, with some satisfaction.

Jeremy overheard, and glanced at them with sudden interest. In the light of his recent failed romance with a photographer named Guy, they now looked quite interesting. He sneered a little more handsomely. They did not notice. They would not have noticed if he had belly-danced past their table with a ruby in his navel.

Alistair was wearing a pained expression. 'You're enjoying this,' he said.

'You've betrayed us all,' said Jonathan, calmly. 'It makes me sick that she's prepared to let you stay. You deserve to suffer – she has.'

Alistair looked sadly at his son. 'You're pitiless, aren't you? Have you no sympathy for human frailty?'

'Not right now, no,' said Jonathan, who was actually finding the act a little hard to maintain. He and Rory had, in fact, discussed at great length whether Alistair should be made to squirm a little, and had decided that he should, although the idea about venereal disease was all Jonathan's own work. 'Did you use a condom?'

'Er – yes,' said Alistair in flabbergasted embarrassment, thinking that these were the sort of questions he should be asking of his sons, not the other way round.

'Every time?' persisted his son.

'Yes, every bloody time!' snapped Alistair, ashamed to realize that he had used them for his own protection rather than Hetty's.

Jonathan relented slightly. 'You're probably quite safe then. Lucy's not completely indiscriminate.'

'How the hell do you know?'

'I know her very well. We slept together last year.'

196

Alistair wished the floor would swallow him up. Now he felt like a pervert. At the next table a Midlands couple were arguing for their right to have custard on the chef's *Pomme Pâtisserie*. Jeremy was too busy trying to eavesdrop to care. When Jonathan and Alistair left, he planned to be at his most charming. They were clearly splitting up, and Alistair was just his type.

'What about AIDS?'

'It's a rare disease, Dad. You're more likely to be eaten by a mad cow on your way home.'

'Statistics mean nothing when it's you,' said Alistair grimly.

Jonathan felt guilty for stirring him up quite so much. 'Talk to Mum,' he said, 'but you don't need a test. Lucy was very low risk, and if you used a condom you're fine. You won't have it.'

Alistair was not consoled. He could see the sense of what Jonathan was saying, but the thought that he had exposed Hetty to such a risk without even considering it was horrific. What a mess he had made.

Later that day Zoë Ormondroyd was due home for half-term, which was something that neither George nor Angela looked forward to, although their reasons differed. Her recent weekend *exeat* had not endeared her to either of them. There had been the affair of the pigs. Zoë had got a lot of mileage, as she would call it, out of that. George dreaded her arrival this time because he knew that she would make fun of the fact that he was going to have his piles done. He knew just what she would say: something along the lines of the cost per pile, sitting on an exclusive pile, all that schoolgirl rubbish. Heaven only knew what she would put on her next placard.

Angela always dreaded her daughter's arrival

because she was a staunch defender of Lady Sybil. This time she hoped to turn the visit to her advantage and enlist Zoë's unwitting help by explaining her own concerns for her mother-in-law, and her planned meeting with John Potter. Nevertheless, she was conscious of feeling nervous.

Zoë also felt nervous. Ever since having her nose pierced, she had been afraid that they would spot the hole. She had masked it with make-up a few times, but the hole had begun to close up and she had had to replace the stud the previous night. Now it would not come out. It was not, therefore, a particularly auspicious moment for anyone when she walked through the door, and the ensuing argument was not improved by George's developing a sudden but intense pain in his bottom.

Angela was torn between horror that her daughter seemed to be turning into a cross between a New Age Traveller and a Turkish prostitute, and concern that the continuing bellowing from George might signify real pain. 'Zoë, dear, please ring John Potter,' she said, hurrying after George, whose progress up the stairs could only be described as painful to watch.

'Hi,' said Zoë into the phone, 'Zoë Ormondroyd here. Could you come? Father's got a pain in his arse.'

John arrived to a sight he would not forget easily. George was in his personal bathroom, leaning over a stool, his trousers round his knees, roaring, 'For God's sake, woman, surely you can see something!'

Poor Angela, meanwhile, being not only squeamish but also terribly embarrassed by bottoms, tried desperately to look as though she was examining his rear, when in fact she had no intention of doing any such thing. 'Oh, Dr Potter, I'm so glad you're here!' she gushed, and John, for once, believed her absolutely.

It took him only a moment to spot George's

thrombosed pile, which was so big that Angela would have been able to see it from the other side of the garden, if her eyes had been open. 'You've bled into a pile, Sir George,' he told George's posterior. 'A very painful condition.'

'You're bloody telling me!' shouted George. 'It feels the size of a golfball.'

'It is,' said John, 'perhaps a little bigger.'

Angela put a hand to her mouth and rushed from the room.

'She's always been delicate,' said Zoë lugubriously.

'Get my daughter out of here!' howled George. 'It's all her fault. It was when I saw that ring she's put through her nose like a bloody native!'

'Father, you're so racist!' shouted Zoë. 'And piles are from being constipated, not from stress, aren't they, Dr Potter?'

'Er, well . . .' John did not want to be caught in a family row. 'I think you should go and see your mother, Zoë. Sir George, let me help you up. I'm sure Sir Oliver Bittern will be delighted to see you in his rooms straight away. Can Wilson drive you?'

'Of course, sir.' The perfect butler, Wilson, was there, unruffled.

'Good, good,' said John, 'and Wilson, while I telephone Sir Oliver, could you possibly get me an ice pack?'

'I took the liberty of preparing one earlier,' said Wilson, 'in case you should need it.'

Sir Oliver Bittern was indeed extremely pleased to hear of Sir George's troubles. It was always a pleasure to earn the undying gratitude of a member of the upper classes, and being paid handsomely for the privilege. He anticipated a few invitations to Glyndebourne and the Cartier Polo out of this one, in addition to his £1,000 fee. Of course, the anaesthetist took two hundred of that, and his NHS houseman would get a tenner for popping over to help, but it was still quite acceptable for a few minutes' work.

Sir George, thanks to the confusing effects of anaesthetic gas and painkillers, remained blissfully unaware that the surgical removal of his thrombosed pile had taken only seconds. He was, in any case, looking forward to a night in a private room with a decent glass of Chablis, particularly as it meant that he could avoid confrontation with Zoë's nose stud and her pile jokes for another twenty-four hours.

Now that the drama was over, Angela was trying to think of a suitable way of explaining George's hospitalization to their friends so as to make it socially acceptable. Sir Oliver was a general surgeon – she would say that George had had a mole removed.

George, who loved to exaggerate his bodily problems, would have been horrified had he known that his pile was being verbally shrunk so dramatically in his absence. Fortunately, he did not know. He was enjoying his Chablis.

Angela was also casting around for a suitable way in which to broach the subject of Lady Sybil's obvious dangerous madness to Zoë. Irritatingly, Lady Sybil was refusing to display any of the necessary characteristics today: she was sitting in the garden with Miss Hawthorn, her companion, drinking tea. Even Angela could make nothing subversive out of this, although she did wonder if there was anything you could put in tea which would cause foaming at the mouth. She was not a well-read woman, but recalled vaguely a reference to someone's ears falling off like figs in something she had read at school. This was clearly a recognized side-effect of such poisons, and Angela did not want bits dropping off Lady Sybil in the house, thank you very much. It was bad enough that her teeth were not her own. Angela hoped fervently that, before she herself reached old age, there would be a cure for it. It did not occur to her that, to her daughter, she was already almost a fossil.

It rained that evening, the kind of heavy, constant downpour which is so much a feature of the early English summer. Alistair sidled into the house. After his lunch with Jonathan he could hardly bear to look Hetty in the face, and sidling seemed appropriate. 'Hello,' he said carefully.

Hetty eyed him in exasperation. 'Oh do stop being so cowed. I can't stand it.'

'I'm sorry.' How was he going to broach this subject?

'Stop apologizing,' said Hetty desperately. She wanted to rebuild and go forward, not endlessly dissect what remained. 'Just take Jess for a walk, please.'

Jess did not want to go for a walk, but Alistair went anyway, with the lead. Hetty sat at the kitchen table and wondered whether to feel better or worse.

The telephone rang. It was Jonathan.

'Are you ringing to check up on me?'

'Yes. Are you OK, Mum? Is Dad with you?'

'No,' said Hetty, 'he's just gone out in the rain to take the lead for a walk. He's not himself.'

'I'm afraid,' said Jonathan, with a touch of remorse, 'that I may be partly responsible for that.'

When he got home, Alistair was soaked, as the French put it so well, to the bone.

Hetty was waiting for him with a bowl of onion soup and a glass of wine. 'Go and get your wet things off,' she said, armed with a warm towel, 'then come here and sit.' Alistair did as he was told. Whilst she was towelling his hair she broached the unbroachable subject. 'Jonathan told me he'd made you worry about AIDS. You know that's ridiculous. Maybe there's an outside

201

chance, but it has to be so unlikely. There's no point worrying. We could just as easily have it from the transfusion I had with Finn. Please don't worry.'

Alistair felt a tear trickle down his nose. How could she be so understanding? 'I'll have to have a test, now that it's in my mind.'

'No you won't. Don't be silly. There are thousands of people out there who've had safe sex with lots of different partners since AIDS. They're not all having tests. Don't make this your way of dealing with the guilt.'

'Is that what I'm doing?' He was becoming slightly mesmerized by the rhythmical rubbing of his head. It reminded him of happy times over the years, when they had done this often. There was silence for a while.

*How could I have contemplated throwing him out?* thought Hetty. *Moments like this take years to create. What is a wife for if not to dry your wet hair and make you French onion soup with cheese in it? What is a husband for if not to pass you a towel when you get soap in your eyes in the bath? Isn't that why people get married, really?*

'They should put it in the Wedding Service,' said Alistair, reading her mind as he always used to. 'Love, honour, cherish and towel dry till death us do part.'

'I suppose,' said Hetty, 'you weren't thinking of making a joke about throwing in the towel?'

'I was,' he said gravely, 'but I decided against it.'

So had she. The fun in marriage is that you both get tuned in to the same frequency, then make the same jokes to one another for ever – and what's more, you both think they're funny. 'We're very lucky,' she said, leaning on him. 'People aren't really capable of promising things until death. The ones who last through are the lucky ones.'

'I'm lucky,' he said, taking her hand. 'Do you think you will be able to forgive me?'

She was silent for so long that he turned round to look at her. She smiled. 'I suppose if I hadn't forgiven you we wouldn't be here like this. The boys think it's too easy, as though forgiveness for a great hurt should take longer to earn than forgiveness for a small one. It isn't like that, though. The forgiveness is something related to me and my feelings for you, not to what you did. It has all been for too long to throw away now.'

'I nearly did, without thinking,' said Alistair, standing to hug her.

'So did I,' said Hetty. 'I'd been thinking some very negative things about us recently. I was considering what I wanted to do. I hadn't reached a conclusion then.'

'But now you have?'

'Now I have.'

They leaned on one another in the glow from the fire. Luke and Finn, creeping down to make sure that they were both still there, nudged one another and crept away again.

'Do you know,' said Hetty, 'I went and got myself revamped a couple of weeks ago. Make-up, hair, the works.'

'Oh God, you mean I didn't notice?'

She grinned. 'You didn't get the chance, I washed it off. It wasn't me. It was when I was thinking, considering my position. It was a way of looking at the options, and I suppose it told me I like things as they are.'

'Do you fancy an early night?' asked Alistair.


They were still awake in Barking Hall. 'Zoë, dear, do come for a chat,' said Angela, for she had prepared her speech.

Zoë shuddered. Anger, fury, disdain – she could handle these, but her mother calling her 'dear' terrified her. She edged her way onto Angela's sofa. 'What?'

Angela chose her words with care. 'I'm very worried about your grandmother.'

'You can't stand her,' said Zoë. She loved Lady Sybil; for as long as she could remember, her grandmother had fed her Opal Fruits behind her nanny's back. The fact that she continued to do it was proof to Zoë that she was fine.

'Now, Zoë, that just isn't fair. Your grandmother and I understand one another very well.'

'Too right,' muttered Zoë thinking, like Greeks and Turks they understand one another.

'Would you just listen, and stop snarling past that ridiculous nose stud!' snapped Angela. 'Your grandmother is much worse. At times she wanders off and she is becoming a danger to herself.'

'I suppose you want her to wear a collar like the dogs,' said Zoë, nastily. The Hall dogs all wore special collars linked to an invisible fence around the property. If they tried to cross it, they received a small electric shock. Passers-by had occasionally been alarmed by the spectacle of a labrador rushing at them, slavering in delight, then yelping, leaping into the air, and running away again. Zoë thought the fence obscene, but Angela hoped that it would frighten people off from using the public footpath in the fields at the back of the Hall.

'Oh, don't be childish,' said Angela, who was fed up with saying 'dear'. It was a term normally used for those people in Harvey Nichols who did not quite qualify for 'darling' but who were not the waiter. 'Your grandmother is going downhill and I fear that we cannot look after her. I plan to speak to Dr Potter about it this afternoon.'

Zoë leaped to her feet. 'You just want to put her in a home!' she accused her mother. 'You've taken over her house and now you're shoving her out of it.'

'Of course I'm not,' flapped Angela desperately. This

just was not working. How could a child who once – ugh, to think of it – gestated inside her, grow up to be so disagreeable? 'John Potter thinks Lady Sybil should have a brain scan. I believe he thinks he may find something serious.'

Zoë blanched and sat down, deflated. 'You mean a tumour? You mean she might die?' She began to cry.

Angela felt a prickling of something unfamiliar. It was guilt, which was why it was unfamiliar. She patted Zoë awkwardly. 'No, not that. He says she'll live for years. I think he just means dementia.'

Zoë was not consoled. 'I'm going to see Gran,' she said, and rushed off, hiccuping.

Angela sighed. She privately hoped that the scan would require the old lady to be in a hospital bed, and that once in, it might be easier to keep her there. After all, someone of her age would have to be settled into a private hospital for something as major as a brain scan. Then everyone would see for themselves how much better it would be for her to have proper nursing care. Angela had done a little research and found the most delightful home. It could even be quite pleasant to visit. They only seemed to have the right sort of people, and she had noticed in the brochure that they kept the incontinence pads in a beautiful Italian cabinet. She smiled to herself. John Potter would be here soon.

John was late, to Angela's great displeasure. The fact that he had been called urgently to see an old lady who had fallen down the stairs cut no ice with her, but she was not about to let him see her annoyance. She needed him on her side. She began with pleasantries, offering John the use of her gardener to trim his lawn on the day of the fête.

John, surprised by her sudden friendliness, concluded that she was after something. He declined gracefully, adding, 'I gather that you are to open the fête,' as Caroline had said something about it.

'Of course,' said Angela, smugly. She was glad to have it confirmed – not that she had ever had any doubts. She looked forward to the humble delegation begging her to officiate. But for now she must get down to business.

John sat patiently while Angela said her piece. He could sense the cogs in her mind spinning, he thought, eating a rather nice piece of fruit cake. She was hoping that the old lady would be admitted to hospital then never leave. He wasn't going to spoil her surprise.

'As you know, Lady Ormondroyd, I have been pressing Sir George to send Lady Sybil for a scan. Whilst she probably does have multi-infarct dementia, I would like to rule out the outside possibility of a chronic subdural haemorrhage.' He was not normally a man who confused his patients with science, but Angela was not a patient, and he felt that in this instance a little confusion would not be a bad thing.

'Is that serious?' she asked carefully, not wishing to appear ignorant.

'Not necessarily,' said John, 'but Lady Sybil is not really capable of giving her informed consent to the investigation, and if she is unco-operative then she might require some sedation. We therefore would need the agreement of Sir George, as her next of kin, and the scan will need to be done as an in-patient.'

Angela felt her glee rising. 'He will consent,' she said. 'I will speak to him.'

John took his leave with raised spirits. Imagine if the old lady did have a subdural clot? Once treated, she could return to full mental health. What a blow that would be for her scheming daughter-in-law!

## Chapter Fourteen

George could not believe the throbbing in his bottom. It was two days since Sir Oliver Bittern had done his worst, but the laxative which he had prescribed had still not helped at all. George was beginning to regret the case of vintage port which he had sent to Sir Oliver's home. He felt that he should have sent half a case, or maybe just a bottle. Angela was not exactly overflowing with sympathy, and as for Zoë, she hadn't stopped making facile remarks since he got home. Fortunately for his dignity, George was not clear about exactly what had been done. The thought of mounting his horse, or his groom, was too painful to contemplate – or at least it had been. *I must be improving*, he thought, *if I'm thinking of that again.*

Angela was a little peeved, in fact, at the break in George's attentions. After all her years of self-imposed sexual deprivation, the rediscovery of the pleasures of the flesh was so enjoyable that she found it hard to imagine why she had denied herself in the first place. Her undignified experience of childbirth had had something to do with it, she reasoned, and then she had realized that none of the ladies with whom she lunched slept willingly with their husbands. Now, though, she suspected them all of lying – apart from the fat ones, who were doubtless covering for their husbands' unwillingness to sleep with them. She, Angela, was not afflicted by fat. She did not even have cellulite. Therefore George's desire should not wane merely because he had had piles. She could not understand how anyone could make such a fuss about such a minor ailment. How could it have possibly been the size of a golfball? He would never have been allowed home the very next day. Nevertheless, by her standards, which were not high, she was sympathetic. Unfortunately for George, her bedside manner was worse than that of those matrons in slapstick comedy films, who smack their patients' broken legs and threaten them with bed baths as punishment for being ill.

Zoë was rather grateful to her father's pile for getting her out of hot water over the nose stud which, in truth, she did not like. That beautician woman in the village had promised to remove it for her, but Zöe wanted to make quite sure that no-one else had any plans to criticize it before she removed it. She was a free spirit, and would remove it when she was ready.

Zoë's free spirit was right now down in the kitchen talking to Cook, so Angela decided to broach the subject of his mother's possible scan to George. 'George, dear?'

'Hmph.' George was contemplating the savoury crackers on which he liked to nibble before dinner.

'John Potter thinks that your mother should have a scan, just to be on the safe side.'

'Mmmm,' said George, still thinking about the crackers. They looked rather sharp, and he didn't want anything going into his body which might have sharp edges when it came out.

'I think there's an outside chance of a brain tumour,' said Angela, who had taken in very little of what John had said.

'What?' George forgot the biscuits and took a handful of peanuts, a far worse move for his bottom. Glad to have his attention, Angela explained.

'I don't know,' said George, compounding his future distress with a few raisins, 'Charles never suggested it.'

'True,' said Angela, 'but John Potter does seem to think that your mother has got a lot worse since Sir Hector died, and that was only just before Charles retired.'

'Still before Potter's time,' said George.

'There's nothing to lose,' cajoled Angela, 'and I am rather worried about her.'

George, by comparison to his daughter and John Potter, was as blind as a bat where Angela was concerned, so he admired her concern for his mother. 'It's very sweet of you to worry, my dear,' he patted her hand reassuringly, 'and of course, you're right. Mother must have a scan. I shall speak to John Potter about it very soon. I shall need to see him in any case.'

Angela did not ask what about. There was no need. You could tell from his facial expression. She really must stop him from eating those nuts.

The Ormondroyds were not alone in having problems. Mrs Groat was terribly upset about her lupins. They were definitely her lupins. She had planted them and nurtured them, tidied them and been their guardian of tender loving care. This made it all the more mortifying, therefore, to find that this year they had seeded over Jessie Bean's side of the fence. Worst of all, Jessie's lupins, owing to a quirk in the lie of the land, had received slightly more sun than Mrs Groat's, and they had flowered first. Mrs Groat muttered and seethed, but did not speak out. She was, by nature, a woman who thrived on muttering and seething. It was her misfortune that she did not recognize when she was thriving.

Jessie, of course, was quite unaware of this grievance. She was not to know that Mrs Groat hovered beside her open front window, ears akimbo, whenever a step sounded on Jessie's path, lest someone should exclaim, 'Aren't your lupins lovely, Jessie?' or, worse still, 'Your lupins are so much nicer than Mrs Groat's.' Poor Mrs Groat. The spirit of competition burned fiercely in her soul, and she would have made a very good Olympic runner. She did not make a very good neighbour.

It was because of her endless eavesdropping that she heard Jessie talking to Jacob as they weeded outside.

'I think that Greta is expecting to open the fête,' she heard Jessie say.

'Surely not,' said Jacob, after a moment's silence, when a particularly determined weed was putting up a fight. 'Why should she think that?'

'I'm not sure,' said Jessie. 'She says that Rose is going to ask her.'

Jacob thought for a while. 'Perhaps you should have a talk to her dear.'

Greta, shaking silently behind her curtain, could bear to hear no more. She should therefore have gone out of earshot, but that was not in her nature. How dared they discuss her as though she wasn't there? It did not occur to her that it was precisely because they thought she wasn't there that they were discussing her. She would show them. She stamped outside. 'Why shouldn't I open the fête?' she demanded. 'Rose wants me to, I have been told. Do you think I am not good enough?'

'Why, Greta!' Jessie was dismayed and horrified. 'I didn't say – I mean I don't think – I mean I meant to say . . .' She became terribly confused, and weeded a lupin by mistake.

'Those are my lupins!' shouted Greta Groat in a fury.

'Now, now,' Jacob came to his wife's defence, 'you are being unreasonable, Greta.'

'I am not!' shouted Greta, who loved a row. That was her advantage. Jessie and Jacob would have preferred being boiled in old chip oil to taking part in a verbal exchange. 'They seeded from mine. The least you can do is look after them.'

'Oh dear,' said Jessie, 'you are taking things the wrong way.'

Rose Bush appeared at the hedge, like the phantom of the opera on opening night. Her ankle was still in plaster, and she had not been the same since one of her nephews had signed himself Jimmy the Stud upon it. Now she was forced to wear trousers to hide it. Rose abhorred trousers except for gardening, so she was having to do an awful lot of gardening to justify their presence. 'I'm so sorry, I heard raised voices,' she said. 'Do you want to tell me what it's all about? I may be able to help.'

Wild horses would not have dragged the truth from Mrs Groat – there was far too much face to be lost. 'We were arguing,' she told Rose, 'about the lupins, about whose they are.'

'I don't know,' said Rose, enjoying fertilizing the row, 'but Jessie's are earlier, and they're a lot taller too, aren't they?'

Jacob cast around frantically for a distraction. To his amazement, one was sent to him like a gift from heaven. It is not often that a coach load of American tourists are compared to a gift from heaven, but then it's not often that they are driven out of Cambridge to see a real English village with a pagan fertility symbol in the churchyard. The coach driver, not knowing exactly where he was, put on his air brakes with a hiss outside the Beans' house. The tourists peered out at the group with lupins, and there were muffled cries of, 'How English!' and 'I must have a shot.'

'Hey, mate,' said the driver to Jacob, 'is this Great Barking?'

'Indeed it is,' said Jacob proudly.

'Well,' said the coach driver, 'we're looking for your penis. Could you tell us where it is?'

Jacob sat down so suddenly on the gravel that it was a while before Rose and Greta, trying to help him up, realized that Jessie could not speak for laughing.

Now that's not something you see every day, thought Rory, as he passed on his way to see his mother. However, the oddness of a group of four apparently hysterical old people seemed to him nothing when compared to the turmoil in his mind.

He found Hetty alone in the kitchen. 'I just popped in,' he said, 'to let you know how my exams are going.'

Hetty looked up from her bill-settling and put down her pen. 'Come and have a cup of tea.'

'Thanks,' he said. 'Is Dad home?'

'Just. He's getting changed to mow the lawn.' Hetty put the kettle on. 'Cake?'

'No, thanks. How are things?'

Hetty sat next to him, put an arm around his shoulders. 'Really very good,' she said. 'All things considered, better than I'd hoped.'

'I'm glad.' Rory fiddled with the sugar bowl.

'What about your exams?'

'They're fine,' said Rory, 'easy.'

Hetty suspected that they were not the reason for his visit. 'You must be glad it's nearly over,' she said, getting up to make the tea.

'Yes. Yes, I am.' He was still fiddling.

'How's Sarah?' she ventured, leading.

'Fine. Wonderful. She's blooming,' said Rory, as expressionless as if delivering a list of vegetables. 'Pregnancy suits her.'

'Are you happy?'

'Yes, of course,' said Rory. 'I love her.' Hetty waited, instinctive. 'I'm so jealous,' he said.

'Of the baby?'

'No. No, of course not the baby. Of the father.'

Alistair, eavesdropping shamelessly at the door, came in. 'Why?'

'Because she's tied to him for ever.'

'Nonsense,' said Alistair. 'He was a roll in the hay, wasn't he? Hardly a lasting passion.'

Rory and Hetty refrained from saying that Alistair should know, although the thought crossed both of their minds in the way that awful things sometimes slip through the minds of most of us.

'Why don't you come for a walk with me?' asked Alistair, putting on his wellies without waiting for an answer.

'All right,' said Rory. 'Thanks for the tea, Mum.'

'It would be a miracle if you had enjoyed it,' said Hetty, 'I haven't poured it yet.'

'Well, it smelt nice,' said Rory. 'Come on, Dad.'

Alistair met Hetty's eyes and she nodded briefly, in an unspoken agreement which needed no words.

They walked down through the village towards the river. The four old people seemed to have gone indoors, but there was a coach parked by the church and a number of people milling around the churchyard.

Alistair cleared his throat when they reached the bridge. 'How do you think of me?'

'Well, you're my father,' began Rory cautiously, looking at the water below them, wondering if he was supposed to say, 'You've been a complete plonker.' He decided the mood did not seem quite to demand that.

'And your brothers?'

Rory could not see where this was leading. He wondered if he was about to get the talk on condoms. At this stage of the game it seemed unlikely.

'Well, I'm sure they think the same. Are you trying to tell me something?'

Alistair watched a drifting stick with a small part of

213

his mind, while the rest sought the right words for Rory. 'If I wasn't your biological father, if someone else was, would you think of me differently?'

'No. Of course not,' said Rory. In the distance he could see Morgan Groat peeing into the river. 'But it's a bit hypothetical. After all, you are my father, you and Mum had been married five years even before Jonathan.' He suddenly wondered if his father was about to accuse Hetty of having affairs. No. Ridiculous.

Alistair took a deep breath. 'When your mother and I were first married, we tried for a baby. After a few years we knew there must be a problem. Eventually, against my will at first, we both had tests. I was sure it was your mother's problem, but it wasn't, it was me.' Rory waited, watching a crayfish in the water. 'It didn't take long to find out, because I have absolutely no viable sperm.'

'Oh, Dad,' said Rory, 'none at all?'

Alistair smiled. 'Most men manage hundreds and millions,' he said. 'I had none. There was nothing they could do.'

'God,' said Rory, 'you must have been devastated.'

'Of course I was,' said Alistair, 'it impugned my manhood. I wanted to leave your mother so that she could find someone else. A man with viable balls, I said. She wouldn't hear of it, of course, said we'd deal with it together.'

'So you are infertile,' said Rory, wanting to be quite clear. His 'O' level biology had concerned fruit flies and locusts rather than human procreation.

'Totally,' said Alistair. Harriet drove past and waved. 'We discussed adoption, and started the process, but even then it took a long time, and there wasn't much chance. Then we read about a clinic which did donor insemination. Your mother left the article for me to read. We went along for a chat, and that decided it. We

214

both wanted your mother to have a child. The counsellors were very good. They explained that this way our baby would still be fifty per cent ours, genetically. The fact that the fifty per cent came from only one of us had to be immaterial. We felt that was right, so we went ahead.'

'All of us?' whispered Rory.

'All of you. The success rate isn't always so good, but for us it worked every time.'

There was a long silence as they walked on. Rory's mind was whirling. He had expected a man-to-man sort of talk, but not a revelation. Should it make a difference, knowing it now? 'Do the others know?' he asked eventually.

'Jonathan does,' said Alistair. 'We agreed long ago that we would tell each of you when the time seemed right. Jonathan was quite OK, I think.'

Rory tried to imagine his parents, young and disappointed, waiting at an infertility clinic. 'Do you think I could have inherited your problem?' he said without thinking.

Alistair laughed aloud. 'That's the nicest thing you've ever said to me,' he said.

Rory laughed with him. It felt surprisingly good. 'Thanks for telling me,' he said.

'I hope you can see why I'm telling you now,' said Alistair. 'Being a father was never about biology for me. If you and Sarah bring up this baby, then you'll be its father as much as I am yours.'

'I see what you mean,' said Rory, feeling much happier now. After a moment's silence he added, 'You and Mum went through quite a lot together, didn't you?'

'Less of the past tense – we haven't finished yet,' said his father, glad to be able to say so.

They returned to Hetty in companionable conversation, picking up Sarah on the way. 'I hope you don't mean literally,' she said when they knocked at the door, 'you'd need a forklift truck.'

'We've come,' said Alistair to Hetty, who had been having a private weep over the onions, always a convenient disguise for tears, 'to help you make our supper.' He saw the tears and felt overwhelmed with love for this woman who had given him so much of herself. 'Don't cry, you're going to be a grandmother.'

'Gosh, so I am,' said Hetty, looking at Sarah. 'Do you mind me being Granny?'

Sarah laughed her infectious laugh. 'It's a bit late if I do,' she said.

Hetty nudged Alistair. 'Granddad,' she said. 'Ha ha.'

Rory, watching them all together, found himself hoping that he and Sarah would have what his parents had.

## Chapter Fifteen

The week before the fête brought unexpected twists of fate to all sorts of people in the village. Most of them were interesting to someone, though not all of them were pleasant for everyone.

On the Sunday there was a good attendance at Communion. Oliver Bush, who had already taken early Communion at Little Barking, and who was duty bound for Evensong at Bumpstaple, tried to calculate how much wine would be required. The margin for error was so much greater with a large congregation, particularly these days, when the head count did not necessarily reflect the numbers who would actually partake of the bread and wine.

It was a glorious day. The gardens of Great Barking were blooming, and the air was sweet with the scent of cut grass. The geese at the Hall were honking, and Jacob had just trimmed the churchyard topiary. Unfortunately he could no longer reach the top of the privet penis, even with the aid of the steps from the vestry, so it was growing ever longer in a manner often promised by small classified advertisements the world over. The rural idyll appeared complete. Alas, appearances are so often deceptive and, beneath the surface, tension brewed gently like toffee simmering in a pan – pretty to look at, but painfully hot to touch.

Angela wished to make clear to the congregation of St Jude's the terrible trouble to which the village's first family were being put on account of the bats. To this end she had decided to put in an appearance in church today, and demonstrate by her watering eyes and delicate cough the immensity of her suffering. Unfortunately her suffering, only five minutes into the service, was quite real, and she was seriously considering leaving early without making her point. She was already beginning to wheeze.

George, meanwhile, was still engaged in the serious contemplation of his bottom. Despite the application of copious amounts of soothing cream, it seemed to him to throb quite unreasonably. He shifted endlessly in his pew, and thought longingly of frozen peas.

Harriet was deeply troubled. The knowledge of Alistair's infidelity towards Hetty, and of her own role in revealing it, weighed heavily upon her soul. She glared at Alistair's broad shoulders across from her, and hated him fiercely.

Jessie Bean was filled with guilt and shame, for it was her week to clean the church and she had forgotten completely. It had been such an awkward and odd few days, preparing to have the fête in the wrong place, Mrs Groat being so tetchy, Rose hobbling and grumbling, and even Harriet acting oddly. She had been so rattled and upset by the atmosphere in the village that she had developed a migraine severe enough to send her to bed on Thursday afternoon. She had stayed there until this morning, something she had never done before, not in twenty years of service to St Jude's. It had taken her mind completely off her usual routine, and had resulted in a true and genuine full week's worth of droppings littering the church. Now her awareness of the ubiquitous bat guano lay on her consciousness like a wet dog on a sofa. How could she have let everyone down? Bat droppings littered the floor, and she dared not look at Mrs Groat.

Mrs Groat, of course, was disgusted. It did not occur

to her that Jessie might have forgotten to clean. It seemed, instead, that the bats had acquired some sort of revolting disease, causing them to poo in previously unheard-of quantities. In twenty years of cleaning up, she had never seen this much guano. They had even dropped it on her pew – in fact, it seemed as though they had particularly dropped it on her pew.

Oliver Bush was unaware of the tension, he was concentrating on his sermon. As it happened, it was a particularly good sermon that day. Hetty and Alistair, observing the proceedings, thought that Oliver put up a very good show of not noticing the agitation, disapproval and ill health of various members of the congregation. Alistair did not listen to the sermon, but Hetty did. It was based on a long allegory of Oliver's experience of getting lost in Rome when Rose was navigating. Hetty was intrigued by the idea of Rose in a country where the tea was not necessarily Earl Grey and the evening meal was unlikely to come with neatly sliced bread and butter.

Oliver worked his way through Rome and its one-way system, and how they had been unable to take the one road they wanted, moving nicely over to the many paths to God and the importance of Jesus Christ in the one situation, and an up-to-date road map in the other.

Rose sat rigid as a comatose stick insect, mentally censoring every word Oliver spoke. She hated it when, as so often, he used extracts from their life together as fuel for his sermons. It seemed to her a gross intrusion into her privacy that even the tiniest things in her life belonged not only to God but also to Oliver's congregations. She feared terribly that Oliver might one day provoke actual titters from the throng. When God made me a vicar's wife, she thought, forgetting that it was a path which she herself had decided upon at an early age, He made sure that I would be tried.

It was fortunately not a long sermon. The birds were singing too gloriously, and the geese honking too noisily, for that. It was a day for mowing the lawn, listening to *Hansel and Gretel* and drinking long, iced drinks in the shade, and the congregation did not want to miss any more ultraviolet radiation than they had to. It was during the prayers just before the Eucharist that disaster struck. Angela Ormondroyd, secure in the family's traditional pew – the one at the front, with the softest kneelers – had been shuffling around trying to get comfortable. This is no easy feat when on ones knees and wheezing, and she was struggling to maintain her balance.

The manner in which you kneel in church is very important. It is not enough merely to slump forward in the pew, true kneeling is essential, at least until great age or arthritis finally restrict you to remaining seated. Nor is it done to kneel right down, cushioning your thighs upon your calves and resting your back against the pew. The only acceptable kneel is the upward kneel, that most unstable of human positions, particularly when performed when balanced on an overstuffed cushion, and those failing to achieve it risk being considered less than devout. It matters little that devoutness is often not the main reason for attendance in church, especially amongst the rural upper classes. The appearance of devoutness, like the appearance of wealth, is everything.

Thus Angela, least devout of women, shuffled and wheezed awkwardly on her kneeler in an attempt to conform to the requirements of St Jude's, and in doing so shuffled right off her cushion onto the hard and unscrubbed floor, where something wet and un-pleasant began at once to seep through her second-best silk stockings. There could be no doubt. It was extract of bat. 'Oh God!' she cried, quite appropriately in the circumstances, and sprang to her feet in panic and disgust. Oliver Bush, midway through exhorting his flock to pray for Queen and Country, was nonplussed. His was not the kind of church in which thirty-somethings occasionally leap to their feet and cry 'Hallelujah!' when the spirit takes them, even though he sometimes rather wished it was. Moreover, if St Jude's had had an evangelical thread, it seemed highly unlikely to suppose that it would manifest itself in the person of Angela Ormondroyd. He allowed his glasses to slip down his nose, which made him look both confused and endearing.

Angela was flapping frantically at her knee and fighting for air. After the first cry of horror her voice had left her, and her wheeze was alarmingly audible. The congregation began to stir and murmur, storing all the details of the unfolding drama for repetition and embellishment in the years to come. George saw with a shock that his wife was in genuine distress. Observing her blotchy, swollen face and desperate beating at her knee, he grasped the cause of the problem surprisingly quickly. Showing a concern for her welfare that no-one, himself included, would have believed he had in him, he cried, 'Help me get her stockings off!' as she collapsed inelegantly into the pew. The next few minutes were a little confused. George swept Angela up against his chest and strode out of the church, with one hand groping at her thigh trying to undo her suspenders, a task he had never before attempted with quite such urgency, although he had not been doing too badly recently.

Zoë, so aghast with embarrassment that her face resembled a ripe Victoria plum in both colour and acidity, hurried out after them with her mother's handbag, crying, 'She's fainted!' for the benefit of anyone who might suspect George's motives for having his hand just where he did.

It was no good trying to continue with the prayers. Oliver Bush admitted defeat and suggested to the congregation that they sat for a moment while Luke Stewart was dispatched with all haste to the Potters' to fetch John.

By the time John got to Angela, she had calmed down a little, and her breathing, though laboured, was easier. Her face was swollen and blotchy, as were all visible parts of her, and she clung to George as though he were her only hope.

'Acute anaphylaxis,' said John, injecting her swiftly. 'What brought this on?'

Angela tried to speak but could only squeak.

'Bats,' said George. 'Bloody bat droppings in church. Saw a specialist last week.'

'Goodness,' John was fiddling with the nebulizer now, 'I wonder why it's suddenly so dramatic.'

'Fsht,' squeaked Angela, pointing at her leg.

'She knelt in it,' said Zoë, torn between embarrassment at the scene in church and relief at finding that there was something genuinely wrong with her mother. Mere hysteria would have been so hard to live down. 'I've cleaned it off.'

'You must go to hospital,' said John firmly, 'we're taking no chances. I'm admitting you to the Royal.'

Angela found her voice. 'Not . . . the . . . NHS . . .' she gasped, images of vast matrons wielding enemas terrifying her into near-relapse.

John was pushing buttons on his phone. 'Sorry, Lady Ormondroyd, but private hospitals aren't for the acutely ill. You could have died.'

'Oh, Angela! Darling!' The full realization of his wife's plight bore down upon George with all the subtlety of a steam locomotive, and he sank to his knees beside her. 'Oh, Angela, if I had lost you . . .' he stopped, overcome. Zoë, who had recently noticed far more than she had let on, and who disapproved of much of it, made a mental note to describe her father's actions in full detail to Lucy Bellingham. With a bit of luck she would leave. One less tart on the payroll, and good riddance that would be. Why, if Zoë had her way, she would live at home, and Father could pay her to be his groom in her spare time.

Inside the church, the congregation had found it very difficult to settle back into the spirit of the Eucharist. No-one could kneel at the altar rail without a detailed inspection of the floor, and Oliver Bush, sensing their detachment, wound up the proceedings as quickly as he could, noting with mild dismay that there seemed, yet again, to be rather a lot of wine left over. It was particularly apt and unfortunate that the closing hymn was 'All things bright and beautiful, all creatures great and small'. The irony was not lost on the congregation, many of whom were puce with repressed laughter by the time they reached the closing prayer.


John Potter drove home cautiously the next day, for it had been a long one, and thought about Angela and the bat droppings. Angela had already left hospital, but doubtless the horror of having been an NHS patient would linger with her for a while. (He was quite right about that, and indeed she had already made an appointment with a Harley Street psychologist to discuss her post-traumatic stress disorder.) As he turned off the main Broomhill road, the vivid no-parking-yellow of a field of oil seed rape caught his eye and made him think of Caroline. She hated the rape. She said that it didn't match Suffolk, which was a cream and pink and green sort of county. Such a yellow was an offence, a blot on the landscape equivalent to the presence of a purple hippopotamus in a Constable original. Most things made John think of Caroline. That was the kind of man he was. When he thought of Caroline, he then thought of sex. It was something he thought of all the more for having less of it. Rather worryingly, he also thought of it more when he had more of it, which raised alarming questions for the future, when you thought about it.

He turned into the drive of Yew Tree Cottage, narrowly missing the twins' push-along dumper truck which had been dumping gravel onto the gravel, and savoured the moment of arriving home. Walking up the drive, the creak of the front door, the smell of Caroline's pot pourri and Henry and Josh's dinner. Such were the simple pleasures of a man's life. Well, those and sex. John shut the door loudly, and listened for the squeal of rushing twins. A terrible urge seized him to shout, 'Darling, I'm home!' but he suppressed it successfully. Caroline hated it, she said it made her feel like a character in an American situation comedy. He found the twins and India seated, zombie-like, in front of the TV, upon which Peter Rabbit and Mr McGregor were having a difference of opinion.

'Hello, children,' he said, waiting for them to cannon into him, begging for hugs. Henry and Josh were not distracted, being fascinated and terrified by Mr McGregor; India began a laboured struggle towards him, as she was just beginning to crawl. All three children looked as though they had been dunked nose-first in tomato sauce.

John picked up India and went to look for Caroline. He found her in the kitchen. She had flour in her hair, on her nose, down her front, and all over the floor. A rather brown cake, which appeared to have sunk dramatically in the middle, sat on the table. Next to it stood the remains of a sponge which someone – or two – had clearly battled with, and lost. Some gingerbread shapes, which might have once been people but which had spread to become humanoid blobs, sat hopefully on a plate. A packet of doilies sat next to them, unopened. The kitchen looked as though Al Capone had been in and shot the Homepride flour man with a machine gun.

'Hi,' said John, carefully. 'I see the twins had pizza.'

Caroline burst into tears.

Later, after they had cleaned up and he had fetched a Chinese takeaway, allowing Caroline to choose the prawn dish which he hated, he felt able to mention the cakes. 'What were they all for, love?'

'The fête.' Caroline, who had thought herself recovered, felt tears hovering in her voice. 'I wanted to make impressive quantities of cakes, but none of them are good enough.'

John put his arms around her. 'Do you really think it matters?'

She sniffed. 'Yes, in this village it does. I have to do my share. I do so want us to belong here, so I was trying to do the right thing. These cakes were my ticket to full membership of Great Barking.'

'Really? As important as that?'

Caroline's lips twitched. 'Well, maybe not quite that important,' she admitted, smiling sheepishly. 'I could always order a few things from the baker.'

'Indeed you could,' said John, admiring the smile, and wondering if India was interested in the same part of Caroline that he was.

'I've got a problem,' said Caroline that evening, as she and John got ready for bed.

'I'm sure I can cure it,' he whispered in her ear.

'You've got a one-track mind,' said Caroline. 'It's like trying to have a serious conversation with one of those telephone sex lines.'

'Oh yes, and how would you know?'

She giggled. 'I just do.'

'Go on then,' he wandered out of the bedroom to run the bath.

Caroline sat on the bed, next to the sleeping India. 'It's Carol Sheldon,' she called. 'She keeps inviting me to a sex-aid evening.'

John reappeared at once. It was amazing how the bath could stir itself during some conversations, but not during others. 'Are you going?'

'Certainly not,' said Caroline primly.

'Why not?'

'Well, for one thing, I hate the idea. I know I'm a bit of a prude but, well, many-headed vibrating things just aren't my cup of tea.'

'How do you know—'

'I read it in *Cosmopolitan*,' she said, 'at the dentist's.'

'Women's porn, that,' said John, 'all G-spots and oral sex.'

He went back to turn off the taps. 'Bath's ready.'

India was well and truly out for the count in the middle of their bed, so Caroline followed him into the bathroom and dipped her toe in the water. 'Turn on the hot tap while I clean my teeth.'

'Hi there, tap,' crooned John, ogling it, 'd'you fancy a bit of rumpy-pumpy?'

'That is such an old joke. Honestly, if your patients could see you now . . .'

He grinned. 'They love me. Anyway, what's the problem over this sex thing?'

'Well, she won't take "no" for an answer,' said Caroline, and rinsed her mouth. 'You see, she wants a magician for her daughter's party.'

'Sounds like a good deal to me,' said John. 'I get paid and you get sexy.'

'I know you think it's funny,' said Caroline, slipping into the bath, 'but I'm embarrassed.'

'I'm sorry,' said John, wondering about getting into the bath with her. The last time he had done so, so much water had overflowed that the lights downstairs had fused. 'Tell her I'll do her magic show free. Just say "no" to the rest. Tell her you're a Buddhist.'

'I don't know . . .' Caroline hated to offend.

'Well, I do. Ask her to cut the twins' hair as payment.'

'She's a beautician,' said Caroline, shaving her armpits with John's razor, 'not a hairdresser.'

'A facial, then.'

Caroline giggled. 'On the twins?'

'That's my razor,' said John.

'Would you prefer me to have hairy armpits?' she asked sweetly. For reasons he did not quite understand himself, John thought hairy armpits on women disgusting. 'I'll buy you a razor.'

'No thanks,' said Caroline smugly, 'I like yours.'

'Why do women always prefer men's things?' complained John.

'Hah. Women don't have things,' said Caroline, and they both dissolved into giggles.


By the next afternoon Sarah's pot had finally been fired. Sarah and Rory were admiring it when there was a knock at the door. Rory grabbed a kimono; Sarah was, for once, wearing one.

'Cooeee!'

'Come in, Jeanette. Rory, this is Jeanette, my agent from London.'

'Hi,' said Rory.

'Goodness,' said Jeanette, 'red hair.'

Rory pulled the kimono together, hastily.

Jeanette, it transpired, was just passing through, but had heard a rumour that Sarah was doing a special commission for the fête. She just had to see it.

'You can keep your hands off,' said Sarah, showing her.

Jeanette looked for a long while, from all directions, then grinned widely. 'Wasted,' she said, 'on these bumpkins. Make them a big urn for their rhododendrons and let me take this one. I know just the spot for it—'

'No chance,' said Sarah, 'this is for the village.'

Jeanette sat on the futon, sipping camomile tea which Rory had brewed. He hoped she wasn't on a wet patch, and sat at the other end.

'Message in it, is there?'

'Do you think there should be?' asked Sarah, blandly.

Her agent considered this. 'Moral repression,' she suggested. 'They must all be repressed here in their tiny village lives, caught up in church council meetings and the WI.'

Sarah draped a cloth over the pot. 'You're joking,' she said. 'This village is a boiling pot of mayhem, desire, lust and passion. I'll wager the seven deadly sins are all being committed within two hundred yards of here right now.'

'I can believe it,' Jeanette giggled and made eyes at Rory. 'I've read Miss Marple. By the way, I suppose that *is* a penis in the churchyard?'

'It must be,' said Sarah, 'although I'm sure it didn't start out that way. Like most penises, it has taken on a life of its own.'

'So. Who are you, Rory?' asked Jeanette.

'I'm Sarah's lover,' he said.

'Well, I'd worked that much out,' she said drily.

Rory blushed.

'Don't embarrass Rory,' said Sarah. 'He's well brought up. Anyway, he's more than my lover. He lives with me. Officially.'

Afterwards Rory reflected that Jeanette had looked

very much like a turbot when her mouth fell open like that.

'Did she see it?' he asked Sarah later, when she was glazing the pot.

'Of course she did,' said Sarah. 'It's like the Emperor's new clothes. Anyone with an eye for shape can see the message in this pot. It's perfect. I do hope someone from the village wins it.'

'Just as long as it's not Mrs Groat,' said Rory, 'or Jessie Bean.'

'Oh, I don't know,' said Sarah, 'it would give them something to think about. In any case, like everyone else, they probably have hidden depths.'

Rory was about to disagree, when he remembered seeing Jessie Bean rolling on the floor with laughter when he and Alistair had walked past that time. He smiled at the memory. 'You could be right. But don't you hate the thought of it going to someone who won't appreciate it?'

Sarah put her brush down and wiped her hands on a cloth. 'No, not really. If I thought like that, I'd never part with anything. A lot of good art is bought by philistines, just as opera houses are filled with the tone-deaf wealthy.'

'I love you,' said Rory.

Sarah knelt down beside him. 'Good,' she said.


Hetty and Alistair had arranged to meet for lunch the next day. She arrived in Cambridge rather early and wandered about a department store, killing time. It was years since she had met Alistair for lunch, and it gave her a warm feeling of anticipation. *If anyone had told me six months ago that my husband would have an affair and I would be able to put it behind me, I never would have believed it*, she thought.

229

The department store reserved its front, downstairs floor space for cosmetics and perfumery, the kind which create their own market out of pure thin air. Hetty had always viewed these little island counters merely as a gauntlet which had to be run in order to reach the relative safety of the stockings and stationery departments behind them. Today, however, she felt attractive and renewed. She had put moisturiser and powder on her face, she had darkened her eyelashes – without teasing them out in the slightest. Carol would have been disappointed. She had tidied her curls, and she felt up to the challenge of Cosmetic Woman, so she browsed. It was not long before she had attracted one. It was when she was reading, with mild disbelief, the claims being made for a series of moisturisers.

'May I help you?' asked the girl. She was about twenty, and her face was devoid of blemish or freckle, for her make-up hid it in a perfect mask. Her blusher, Hetty noticed, was applied exactly as Carol would have advised, and her eyelashes had been teased apart, giving her that vaguely surprised expression Hetty had so disliked.

'I was just looking,' said Hetty, determined not to be scared away. 'I was surprised that there seemed to be five different moisturisers in the range for my skin type. Would I need them all?'

'Well, they are designed to be used together, but you could probably get away with three,' said the girl, sizing Hetty up and mentally classifying her as a non-gold credit card.

Hetty said, 'Oh, yes,' in a leading way, and the girl continued, encouraged.

'There is a special youth action cream for daytime,' she said, 'then there's the replenishing night cream, with special placental extracts, which—'

'What?'

'Placental extract. You see the placenta is a valuable source of—'

'What kind of placenta?'

The girl, Sandra, parried. She had not been asked this before, and could not recall seeing it in the training manual. She hazarded a guess that it could be goat placenta, but it was definitely highly nutritious.

'What a lot of tosh,' said Hetty, 'placenta on your face.'

'Well, we do have a super eye care cream. That doesn't have placenta in it,' said Sandra, who had been trained not to give up.

'Does it have spam?' asked Hetty, who had once been able to quote Monty Python word for word.

Sandra knew a hopeless case when it made obscure jokes at her. She sniffed. 'Well, of course, it is laboratory tested, but then if you don't want a quality product . . .'
She spotted a likely looking woman with highlighted hair and a face like a leather boot on the other side of her island. Adjusting her smile, she made off.

Hetty grinned to herself and strolled away. Far from feeling intimidated and wrinkly, as she usually did in these places, she felt worldly, mature and far above the spreading of any species of placenta on her face and neck. It was time to meet Alistair.

Jeremy, the waiter at 'Pepes', was disappointed to see Alistair with a woman. He developed a visual field defect in their direction.

'This is a posh place,' said Hetty, 'but they've forgotten the salt.'

'Sssh,' said Alistair, 'they don't put it out. The food is meant to be perfect.'

'Perhaps I should try that at home,' said Hetty, 'but in any case, I can't believe that a man who drowns his chips in vinegar, salt and ketchup at home could live without salt on the table.'

Jeremy winced. He could hear her clearly, and they sounded awfully married.

'Do you know,' whispered Alistair to Hetty conspiratorially, 'I really rather fancy a sandwich down by the river.'

'So do I,' she said, 'come on.'

Jeremy was relieved to see them sneak away, although he pretended not to notice.

Harriet, too, was having an unusual week. She had made successful contact with the Cambridge branch of the Save Our Bats Society. SOBS had initially been formed to try to save a colony of Daubenton's bats roosting in a disused tower of the library, and had hence started out as the Save Our Daubentons Society, but this had swiftly been changed to avoid embarrassment. The bat people, as she liked to call them, had been very helpful. It was quite clear, they had explained, that the bats in St Jude's were protected by law and could not be touched. They offered to send someone to give a lecture, but Harriet was not sure she dared go that far, yet.

'Well,' the man had said nicely, 'shall I just come along and chat to you about it?'

'I wouldn't want to trouble you,' Harriet had fluffed, as she spent her entire life trying not to trouble anyone.

'No trouble at all,' the voice had boomed, 'be delighted.'

And on Thursday Harriet, too, was delighted, for when Lionel Frobisher turned up, he was wonderful. He was tall, white-haired, an ex-army colonel, widowed for many years, and with the most twinkling blue eyes that she had ever seen. They had tea and crumpets, walked around the church, and generally enjoyed a very pleasant afternoon. Harriet was particularly proud that she managed not to blush when he invited her for lunch in Grantchester, and was quite overwhelmed when he promised to come to the fête.

Rose was determined that the plaster would be off her ankle before Saturday. They tried to tell her that the plaster should remain for another week. Clearly they had no grasp of the complex requirements of being a vicar's wife. She cut off the plaster herself with a pair of kitchen scissors on the Thursday afternoon. Oh, what a wonderful feeling it is when a plaster comes off. To scratch, really scratch, an itch which has been many days in its brewing and fermentation must surely be one of the greatest pleasures known to man, on a par with a drink of cold water after profound thirst, and with various lavatorial activities which do not bear repeating. Rose allowed herself a really good scratch, then changed into one of her neat summer dresses and a pair of medium support stockings in medium size. She always bought medium. Small smacked of vanity and large of extravagant self-indulgence. The offending plaster she put on the bonfire which she had been making in the garden. She had some vague idea that itinerant drug addicts, who found uses for discarded syringes and tablets, might steal it if she did not destroy it. Rose had very little understanding of the problems and needs of the addicted.

## Chapter Sixteen

*Perhaps*, thought Caroline on the Thursday evening, sitting on Carol Sheldon's overstuffed floral sofa with a glass of sherry and India, *perhaps I should not have brought my baby*. Down on the floor, Carol was starting a race between two battery-driven objects which she had christened Stan the Sausage and Olly the Octopus. Caroline decided that whilst Stan's name was self-explanatory, Olly's name presumably related to the ridiculous number of operating appendages he possessed. He had three, which was, admittedly, somewhat fewer than an octopus, but was surely just as pointless. Caroline felt that God had clearly had a night of peculiar extravagance when He designed the octopus – or perhaps He drew up the plans at the very end of the Sixth Day.

'Honestly,' Carol was saying as the two other ladies giggled in pretended outrage, 'they really will move on this carpet. It only works on Axminster. Look!' Indeed she was proved correct. Caroline watched in unwilling fascination as the two unpleasant pink objects inched along Carol's hearth rug, buzzing in a manner presumably intended to excite. She found it hard to imagine a less appealing sexual toy than Stan, except possibly Olly.

Trish and Alison, Carol's two other hapless victims, were now quite overcome with laughter. Caroline, who had felt out of things ever since she arrived late, was enveloped by the dreadful sensation of being the only person in a room who is not at all amused. She wished fervently that she had not allowed herself to be coerced into coming. She had run into Carol Sheldon earlier that day, when trying to get the twins fitted for shoes in Broomhill. Henry and Josh had staunchly defended one another from what they perceived as attempted assault by the shop assistant, and as a result Henry had kicked her so hard on the chin that she had been reduced to tears. Carol, who had been purchasing truly impractical pink fluffy mules in the adult department, had heard the commotion and come over to help. Embarrassed and hot, Caroline had then felt obliged to accept the proffered invitation. Now here she was, viewing sexy toys, sexy lingerie and manuals of sexual positions with all the enjoyment of a turkey at a Christmas feast. It struck her that if Carol could hold these parties and yet still be a pillar of the village, then she, Caroline, was hardly going to be blackballed for failing to make a decent quota of cakes for the fête. Mind you, Carol could probably produce gingerbread men who did not resemble the Michelin man after a bout with a steamroller. Who could say what relative importance might be given to sex toys *vis à vis* gingerbread men? Villages could, after all, be very odd.

'This is quite an interesting one,' said Carol in her ear.

'What is it?' Caroline took the plastic egg, noticing absently that Stan had won the race, and that Trish had apparently therefore won Stan. The egg was smooth and plastic and, unsurprisingly, pink. Caroline wondered if a plastic naked woman would pop out at the touch of a button, whilst the device played 'Happy Birthday'. It would be on a par with what she had seen so far.

Carol flicked a switch on the egg. 'You can wear it to the supermarket,' she said, 'it makes queuing so much more fun.'

Caroline dropped the egg as it began to vibrate threateningly in her hand. 'You mean it's a vibrator?'

'Oh, do let me see!' cried Trish, fascinated. India started to make grunty, nipple-seeking noises. Caroline found a rusk and tried to persuade her to chew on it. All evening she had been telling herself that this whole event was just a bit of fun, and no-one would really be seen dead buying any of this stuff. Now, however, Trish and Alison were both ordering eggs. She fervently hoped that she was never behind them in the supermarket queue.

'More sherry, Caroline?'

'Er, no, I haven't finished this, thank you.' Caroline disliked sherry, and would have preferred juice, as breastfeeding made her terribly thirsty. Carol had, however, been horrified at her request for something long and soft; Trish and Alison, already primed by two bottles of white wine and a catalogue of minimalist underwear, had laughed loudly and lewdly. Clearly the consumption of considerable quantities of alcohol was essential to the success of these parties, so she had accepted the sherry. Sipping it now, she wondered whether Carol did the make-up of both Trish and Alison. They seemed to have identical eyelashes.

*I really should make more effort*, she thought, swallowing the rest of her drink in a determined gulp. *I really have to buy something*. India wriggled and griped in her arms, feeling as cross as any baby would when she asks for milk and is given tasteless biscuit which turns to mush when sucked. Caroline picked up the nearest catalogue, deciding to pick a page at random and purchase something from it for John.


'You ordered a string vest? How can that be titillating?'

'Some women think so, apparently,' said Caroline,

stroking India's hair as the baby snored gently between them on the bed.

'You don't,' said John, sure of his ground because she had thrown all his vests away when they married.

'Well, no,' said Caroline, 'but I had to buy something in a hurry, and it was the first thing I found which didn't need a battery.'

'Why did you have to leave in a hurry?' asked John. 'Embarrassment?' He knew his wife – she must have hated the evening.

'Yes,' said Caroline, 'they were all frightfully embarrassed.'

'*They* were?'

'Yes, it was when I started breastfeeding. Oh John, it was so funny – they were playing with vibrators and yet they didn't know where to look when India fed.' She started to laugh.

John thought, as he did so often, that six years of medical school and five of marriage had not helped him to understand women. Women were just odd.


John had arranged Lady Sybil's brain scan for the following week. George had felt that a few days' delay was best, but Angela was anxious to go ahead. She was clearly very worried about his mother. Angela's sudden illness, short-lived though it was, had had a profound effect on George. He had realized how desperately he did not want to lose her, and he was not certain that she would wholeheartedly approve of his minor tampering with certain members of staff. Not now that she was interested in him herself. Then there was this class thing again, of course. In the old days, when servants were servants and one never knew their names, let alone their Godparents, then it would have been fine, but now . . .

The temptations of the flesh, however, are great at

times, and George, like a smoker trying to give up tobacco, could not help wanting just one more. He was, at times, quite firm in his resolution that the last occasion had been exactly that. The problem was that, at times, he was firmer inside his plus twos than in his mind, and at such times Lucy's dimples – she had four, if you included the two on her face – proved too great a temptation.

On the night before the fête, Angela was much irritated by Zoë and her endless nagging about school. George had sometimes wondered how such a child could be his – not in any serious way, of course, for Angela had never seemed terribly keen on sex in those days. Times had certainly changed, he thought, smirking a little. Zoë had been Angela's only pregnancy. She had vowed 'never again', and George had accepted that his daughter would be his sole heir. Poor Angela – she had planned a Caesarean section in a nice private hospital, but had gone into labour during the Earl of Watton's anniversary banquet. She had hidden what was happening from everyone, but then this had eventually been rendered impossible when her waters broke just as the cheese was brought in. She had not eaten Stilton since.

Zoë had been the property of nannies largely from that point on. Delightful girls, some of them; he smiled at the memory. Angela had assumed that her daughter would turn into a replica of herself, but she could hardly have been more wrong. Zoë thought herself a Marxist. She did not wear pearls, did not approve of field sports, called the servants by their first names and refused to be called 'Miss'. It was a mystery, the way she had turned out.

Since Zoë's presence was occupying Angela, George decided to slip out to the stables in the hope of slipping into someone a little more comfortable. Lucy was there, grooming Sir Hector. He did not notice Zoë as he hurried into the stable block, which was really rather unfortunate, as she saw him. She fiddled with her nose stud as she went indoors, thinking. The noises she had subsequently heard coming from the stable had been self-explanatory – it was simply a matter of how she could use the information to her advantage. Actual dates and times were so much more useful than mere suspicions, so she was sure she was in a powerful position.

Zoë was not the only person who saw something unexpected that evening and benefited from it. The other person whose life was about to be altered unexpectedly was Morgan Groat. Morgan had a large prostate, and unfortunately it went everywhere with him. In the language of doctors, which often makes odd and unappetizing references to food, it was the size of a grapefruit, and this meant that Morgan's bladder seemed to him to have the capacity of an egg cup. He was, therefore, often to be found emptying it into the river. He was a small man, apart from his prostate. He had a shiningly bald head and wore little round glasses. His teeth, though, were still his own, and when he smiled his face lit up with the sweetness of it. Unfortunately he was not often seen to smile, for he was a man who lived in fear. He feared losing his fishing licence because of peeing into the river, he feared needing an emergency urinary catheter passed by a young, blonde, nubile doctor with cool hands and a warm smile and, above all, he feared the wrath of his wife. After all, if Mrs Groat's tongue had been any sharper she would not have required teeth, and Morgan would have faced the seven trials of Hercules rather than a tongue-lashing from Greta.

As a result of this fear, Morgan spent much of his time alone, fishing the ottery banks of the River Running, and as he fished, he dreamed. He dreamed the dreams of a man who, in his life, has not had nearly as much sex as he needed, and who would like to have had far more sex than he needed. Most of us build our dreams from images of things we have seen or read, but Morgan had seen very little in his life, so his fantasies lacked much visual form, and he longed to improve this state of affairs. Sadly for him, the kind of films and magazines he might have liked had never come his way, and even if they had, his high myopia would have turned even the most explicit of images into a blur, with all the sex appeal of a gardening magazine.

Morgan's erotic experiences had been almost zero in recent years. His sole glimpse of Sarah Struther's tanned and extravagant breasts had been an oasis in a desert of visual deprivation, aided by the fact that she had been at exactly the right distance for his spectacles to focus both of her nipples sharply and unmistakably upon his delighted retinae. Since that occasion, some twelve months ago now, Morgan had spent a great deal of his time to-ing and fro-ing past Sarah's kitchen window with his fishing tackle, and, indeed, his personal tackle, on standby, hoping for another glimpse. Alas, her potting shed had no windows, so he was denied the kind of view which had so alarmed Rose. He had been denied any kind of view, but he was a man who lived in hope. This meant that he now always fished the same stretch of river and the fish, even with the limited reasoning power that fish have, seemed to have cottoned on.

Today was to be Morgan's lucky day, in a manner which Rose would have recognized. He was heading home for tea, taking his usual short cut through Sarah's garden and past her potting shed. Sarah and Rory were

240

in the studio, and Rory was also in Sarah. The day had been warm, and the evening was gentle, with a soft sun which had turned the glass-roofed studio into a little greenhouse. The soft breezes which stroked the hollyhocks were so welcome to their heated bodies that they had left the door wide open.

Morgan, walking quietly past the kitchen window, heard a sudden moan and, telling himself that someone – naked – might be in pain, trotted across the lawn to investigate. Once more, his spectacles served him well. They, and he, focussed clearly. They focussed on naked bodies, on entangled brown limbs and white limbs and softly dimpled skin. They focussed on the way in which breasts, large breasts, move when they are gently rocking. Then, not daring to outstay his welcome, lest he should be seen and thought a voyeur, he left.

His mind was filled with hitherto forbidden delights. That position, that view, such things had previously been beyond his experience. As he walked home, strange feelings came upon him, and he walked like a man with a purpose, casting his fishing tackle into the Potters' hedge as he passed. They were strange feelings, but they were not completely unfamiliar, they just had not been used for a long time. They were also extremely pleasant, and he was determined that they should not go to waste. Morgan felt that he had had a vision in Sarah Struther's garden. It filled his mind, his soul, and certain other bits of his body until, despite his prostate, he felt young and powerful, not at all the kind of man who lives in fear of his wife.

Mrs Groat was in a rather nervous mood. The fête, after all, was tomorrow, less than twenty-four hours away, and it was much on her mind. She had not felt quite herself since Sunday's incident in church. The huge volume of bat droppings had eventually set her wondering whether not only had Jessie failed to clean, but whether she herself could also have forgotten the previous week. If she had thought of this, then surely so had Rose, and after all, Rose had not yet clearly asked her to open the Great Event. Now, so close to the day, the lack of faith which Jacob and Jessie had displayed in her chances of being asked to open it was eating into her confidence. Worse, there lurked the awful suspicion that Rose might have no intention of asking her, that she might be planning to do it herself. Her one hope was that Rose was planning to spring it on her at the last minute, and so spare her nerves. After all, Rose's own name had not been on the original list which Greta had seen at that fête meeting, and she had told Harriet that she would ask Greta, hadn't she?

It was perhaps on account of all this mental turmoil that her guard was down. Indeed, her guard had never really needed to be up as far as her husband was concerned. Morgan's sexuality had not reared its ugly head – an unfortunate way of putting it, but apt – in the marital bed for rather a long time. In fact, for most of their sexually active married life, foreplay had consisted entirely of Morgan's saying, 'Do you mind if I . . .' on Saturday nights, and Greta had usually attempted to sleep through the proceedings. Tonight, however, the tiny little spark which had been set off in Morgan by his glimpse of Sarah and Rory, had been fanned into a huge, roaring flame, filling his entire mind and body with the realization of hitherto undreamed-of possibilities. This was why Greta Groat, at first with surprise, then with outrage, then with interest, and finally with genuine enjoyment, found herself experiencing marital relations with Morgan in a position which would never have occurred to her even if she had thought about it, and she never had. A crude observer might have made a comment about Morgan having abandoned one kind of rod in order, with far greater success, to employ another, but fortunately no-one quite that crude was present.

## Chapter Seventeen

At last, the day had arrived. The tables were laid out ready for the fête, and Caroline and John's garden had not looked so tidy since before they had moved in. Rose had directed the laying out of tables, keeping a nervous eye on Solomon, who had moved into an aviary in the garden on the advice of the Broomhill vet. (He spent a lot of time hanging by his beak and one claw from the chicken wire, as near to her as he could get, and she felt it was quite clear that he intended to rip his way out of the cage and tear her limb from limb. It was just a matter of when.) The tables were laid out in accordance with the strict hierarchical rules of the fête, which Rose kept fiercely alive. During her childhood in the village, the fête had been a truly grand affair. Occasions of any sort had been far fewer in the lives of the villagers in those days, for many of them hardly left their village from year to year. All attended church, so the fête had been up there with the great occasions of life: birth, baptism, marriage, burial, adultery. In those days, the importance given to which stall one should man, and exactly where it should be placed relative to the other stalls, had been infinitely great. Your entire position on the ladder of social status could rest upon whether you sold the tarts or the fruit cakes, and whether your position on the white elephant stall was, or was not, physically nearer to the entrance of the Hall than that of your neighbour behind the tombola.

Morgan Groat and John Potter were struggling to fix

the bunting to the apple trees. As is often the way with village fêtes, it had taken considerable excited discussion before the exact siting of the bunting had been settled upon. Morgan, who had the suffering patience of the unsuccessful fisherman, had tried every possible permutation of tree and bunting until Rose had at last been satisfied. John, who was short on patience as he saved it all up for the surgery, had eventually sat down on the grass, exasperated.

Now, at last, it was done. The garden was a flurry of activity as each member of the Committee tried to make their stall tempting and attractive. For some, this was more difficult than for others; there is a limit to how attractive a pile of old knitting patterns or a china plate bearing a photograph of a pop star can be made. Nevertheless, the importance of being said to have done a good job was not to be overestimated, even these days. It could even – hope above all hopes – lead to a chance to draw the second winning raffle ticket. The rector, of course, always drew the first, after making his usual joke about the church and gambling.

Hetty was putting out the white elephants, helped by Caroline. 'Some of these things,' said Hetty cheerfully, 'have been on this stall at every Barking fête since rationing ended.'

'You mean they don't ever get bought?'

'Oh, no, they always get bought, that's the point; even the cruet sets. They just come back the following year. So many people feel obliged to buy something at every stall that there isn't enough stuff they really want, so they buy what they don't want and then give it back twelve months later.'

Caroline suddenly discovered a long-forgotten memory of a box in her mother's attic labelled 'Fête Things' – or had there been two boxes? Yes, her mother would have had two, to alternate which was given and bought back every year. That way none need be offended. That was a good idea. She smiled to herself, thinking that it was the first time she had ever actually thought of her mother as having good ideas. 'It was ever thus,' she said wryly to Hetty. 'Don't you ever think it would save a whole lot of fuss if all the same old folk who come and spend money on things they don't want just turned up, gave us five pounds and had a cup of tea?'

'Ssh,' said Hetty, giggling, – it surprised her how much she giggled these days – 'such subversive suggestions could get you thrown out! In any case, it would spoil the fun. After all, half the joy is in trying to find something that you can bear to buy on the white elephant stall. People enjoy a challenge.'

'I suppose,' said Caroline, 'that you don't have to buy from the stall you're manning?'

Hetty's grin widened. 'You're kidding. I have to loudly persuade Alistair to put in five pounds for everything that's left.' This year she had noticed a particularly grotesque money-box which was a china pig in school uniform, and she did so want Alistair to have it.

'Oh, look,' said Caroline, 'a real white elephant.'

'It's a kind of tradition,' said Hetty. 'I always make one. If anyone guesses his name they win him.'

'Does anyone know his name?'

'Only me.' Hetty had a soft spot for soft toys, even those she had made herself. She could not have borne her elephant to go to someone who might not love him. She smiled to herself. The name was not yet chosen, only the recipient. India Potter should win the elephant this year. She finished unpacking the box of white elephants provided by Barking Hall. It proved interesting . . .

*   *   *

245

Some months earlier, Angela had been to see a beauty consultant and had been sold, at great expense, a bosom-enhancing programme. Envy was not a part of Angela's make-up, as her sense of superiority was too great to allow it, but she did regret the size and shape of her bosoms – not, of course, that she would wish to be cursed with a battering ram type of chest like poor Lucy, the English aristocracy were, she felt smugly, genetically plagued by bosoms and body fat. That's what happened when you in-bred for centuries. She did, however, believe in self-improvement, and Camilla, her personal beautician at the Sloane Foundation of Youth Institute, had insisted that two cup sizes and considerable uplift could be achieved by the industrious use of this unusual equipment.

The oils were innocuous enough, and she had been applying them faithfully every morning. The fly in the soup, as it were, was the object which was meant to simultaneously firm, tone and enlarge, not to mention hoist skywards, her modest attributes. It looked like a plastic pith helmet attached to a length of hose, which had to be plugged onto the cold tap. Some devilish device within the pith helmet then arranged for a rotating jet of freezing spray to be applied to the unsuspecting breast. The shock of it was quite intense, particularly the first time, and this water torture was meant to be continued indefinitely, morning and night.

Angela was terribly concerned that Wilson or the cleaners might find her pith helmet. It certainly had the appearance of something which some of the odder members of the human race might derive considerable pleasure from, and whilst she always used it behind locked doors, its size made it difficult to conceal. However, she was now convinced that it was not doing anything for her bustline. She had therefore decided to put it in a box and give it to the village fête, well hidden in a box of objects for the white elephant stall. Let someone else make of it what they would.

It sat now, unidentified and unpriced, amidst the white elephants, a testimony to Angela's relentless search for a C-cup. People took guesses all morning as to what it might be. Hetty had refused to discuss it, as she planned to give it to the person who, in her estimation, having paid their ten pence, made the most imaginative guess as to its original purpose.

Harriet, carefully arranging jars and bottles for the tombola, glanced over at Hetty anxiously. She was smiling, and Alistair seemed still to be living at home. Could she have read too much into what she had seen pass between Alistair and Lucy that evening? Surely Hetty and Alistair could not still be together, and apparently so happy, if what she had suspected were true? She had never experienced the ebb and flow of compromise and forgiveness of real relationships. She lived in a world of formula romances, in which tall arrogant men named Grant and Piers swept virginal Alices and Verities off their tiny, perfect feet into a life of sweet fulfilling sex and intergalactic orgasm, which was never described, only subtly implied. Her most recent read had concluded with the immortal words, 'he carried her up into the heavens until, amidst an explosion of cascading stars, she understood fully the power of their passion and the glory of their love.' Imbued as she was with this rose-tinted view of love, Harriet really had very little understanding of what Hetty would call life after orgasm, the day-to-day business of sharing one's life with someone whose bodily hair was differently arranged to one's own. To Harriet, unfaithfulness was a disaster from which one could not recover, it was a terminal disease in a marriage. She puzzled over Hetty's smiles.

The hoop-la stand, next to Harriet, was Jacob's

speciality. It had originally come from a fairground, and therefore had been fiendishly designed so that the hoop would never fit neatly around the post. Jacob, a kind and fair man, had laboured hard with a block and sandpaper to remedy this state of affairs, and regulars of the Barking fête now knew which pedestals were particularly easy.

Mrs Groat was setting out the cake stall. Normally this task was accomplished with her usual gloomy countenance, as she compared the cakes of the various contributing village ladies, and assessed whose should be sold whole, whose cut up and sold by the slice – a great honour – and whose retained in order that the masses might attempt to guess its weight – the greatest honour of all. This year, something very odd seemed to have happened to Mrs Groat. She was smiling to herself as she laid out the cakes, singing a little song as she randomly selected Hetty's fruit cake to be the unknown weight. She even skipped slightly through Caroline's front door on her way to fill up the tea urn for Jessie. It was very odd indeed. Rose and Jessie, who knew Mrs Groat as well as anyone, were quite alarmed. They both felt that Greta was behaving terribly strangely, but neither dared draw attention to the fact, lest it should make her worse. They therefore skirted her cautiously, warily, avoiding being drawn into conversation on the merits of Carol Sheldon's chocolate cake as against Harriet's lemon madeira. They need not have worried. Mrs Groat, having found nirvana via a most unexpected route the previous night, was not about to leave it over a lemon madeira cake. The truth was that over the years she had simply forgotten about sex. She had effectively been switched off at the mains, so there had been no point in plugging anything in, so to speak. Last night, though, Morgan Groat had put the entire power of the National Grid through her in erotic terms, and with the increased circulation to certain parts, memory had also returned. There was no doubt Greta Groat was all woman, and she was humming a selection from *South Pacific* to prove it.

Caroline had left the twins with John, who was setting up his magic tricks ready for the show. India was being molly-coddled by a cooing Carol Sheldon, whose bookstall was neatly amassed with paperback romances, their coloured spines arranged in visually pleasing order like a Dulux colour chart. India was gurgling happily and hoping for a chance to rip off and eat one of Carol's dangling earrings.

Alistair appeared around the corner of the house with the lawnmower. 'Finished!' he called to Caroline and Hetty, and headed for the garden shed.

'He's quite domesticated, isn't he?' said Caroline, suddenly noticing the particular camaraderie that Hetty and Alistair, as a couple, seemed to exude. It was strange that she hadn't noticed it before.

'Not always,' said Hetty with a smile, glad that she had forgiven him. Her mother had told her that she was crazy, Jonathan thought that she should have extracted more penance, but at least Rory seemed to understand. Perhaps because he was in love himself, he understood that she was still in love with Alistair, with the Alistair she had married and also the Alistair that he was now, after all their years together. To other women, the very fact of all those years might have made the betrayal too great, but to Hetty they were too great a prize to give up. She and Alistair were mutually dependent, they had grown together like two fruit trees planted close; to pull them apart now would leave them both looking and feeling unbalanced. She had known there was no point in carrying on if she could not forgive him, but she was terribly happy to discover that she already had.

Alistair reappeared from behind the shed. He came up behind her and put his arms around her. He knew that he was forgiven. He could not remain tentative and apologetic, and did not wish to try. He was the old Alistair, confident, interested and sexy.

Mrs Groat appeared, chuckling, from the door of the house, carrying a plate which bore what looked like the remains of a cherry cake. Josh and Henry trailed behind her, the white icing smeared across their faces providing clear evidence of their guilt. Caroline and Hetty looked at one another. A rush of thoughts raced through Caroline's mind rapidly, like flickering images on cinefilm. Whose cake was it? Would her name be mud? Would Rose notice? Would she ever live it down? Would the twins throw up? What would Mrs Groat do to her? She started to shake silently.

'Would your parrot,' called Mrs Groat as she approached them, 'like the last few of my cherries?'

Hetty and Caroline fought valiantly but lost, and collapsed in waves of hysterical laughter. To their surprise, when they had recovered enough to look, Mrs Groat was down there laughing with them.

Rose Bush looked over in horror. Was Greta drunk? Poor dear Hetty had been under a lot of strain recently, and Caroline Potter, well, she did have twins – it must affect the mind. Mrs Groat, though, had always been the kind of woman upon whom one could depend to remain truly dour, whatever the circumstances. Indeed, her dourness had often been an asset at rectory tea parties when the rural dean's wife, as she was so wont to do, got the giggles.

Rory appeared at Rose's elbow. 'Marijuana, I should think,' he said gravely.

'I beg your pardon?' said Rose weakly.

'Very common amongst the middle classes,' said Rory. 'You know, it just looks like any old plant.'

Rose, rushing over to her plant stand to see whether anything on it looked particularly subversive, was thus distracted from the arrival of Sarah Struther's pot. Sarah was able to place The Pot upon its prepared table without anyone present catching a glimpse of it. She propped Rory's painting behind it, and covered both with a huge green tartan rug; then she sidled up to Rory. 'Keep an eye on it,' she said to him.

'I shall guard it,' said Rory, 'with my life. Actually I plan to offer Finn a fiver to stand here like a guard dog. Hey, Finn!'

Everything seemed to be ready. Even the PA system, a veteran of fêtes and village hall functions, which could be relied upon to whistle horribly whenever anyone attempted to use it, was set up and switched on.

Rose, at last able to fulfil a function which, in her eyes at least, gave her some standing, invited everyone to come and have a sandwich on the vicarage lawn before returning to man their posts against the onslaught. She had laid out and watered the plant-stand cuttings. None of them would grow, of course, for as everyone knows, only stolen cuttings ever grow, but at a fête that does not matter. Now everyone, excepting only Finn and the Potters, left obediently, and after a few minutes the garden was virtually empty.

John held India, who had the frustrated attitude of one who has failed in her quest to eat an earring and is now faced with a father who does not wear any. She struggled and clutched at hairs. Henry and Josh, horribly full of Mrs Groat's cherry cake, were chasing one another around the lawn on their ride-on toys, and things seemed to be under control. 'Well,' said John, 'who would have thought it?'

'I know. It actually does look like a village fête ought to look, like something out of a nineteen fifties drama on TV.'

'I'll put the twins upstairs for a nap,' said John, handing India and her earring fetish to Caroline.

'Ow!' said Caroline. 'That's my pearl stud.'

India grinned.

Henry and Josh did not want a nap. Henry, in fact, wanted to poo, so the whole process of settling them down took John quite some time. While he was gone, Caroline wandered around the garden with India, nodding at Finn, who lounged near Sarah's covered pot, as she went. The garden was looking beautiful. It should do – it was her first ever proper garden, and ever since her offer to host the fête had been accepted she had spent hours at the garden centre, buying things which didn't have to be grown, only put somewhere. Poor Caroline had not yet realized that plants, having a will and – sometimes malevolent – plan of their own, grow anyway, so that in a few years' time the neat garden would be a jungle of towering shrubs and trees. She leaned over, carefully balancing India, and dead-headed a couple of roses which were a little too ragged for the fête, although in normal circumstances they would have been fine for another week. Then she stood back, silently satisfied. Surely this was it. *We are accepted*, she thought, *we are a part of Great Barking. This is home.* She felt a real sense of belonging. Today would be worth it even if, as Rose had warned, every teenager from Great and Little Barking and Bumpstaple used an entire roll of soft lavatory paper. It would be worth it because it brought acceptance, she could be herself and still belong. She didn't have to feel guilty for being bright, as she did amongst her relatives, or guilty for not working, as she did amongst her old university friends. In village life, she thought, there is a place for everyone, just as long as they listen to Radio Four rather than Radio One and don't have a satellite dish.

Caroline laughed with sudden insight as India

planted a wet kiss on her cheek. 'Do you know, I think I'm becoming just like your grandmother,' she told the baby, thinking of how much time she had wasted worrying about being different. 'You can never escape your genes, so you may as well give in now, and I'll put your name down to man the white elephant stall in twenty years' time.'

India gurgled then wriggled ecstatically as John appeared. 'Fancy a quickie, me darlin'?' he croaked in Caroline's ear.

Contentment had worked its magic on Caroline. 'Yes I do. Let's go inside,' she said, and they went indoors.

Finn, left alone with the readied fête, wandered over to the cake stall for some lunch.

## Chapter Eighteen

The most important moment in Great Barking's history, since Boadicea and her Iceni faced the Roman Legion in a field a mile north of St Jude's, had arrived. Some might argue that events had been less confused on that occasion, as there were then only two sides, and they did not both wear pink, not to mention the fact that one side had blades on their chariot wheels, making it fairly clear exactly what sort of business they meant.

The confusion over who was to open the fête had managed to grow from a minor misunderstanding to something with the potential for fiasco. As in all the best fiascos, all sorts of people had had a hand in it – the main contributing factors being the immodesty of the three contenders, and the assumption by everyone else that 'someone' would sort things out. Only the woman at the dry cleaners had thought that something was amiss, for she did not often have three pink suits collected on the same day. She was, however, far too engrossed in *Drip Dry*, the fun magazine for dry-cleaning staff everywhere, to think much about it.

The microphone, skilfully rigged by Morgan Groat to give maximum shriek for minimum input, stood conspicuous and silent as the gallows. An occasional passer-by might not particularly have noticed its looming presence, but to certain of those gathered in the garden it dominated the proceedings entirely.

Angela Ormondroyd, Rose Bush and Greta Groat were all awaiting their moment of glory. Angela looked forward to asserting her position as undisputed Lady of the Manor, receiving admiring and envious glances from what she saw as the lowly villagers, and accepting their gracious thanks for her contribution. Rose looked forward to credit finally being delivered where it had been overdue for many years: to her, the organizer of so many past fêtes. For Greta Groat, admittedly floating on a cloud of fulfilment somewhat unfamiliar to her previous persona, the chance to stand up there, nodding and smiling, and to be applauded by the crowd would be reward enough for her years of service to the church and the village. She did not require envy or gratitude, merely recognition.

As the three ladies eyed the microphone greedily, looking at their watches and at the empty podium, and realizing that the time was ripe, they also, as if at some secret signal, became aware of one another. Three women in three pink suits. Three women sharing one ultimate ambition. No-one wanted to rush forward too hastily; each lady wished to capture her prize with dignity and aplomb, and each still hoped that she was mistaken in her suspicion that the others had the same thing in mind.

To the untutored eye, it seemed that a bevy of middle-aged ladies in vivid pink suits were circling the podium gently like manatees drifting in a pool. There, though, the resemblance ended. Manatees are simple creatures who think only of food and sex, and are quite lacking in aggression, whereas here, war was being silently declared. Oliver Bush and Caroline Potter, standing together surveying the scene, were both aware of the commencement of battle, and they each came to the same conclusion as to what was going on. They also, unfortunately for them, both had the same idea as to how to prevent disaster.

Their mutual idea was to seize the microphone first,

thus preventing the ladies from coming together in a Vesuvian eruption of pink, then to introduce one or another lady as speaker and thus defuse the contest. Of course, all that they actually did was increase by two the number of people now converging on the microphone.

The next few seconds were a little confused. In fact, only the photographer from the *Broomhill Gazette* entirely followed events, and that was only because he was able to look at the photographs afterwards. As Oliver Bush hurried up and took hold of the microphone, marginally ahead of the fray, Mrs Groat cannoned forward in a rush of crimplene to intercept him. As he turned, half startled by the fast-approaching pink blur to one side, Angela, closing rapidly from the left, caught her stiletto heel in the microphone cable and flew headlong into Rose. The 'I say!' from Oliver, as he witnessed her flight, was entirely drowned out by the shriek from the microphone as it was whisked out of his hand and hurled into the bran tub. There was a loud 'thunk', then a silence broken only by Solomon, squawking like a demented old wizard. Oliver Bush and Greta Groat sat, dazed, on the right side of the podium. Oliver had fallen backwards onto her and they were both quite unable to get to their feet, waving their arms and legs vaguely in combination like a mutant tortoise. Greta was giggling weakly, which did not help.

Jacob picked the microphone out of the tub and tapped it gently. It seemed to be working. He wondered who to give it to; he was unable to tell all the pink people apart, so it was likely to be a fairly random decision. Angela, whose Marks and Spencer underwear had been irrevocably exposed, had landed awkwardly on one ankle and remained grounded to the left of the podium, recovering her breath. She and Rose had impacted upon one another and then bounced apart, like those perfect round bodies in mathematics which rebound off one another in directions which have to be calculated on A-level maths papers.

Rose, in whose day questions on the coefficient of restitution had not been set in maths, had tottered backwards following her impact with Angela, and had landed on Hetty's stall where she floundered still, a pink elephant amid the white ones. She was doubly unfortunate in that India Potter, to whom a supine adult meant fun, had crawled away from John and pinned her to the ground. It was her first successful crawl and she was delighted with herself. Her enthusiastically bouncing presence on Rose's abdomen placed such an excruciating load on her bladder that she dared not move. She was no longer in contention.

Caroline had come off best. The collisions had not involved her, and she had reached the podium unscathed, only to discover that the microphone had gone. She looked around. Jacob was holding it, hoping someone would tell him what to do with it. There seemed to be no-one to open the fête, and the crowd were becoming restive and eager to spend. Greta was unable to get to her feet with her modesty intact, as Oliver was kneeling on her skirt. She was also handicapped by the fact that she was wearing red silk camiknickers and had no wish to reveal them. Angela was also restrained as her suspenders had all pinged open on the right leg, so she had wisely decided not to stand up quite yet. Rose strove desperately to avoid catastrophe while India gurgled happily.

Most of the crowd were engaged in observing the state of Angela's underclothes, so it was only Caroline, from her vantage point on the podium, who noticed Lady Sybil Ormondroyd walk through the garden gates. The old lady wore her habitual pleasantly-questioning expression, with her head slightly to one side. She also wore a blue suit and hat, and white gloves, which was quite a relief to the eye after all the magenta ladies. She walked carefully up the drive and, as she did so, looked up and saw the red, blue and white bunting strung between the trees. Then an odd thing happened.

Caroline had rather objected to the bunting, but she had not liked to say so. It was old and tatty and had seen better days, most of them, she imagined, before the present Queen was crowned. She thought it looked rather tacky in her trees. Now though, for the first time since she had seen her, Caroline saw Lady Sybil's expression change. Her faded blue eyes seemed to harden and clear, the lyrical tilt of her head to starboard was corrected. Her smile became gracious rather than vacant. She focussed, and there was suddenly someone there behind the eyes.

She strode across the flower bed between the white elephant stall with the floundering Rose and Jacob Bean's hoop-la, straight to the podium with its forlorn and lonely microphone stand. 'Jacob, dear,' she said, quite clearly, 'may I have the microphone?'

Silence fell at once upon those who could see what was happening, then diffused through the rest. Miss Hawthorn, hurrying up the drive in search of her escaped charge, stopped in her tracks, hand to her mouth. Hetty looked delighted, Angela horrified and Greta oddly satisfied. Rose wore the expression of one who has just lost control of her bodily functions. She had not, as it happened, but the expression was there all the same.

'Ladies and Gentlemen,' said Lady Sybil, as she had done for more than forty years, 'thank you all so much for coming along today to support our village fête. I am so pleased that the weather is on our side. As you know, our village church is always in need of funds, and that is particularly true this year, so may I urge you all to give generously? Finally, I must also take this opportunity to thank everyone who has worked so hard to get everything ready, and those who have donated their time, skill and possessions. It now gives me great pleasure to declare the Great Barking Fête open.' She put the microphone down. It had been a perfect speech – it should have been, for she had made it, unchanged, forty-two times.

Miss Hawthorn and Sir George reached her at the same moment, just as the applause died down and the serious shoppers rushed to buy their chosen gifts from the white elephant stall.

'Mother,' said George, hardly able to believe it, 'are you feeling better?'

'Lady Sybil,' said Miss Hawthorn, who was wiser than George (not a difficult achievement), 'what are you doing?'

Lady Sybil turned unfocussed blue eyes from one to the other. 'Who are you people?' she asked them. 'Can I put five pounds each way on Red Rum?'

Caroline, watching, sighed. 'I thought perhaps she'd recovered.'

'No such luck,' said John, thoughtfully. 'Demented patients can appear surprisingly normal at times when the surroundings are familiar. Mind you—'

'It was when she saw the bunting,' said Caroline, 'her face just seemed to clear.' John said nothing, but he was glad Sir George had agreed to the scan. He was sure that Lady Sybil was not as she seemed.

Angela, whose pride had been terribly wounded, decided that the only thing to do was to make a remarkable recovery. Fortunately nobody who counted was here yet. Finding her feet, she sought out George. 'George! Whatever is Hawthorn doing letting your mother get away like that?'

George, watching Miss Hawthorn escort Lady Sybil

away, frowned. 'She's not a prisoner, Angela, she would have been fine if the fête had been at the Hall.'

Angela sensed her advantage slipping a little. 'Now, George, dear, we agreed it was for the best.' She stroked his arm.

George, who was not a clever man, was not sure that he remembered it being for the best, exactly. He had, however, just spotted Lucy dimpling at him and was anxious that Angela should not notice. He and Lucy had finally said their good-byes on Friday, but the boat could still be rocked. 'Come along, dear,' he said chirpily, 'we should circulate.'

They headed stoically for the plant stall, which Angela always felt was the least of all evils. In a previous year, when only Lady-of-the-Hall-in-Waiting, she had managed to win a huge jar of boiled sweets at the Great Barking Fête, by virtue of guessing how many were in it. It had been particularly surprising as she had attempted to hazard a wildly inaccurate guess – but that, of course, is so often the secret of success.

Now that the uncomfortable business of the speech was over, the real business of the fête began. It was desperately important to each stallholder that their stall should make more than it had the previous year. This is true of all fêtes, and in this respect inflation is a blessing, for without it a considerable amount of face could have been lost.

Harriet was very happy. She floated in the manner which only elderly ladies in chiffon skirts who suddenly feel twenty-five again can float. The reason for her elevation above ground level was the presence of Lionel Frobisher, the man from SOBS. The good Colonel was so captivated by Harriet that he had turned up almost as soon after two o'clock as decency allowed, and he was now proving a great asset in the running of the tombola.

'Roll up! Roll up!' he cried. 'Come and take your chance!' Harriet, who hated drawing attention to herself, found herself loving the jollity and even joining in with the kind of fairground banter which normally sent her scurrying for the nearest ladies' room.

Jessie, rendered more or less redundant by this partnership, had gone to help Greta with the teas. Such was the heat of the day that the demand was huge. No-one has ever adequately explained why, on the hottest of days, the English choose to be refreshed by tiny sips of the hottest of brews, but it is a fact of country life that, were iced tea to be offered instead, it would be met by cries of derision and disbelief, and only children drink squash.

Carol Sheldon's books were going well. This was at least in part due to the fact that she had bought all the bodice rippers herself and stashed them in a box under the table. She always enjoyed watching what other people bought, and prided herself on being able to choose the right book for anyone who should stop by her stall. This year she had earmarked a book on fishing for Morgan Groat, *A hundred and one cakes and biscuits* for Rose, and a battered *Rubaiyat of Omar Khayyam* for Oliver. Fortunately Rose was unaware that this last choice was a poem in praise of alcohol, and had the impression that it was a spiritual text. Carol had also chosen a book for Harriet – a formula romance which she had checked to make sure there were no references to any parts of people which hardened or throbbed, for those she kept herself.

The white elephant stall was always a crowd-puller. Hetty had a certain amount of assistance from Caroline, whose attention was endlessly being demanded by India. At least Henry and Josh were still asleep.

Someone bought the china pig which Hetty had ear-marked for Alistair very early on. It seemed, said the woman who bought it – an antiques dealer from Saffron Walden – that these things were going to become quite collectable, and she paid them two pounds for it, even though they only wanted fifty pence. They were overwhelmed by her generosity, although they would perhaps not have been had they known that the pig was already in demand and would be sold the following day for thirty pounds. That, though, is the nature of village fêtes.

There were lots of guesses at the name of the stuffed elephant, everything from the wildly unpredictable 'Elephant' to the oddly amusing 'Debbie'. Hetty just smiled when Caroline asked if anyone had won yet, and persuaded her to have a go on India's behalf.

Jacob's hoop-la was always a great success, not least because he was far more generous with the awarding of prizes than any fairground hustler could ever afford to be. No-one minded that the prizes were small chocolate bars and that everyone won – it was one of those rare exceptions to the rule, in that it was the winning that was important rather than how one played the game.

It was a bustling, happy scene, with villagers running their stalls in a spirit of friendly competition, and spare spouses passing from stall to stall to gently harass them. It was, thought Caroline, a scene to swell your heart with pride. No-one was arguing, no-one was being bitchy or nasty. It was, to her, a scene showing how much a village can achieve when they have a mind to.

Angela was at first delighted when Marsha Millington turned up with Professor Quincey, particularly as they had missed the débâcle at the beginning. They greeted one another like old friends, Angela unwittingly sending Marsha into a red hot rage by inquiring after the progress of her rash. It was intended as an innocent and friendly question, but to Marsha it was imbued with hidden threat and was therefore highly malicious. Professor Quincey, a model of decorum, said nothing, but Marsha was sure that he dropped her arm as soon as he could without causing offence. She feared that Angela knew why. Quelling the urge to hyperventilate, she assumed a gracious expression.

'Everything looks so quaint, my dear,' she said, patting Angela's arm and smiling without using her eyes.

'We're so pleased that you could come – so clever of you to bring the dear Professor,' said Angela, hoping for a good write-up and adopting her friendliest tone.

*She knows*, thought Marsha, vowing revenge, *she knows what I've got, and she's enjoying it.* The paranoid and the suspicious are well known for sensing betrayal at every turn, and Marsha did, after all, have a socially unacceptable condition. Angela was still being charming. 'It means such a lot to the village if we all show a little willing. That's why George and I are so involved.'

Rose, within earshot, snorted. Marsha did not notice. She was trying to decide how best to get back at Angela for so clearly enjoying her distress. She must make sure no-one would listen to Angela, who was clearly planning to betray her awful secret. She must discredit Angela before this could happen, *And who could be better placed than I*, she thought, *for the engineering of social death?*

The cake-whose-weight-must-be-guessed had been abandoned. Mrs Groat had decided that it was a project doomed to failure, and that more money could be made by selling the cake in pieces. She was so laid back, as Finn would say, that she was horizontal. She had taken her failure to open the fête in a surprisingly phlegmatic way, and was still a more cheerful and smiling Greta Groat than anyone could remember since the day when the Ormondroyds' geese got out and ate Jessie Bean's dahlias.

The donkey rides were always a great success. Zoë Ormondroyd was responsible for their front ends – feeding them, leading them and petting them – while Luke Stewart got the rear end or, as he put it, the bum job. All proceeds were to be spread on Caroline's roses, despite Rose's earlier, and entirely serious, suggestion that they should sell it by the shovelful. She only really gave up the idea when Carol Sheldon pointed out that the sale of donkey droppings at Great Barking Fête might lead to an undesirable headline in the *Broomhill Gazette*. The donkeys, a pair named Hector and Lysander, were friendly and docile. The children of the village, who were far too middle class ever to have known the pleasures of donkey rides on the beach at Blackpool, queued endlessly to be led up to the river and back again. Zoë led them happily. The job which she had initially spurned as uncool had suddenly become so cool it was almost frozen, due to the presence of the unusually handsome Luke trailing along behind with his shovel, regaling her with the entire St Joseph's High School repertoire of toilet humour as he did so. An interesting follow-on from this lavatorial conversation was the acquisition, by large numbers of small local children, of words which would otherwise not have entered their vocabularies until they went to Bumpstaple Youth Club at the age of ten.

Zoë was entranced. Her experience of the opposite sex had been severely limited. The headmistress of Butterton was a terrifying woman, built like a tank and with a voice which could rattle china at twenty yards, so local boys fled at the sight of a girl in uniform in Butterton village. Zoë had had more conversations with the pop stars sellotaped to her dormitory wall than with any flesh-and-blood presentable male. She and her room-mates had fantasized endlessly about boys far less handsome than Luke. Zoë had now lost her heart and her head in one fell swoop.

# Chapter Nineteen

Jacob Bean was very pleased with the plant irrigator which he had bought on the white elephant stall. Dear Hetty had had no idea what it was meant for, but he had guessed that it was for irrigating seedlings. She judged his the best guess, so he had won it. He later found that it gave out a wonderful rotating spray for his sweet peas. Hetty had not given Jacob the leaflet which she had discovered with the breast massager, and derived huge pleasure from the whole affair. She was quite unable to look at Angela without imagining her linked up to a variety of hoses and plungers. The most interesting thing of all was, not the number and variety of wrong guesses as to its use – everything from self-watering plant pot to colon-irrigator, whatever that was – but the number of people who had clearly known exactly what it was. An awful lot of members of the WI had guessed correctly, though. Hetty couldn't honestly say that any of them were particularly notable for the size or gravitational resistance of their bosoms, which just went to show that hope and vanity together can sell anything to anyone.

Things were going very well. Everything worth having from the white elephant stall had been bought in the first five minutes by the regular fête-sweepers from Broomhill. These treasure hunters lived in the ever-lasting hope that a hitherto-unknown Da Vinci sketch, or something by Clarice Cliffe, might be unwittingly donated by some myopic spinster, to be sold for less than a pound to those with The Eye. None of them really had The Eye, of course, for if they had then they might have bought raffle tickets for Sarah's mysterious, and still hidden, vase. Her fame as a contemporary artist gave them a far higher chance of financial gain than did the rapid purchase of ten unmatched saucers which they could take home and look up in the *Guide to Antique Porcelain*. Human nature, though, is composed more of avarice than of common sense, and they did not come to the fête to waste their money on raffle tickets. Therefore they had now gone. For those who remained, a mixture of villagers, friends and interested parties from neighbouring villages – comparing fêtes was an absorbing rural pursuit, adding subtle overtones to the desirability, or otherwise, of living in one village rather than another – the highlights were only just beginning. Most people were sitting on the grass with polystyrene cups of tea and melting choc-ices, and it was time for John Potter's magic show.

John had put a great deal of time into thinking about what he could do for a group of such varied ages, and such varied degrees of visual acuity. He had come up with a neat performance centred on his home-made conjuror's table, a purple affair bearing a shining gold dragon. Some of the Fête Committee had not been entirely sure that a magic show was the thing for a fête. In fact, if they had been familiar with the word 'naff' then they might have thought it, but since words like 'naff' tend to be largely the province of those to whom they apply, they had not. Mrs Groat – at least, the Mrs Groat that everyone had known before today – had feared that conjuring might be a little downmarket for Great Barking, and Rose had worried that the whole thing had overtones of music hall and a rather common class of person. But everyone else's enthusiasm had kept them quiet, and the result was a performance which proved once and for all that petty snobbery is a fool's game, and everyone loves a magician.

Henry and Josh, woken from their nap, were delighted to sit at the front as John, assisted by various eager children and Oliver Bush, ran through a varied repertoire of disappearing silks, hatless clowns whose headgear reappeared mysteriously, linking rings, disappearing ghosts, wobbly wands and the sudden production of a furry parrot from his top hat, accompanied by the immortal line, 'A bird in the hat is worth two in the bush.' It was, there could be no doubt, a triumph. Indeed it was quite possible that, even at that moment, local estate agents were rearranging their window displays to alter Great Barking's desirability status in the scheme of things: 'A delightfully picturesque village boasting an active *and varied* community life'.

Completely forgetting that she had ever entertained doubts about the show, Rose was particularly pleased to notice that Audrey Mainwaring from Little Barking was visibly grinding her premolars, and that the archdeacon's wife had arrived just in time to see the whole thing. This would surely merit a mention in the bishop's monthly epistle to his flock.

Greta Groat was happy anyway, magic or no magic. She had spent much of the show holding Morgan's hand. Just now, though, Morgan and his prostate had headed off to the Potters' curious downstairs lavatory. It was curious because it was full of medical magazines which discussed the treatment of enlarged prostates in incredibly frank terms. Reading them gave Morgan hope, and he kept returning for another paragraph. While he read, Greta sat alone, gazing dreamily into the middle distance as she ran through her mind, item by item, some of the more intimate events of the previous night.

After the magic show, when the Fête Committee were absolutely sure that all present had spent every penny that they were likely to spend, Oliver Bush called their attention for the unveiling of Sarah's pot, the first prize in the raffle. To scattered applause, and Rose's overwhelming anxiety, the cover was whisked away, revealing the pot and the picture which accompanied it. The pot was splendid. It was organ-like, gothic, complex and clever. It made one think of church, of music, of pipes and stops and angels. It seemed to reach towards heaven. It was magnificent. Rory's picture was a joyful abstract of greens and turquoises which somehow suggested the sky, the earth, and summer in all its glory.

There were admiring murmurs from those who understood art, and exclamations of wonder from those who wished those who understood art to understand that they, too, could appreciate the modern movement. There were also the usual unappreciative mutterings from the culturally challenged, along the lines of, 'My Charlotte made one like that for her GCSE'. Rose alone sighed a huge sigh of relief. The pot was not rude. Sarah might be a sinful woman, but clearly that did not mean that she would sculpt an offensive pot.

It is one of the dilemmas of village fêtes that the faithful few who organize them always end up buying most of the raffle tickets. There is, therefore, always a very real risk that one of them will win the prize, and allegations of rigging may then follow. Rose had always tried to avoid such a scenario by not actually putting the stubs of tickets bought by members of the committee into the draw. Unfortunately, on this occasion, Jessie had found these stubs discarded on the tea stall, and had helpfully put them in for her. So it was that Caroline won the pot and the picture, which Sarah had, most unreasonably, Rose felt, insisted should be part of the same prize. The photographer from the *Broomhill Gazette* photographed Rose presenting the prize. Rose smoothed her pink suit, then dutifully handed Caroline the pot, wearing an expression of delight that looked only slightly strained about the eyes. The photographer was also delighted, particularly when he looked at his proofs later that day. The angle at which he had photographed the pot could not have been more perfect, and he had not even realized its shape at the time. It was one of those things which needed a second look. He telephoned the deputy editor to suggest that the headline should be altered from, 'Fête Raises Money For Church Roof And Organ Repair' to 'Pot Saved My Husband's Organ, Says Vicar's Wife'. He had ambitions towards the national tabloids, and would have liked to put, 'Vicar's Wife In Sex Slavery Orgy', but perhaps that might be going a bit far.

Once the presentation was over, those who remained were obliged to circle from stall to stall, making certain that everything had been bought, and Oliver announced a few more raffle prizes of bottles and book tokens, awarding the stuffed white elephant to India Potter for her guess of 'Lont'.

Alistair, whose gentle rapport with Hetty still mystified Harriet, was persuaded to hand over ten pounds for a one-eyed nodding dog which no-one could remember actually having seen on Hetty's stall. 'I shall put it,' he told Hetty, 'on the window ledge next to our bed. Then you can look at it all the time.'

Hetty giggled. 'I plan to have my eyes closed,' she said, and his heart lifted.

Caroline liked their banter, their obvious happiness together. She watched them surreptitiously when she wasn't chasing the twins. They were almost honey-moonish, and Hetty seemed to have a glow about her at the moment which made her quite beautiful.

Lucy Bellingham had noticed the glow, too. She was a nice girl at heart, despite behaving like a strumpet, and she couldn't honestly see why he would want to mess about when he had a wife like Hetty. *But then, I am young*, she thought, *and quite striking. Good hips.* She wiggled them a little and smiled a smug smile. Professor Quincey noticed the smile and the wiggle and caught up with her as she headed for the gate.

Sir George Ormondroyd observed their departure with a mixture of wry amusement and relief. He had been a little concerned that there might be a price to pay for his indiscretion, but he was glad to find that he was wrong. In this, sadly, he was incorrect. There was to be a price to pay, but it was not Lucy who would levy it.

The donkey rides, which had stopped for the duration of the magic show, had recommenced. Hector and Lysander, who had been witness to some fairly thorough groping between Zoë and Luke during their break, had become rather frisky, and by the time Henry and Josh had their rides, they were almost managing a brisk trot. Caroline, following behind, was quite alarmed – she had deliberately waited till she thought the donkeys would be tired. The twins, despite their tender years, loved it, and shrieked gleefully all the way to the ford and back.

'Mummymummymummylookme!'

'Mummy Enry in river!'

Then Josh made the connection between large grey animals and thunder.

'Mummymummy. Josh on lont!'

'Mummy. Enry ride lont in 'ky.'

'What are they saying?' Zoë asked Caroline.

'Oh, nothing,' Caroline smiled, sure that they wouldn't be afraid of thunder again.

Just ahead of them, Lucy and Professor Quincey emerged from the Potters' garden.

'My cousin Sebastian used to fancy her,' Zoë said to Luke, wondering fearfully whether he did too. It would be awful if, now, having found the boy of her dreams, she discovered that he fancied just anyone.

'What a tart,' said Luke, delighting her. 'My dad had an affair with her, but Mum's forgiven him.' It made him feel very adult, telling Zoë that so nonchalantly.

'*Did* he?' Zoë was thoughtful. 'My mother would never forgive my father. It wouldn't be his doing it that would bother her, it would be other people finding out.' Her face lit up. 'Hey, I know how I can swing things to leave Butterton and come to St Joseph's High.'

Luke beamed and then blanched. 'That's great,' he said, wondering how on earth he was going to explain this to Katy Hoskins. Probably the same way he had explained Katy to Tammy Baker. He cheered up at once. He'd been planning to finish with Katy anyway – she was pressuring him for sex.

'I shall sort it out at once,' said Zoë, and rushed off, leaving him holding Hector and Lysander while Caroline hauled the protesting twins off their backs.

George, standing with Angela and Marsha, was unaware that his Nemesis approached. There was something about Marsha's smile – it was making Angela rather nervous.

'Father!' cried Zoë, rushing up to them. 'Father, I've met a really neat boy, and he's at St Joseph's High. Isn't that great?'

'This is Zoë,' said Angela faintly to Marsha, who had homed in. 'She's on half term from Butterton.'

'Really?' said Marsha. 'Tell me, Zoë, is it true that they grow hashish in the sixth form common room?'

Zoë ignored her. 'I'm leaving Butterton,' she said, 'aren't I, Dad?'

'What?' blustered George, uncertain as to whether this 'dad' word could actually refer to him.

'You remember,' insisted Zoë, 'we were talking about it in the stable last night.' She looked him in the eye.

George swallowed hard, remembering exactly what he had been doing in the stable on the previous night, and to whom. The presence of his hunter had certainly made it memorable, especially as Lucy had mounted them both for his enjoyment. They were all looking at him. 'Er – yes,' he said desperately. 'Angela, darling, I promised that we would talk about it.'

It was Angela's turn now for concern. Marsha seemed to be hovering like a vulture. 'Of course, dear, if that's what Zoë wants,' she said quickly. Zoë smiled smugly and went off to find Luke again.

Marsha raised an eyebrow.

'We believe,' said Angela rather faintly, 'that Zoë should have a say in choosing her high school.' God, her accent was slipping and she sounded horribly like a Liberal American. There was a risk of being taken for a Democrat.

'Of course, I understand.' Marsha smiled. Now she had a smile like a piranha in a swimming pool.

After it was all over, Caroline lay on the sofa, exhausted, wearing her dressing gown but not her diaphragm. John had said it was the thinking woman's answer to condoms, but when she had opened the packet from the pharmacy and seen that the thinking woman's answer was that awful sex-party pink, she had decided to give up thinking and had thrown it away. The children were all asleep, including India, who was in her own cot at last. John sat at the other end of the sofa, massaging her feet and feeling replete and sexually satisfied. It had been a good day.

Sarah's pot sat on the coffee table, and Rory's picture

273

hung above the mantelpiece. Caroline loved them. John, who wouldn't have gone quite that far about anything which wasn't edible or a magic trick, was fairly impressed.

'It's too good to put flowers in,' said Caroline, eyeing the pot.

'I don't see how you could, there are too many separate pipey bits,' said John. Then he frowned, staring at it.

Caroline was thinking of Hetty's suggestion that, should she wish, an arrangement of branches and individual flowers in some of the pipes would look rather unusual and Japanese. She was startled when John began to laugh. 'What is it?' she asked.

'Come here.' He moved her onto his lap. Caroline moved carefully. She secretly hoped that at this very moment sperm was meeting egg, and she didn't want to disorientate them by altering their perception of gravity. 'Look,' he said.

Caroline looked. She saw the pot from a slightly different angle, and said so.

'Now look again,' said John, 'de-focus and try to look past it.'

Caroline did. 'God,' she said, 'it's a willy, isn't it?'

'It certainly is,' said John. 'I wonder who the model is? No-one I know,' he dissolved again into laughter.

Caroline still could not believe it. 'You don't think it was deliberate, do you?'

'Of course it was,' said John, delighted. 'Don't you see, it was meant to represent an organ and it does – in every sense. I love it.'

Caroline hoped that such a potent fertility symbol would do the trick for her, but a bit of practical help wouldn't go amiss, so perhaps a top-up was in order. She wriggled on John's lap.

\*     \*     \*

It was a further forty-eight hours before the rest of the village saw what John and Caroline had seen, for this was the length of time it took for the weekly issue of the *Broomhill Gazette* to hit their doormats. Once this occurred, they could not fail to see it. Like a monster in the wallpaper, once seen, a thing like that can never again be unseen, and the village's perception of The Pot, and Rose, who was clearly associated with it, was altered irrevocably. Previously Rose had been seen as almost clergy, whereas Sarah had been seen as arty and peculiar. Now, though, Rose and Sarah were inextricably linked, they were the sort of people you thought of in the same breath, the breath in which you also thought of naughtiness, art and penises.

The deputy editor had been bored on the day of the fête. He had worked on the *Broomhill Gazette* for nearly thirty years, starting as a tea boy. In all of that time, sad to say, the job had brought him very little professional satisfaction. The average local stories tended to lack what he regarded as the key ingredients for selling copies: breasts, sex, corruption, vicars and breasts again. Now at last he had had his chance. He had captioned the photograph himself in the end, and was particularly proud of 'It's My Husband's Organ All Right, Says Local Vicar's Wife'. It might be simple, but it sprang out of the page, and, with a little touching up so, too, did the photograph.

# *Epilogue*

The medical student was really very attractive, which was why Mr James Grace, consultant neurosurgeon, had brought her with him to observe proceedings at the private hospital. She was named Rebecca, and she had been extremely proud to be asked along by the great man himself. It had been particularly pleasing to be offered a ride in Mr Grace's silver XJS and then to put on the neatly ironed theatre greens at the private hospital, rather than the NHS ones which were always crumpled, and whose flies never stayed shut.

'This,' said Mr Grace to Rebecca and the anaesthetist, 'is Lady Sybil Ormondroyd.'

Lady Sybil Ormondroyd sat, looking frail and genteel in her hospital bed, watching them.

'Good afternoon, Lady Sybil,' said Rebecca.

Lady Sybil took a deep breath and began to sing in a cracked but tuneful voice. 'Early one morning, just as the sun was rising, I saw a couple at it in the valley below.'

Rebecca gaped. The anaesthetist, who was named Duncan McDonald, choked, and Mr Grace cleared his throat quellingly. 'Lady Sybil is our patient. A scan earlier today revealed her to have a chronic subdural haemorrhage. What can you tell me about chronic subdural haemorrhage?'

'Well,' said Rebecca, 'it is a blood clot around the brain, usually in the elderly. It comes on very slowly, and can look very like dementia. The clot can be removed by making small holes in the skull.'

'Oh. Very good,' said Mr Grace, rather taken aback. In his day, medical students had never known anything other than which varieties of real ale were in stock in which college bar at any one time. 'And what do we expect when we do so?'

'Oh what a whopper, I've come a cropper, How could you use a poor maiden so?' sang Lady Sybil.

'Some recovery,' said Rebecca, trying valiantly to concentrate, 'as soon as the patient wakes.'

'Hmm, yes, very good,' said Mr Grace again. What was the world coming to when medical students knew what was what? 'Let's get on then, Sister.'

'Yes, Mr Grace. Sir George is waiting in the office for a chat.'

'Of course, of course.' Mr Grace hurried off. These paying guests liked to feel that they had had a bit of obsequiousness for their money.

Lady Sybil was still singing. 'Oh, gay is our butler, and fresh is our gardener, But our groom Alfonso is hung like a horse, Please let him choose me, amuse me and use me, I'm not a very good girl and I never show remorse.'

'I must write that down,' said Rebecca.

Lady Sybil fixed her with eyes like gimlets. 'I keep telling you that I don't want any black pudding,' she said.

Theatre was always rather hushed when the patient was conscious, even though in this case she could be said not to be all there. Mr Grace normally liked to play Vivaldi, but it had been rather spoiled by Lady Sybil's singing, so he had had Sister turn it off.

Duncan McDonald was a man who played things so safe that he never ceased to marvel at his own daring in getting out of bed in the morning. 'At her age,' he said, 'I feel that a local anaesthetic would be safest.'

'I do agree,' said Mr Grace, thinking that this would

277

mean less of a fee to the anaesthetist, who had only provided his advice.

Lady Sybil was draped with a series of sterile green towels. 'While shepherds watched their sets by night, All tuned to BBC, The angel of the Lord came down And turned to ITV,' she sang from beneath them.

'Isn't she sweet?' said one of the theatre nurses.

'She was a baker's daughter and she really was a tart, She kept her feet together but she left her knees apart . . .'

'Can't you turn her down?' asked Sister, who disapproved of vulgarity, even from the gentry.

'Now, now,' said Mr Grace, 'not long.'

Sister draped even more green towels over her until she resembled a camouflaged army bunker, then Mr Grace, with a certain flair, injected local anaesthetic into her scalp.

'In Dublin's fair city, where the girls are so pretty . . .'

Mr Grace was handed his hand drill by Sister, and began to drill.

'There was none who could go like sweet Molly Malone . . .'

Rebecca held her breath.

'I am drilling,' said Mr Grace, 'two holes.'

'It's horrible,' whispered one of the theatre nurses. 'Like something out of *Frankenstein*.'

'Be it Tom, Dick or Freddy, young Molly was ready, And everyone knew it, they all heard her moan.'

'There,' said Mr Grace. There was a moment's silence, then the heap of green towels moved.

'Oh my goodness,' said Lady Sybil from underneath them, 'what on earth is going on? A truly pompous ass has been drilling holes in my head!'

Sister moved some of the towels aside. 'Hello, dear,' she said gently, 'you've had an operation, but it's nearly all over.'

'Don't patronize me, young woman,' said Lady Sybil, 'I am well aware of what is going on. You people can all stop staring – I may be old but I still have all my faculties. Clear off, the lot of you!'

Rebecca fled, followed closely by Duncan McDonald, who planned to invite her for a sandwich.

'What a shame,' whispered one of the theatre nurses to the other, 'I was quite looking forward to the next verse.'

Sister glared.


'Cured?' squeaked Angela. 'How can she be cured?'

'She is, you should see her,' said George, his words falling over one another in his enthusiasm. 'She's sitting up in bed, ordering the nurses around and criticizing the wine list. She's coming home tomorrow. Must go – I'll be home shortly. I just had to tell you the good news.'

Angela stared at the purring receiver. 'I think,' she said to herself, 'that I shall spend some time in town.'

'I don't think you will, Mother,' said Zoë behind her. 'Look. *Tatler* again.' She waved the latest copy of the magazine at Angela, who seized it greedily.

On the social pages, next to the usual photographs of the great, the rich and the fashionable sipping champagne, there was a picture of herself at the fête, lying on her back on the grass. Her underwear was clearly visible. She sat down.

Zoë grinned. 'Do you want to hear what it says?'

Angela's lips moved, but no sound came out. Zoë took this as a yes. 'It says, "Lady Ormondroyd supports a well known chain store when attending her local village fête." Could this be the first sign of poverty in the upper classes, or is it perhaps an American trait?'

Angela knew that she had reached the nadir. She took

the telephone off its hook. 'That Millington woman,' she said, 'is an asshole. She should be shot.'

Zoë, feeling a little sorry for her mother, said, 'She needs a shot. Penicillin, I should say.'

'What do you mean?' Angela lifted her head slightly.

Zoë grinned. 'She went out with Anna Grant-Smythe's father. She gave him a nasty present.'

'What present?' Excitement crept into Angela's voice.

'Well,' said Zoë, 'she came out in this rash. She showed Anna. She took it to some posh chap in Harley Street, and it turned out to be gonorrhoea. Anna hates her, so she told me.'

*It is amazing*, thought Angela, *how, just when they have crushed you into the bottom of a hole, God hands you a missile launcher*. 'We must ask Anna to tea,' she said.


Hetty felt that she saw love everywhere these days. She was sure that Harriet and Lionel were made for one another, and it was surely only a matter of time before they saw it themselves. Her own marriage had risen, phoenix-like, from the ashes of its crisis, and like most people who find themselves in love, she and Alistair wanted everyone to feel as they did. Their walks were taken together these days, however hard it was raining, and when they made male-bonding-type jokes at work now, Alistair recounted anecdotes about his wife and children. He had found that this had an instant and deflating effect on those peculiarly sexual innuendoes beloved of single-sex groups of workers anywhere. He had also completely failed to notice that his secretary had been making eyes at him.

\* \* \*

Oliver Bush was left facing something of a dilemma. In the months since the fête, the problem had become apparent, even to him. Was it morally wrong of him not to have the offending privet bush cut down? On the one hand, the regular busloads of sightseers from Cambridge were bringing valuable donations to the church collection box, on the other, was it right for the church to profit from a pagan fertility symbol? Of course it had never been *intended* as a pagan fertility symbol, poor Jacob had trimmed and pruned it in all innocence, but that, nevertheless, was how it was now perceived. The numbers of tourists could no longer be ignored. Rose, of course, was terribly upset. It was surely only a matter of time before she became widely known as the wife of the vicar with the penis. This would be even worse than being known as the wife of the vicar with the organ, which she had had to suffer for a while, so she knew what could be in store. She would never again be able to hold up her head at the deanery tea party, and as for the bishop's wife . . .

Jessie was not particularly upset about it. As she said, a maypole was a fertility symbol, too, and they had had one on the green for years, and the gargoyles on the church represented the old English green man. She was secretly rather proud that her husband was the creator of this controversial and interesting piece of modern art.

Greta Groat was not upset about it either. The old Greta Groat would probably have rushed out at first light and ripped it up with her teeth, but the new Greta was a far more tolerant and amused sort of woman. Morgan was likewise unruffled by the prospect of living in a village with an organ of its own, quite apart from the one inside St Jude's.

No-one else took the matter seriously, apart from Harriet, who was too embarrassed to complain, as this would involve admitting that she knew what a penis looked like in the first place. Hetty and Alistair found it funny, and Sarah loved it. She believed it to be an example of true art, created in innocence and without contrivance. John and Caroline were too busy with her morning sickness to notice, and Carol Sheldon hoped that the publicity would bring tourists to her salon. It had not occurred to her that a coach-load of American tourists on a cultural tour of East Anglia were unlikely to stop in Broomhill for an eyelash tint. They all bought postcards from the village shop, and the landlord of the pub was even better off, as he served them lunch. No-one seemed to have lost out. What was Oliver to do? He resolved to speak to the bishop.

The bishop was even more cerebral than Oliver, and he was a sweetly innocent man, despite his years of inner city work in the sixties. He and Oliver paced around the base of the privet penis discussing it, wholly oblivious to the fact that they were featuring on count-less strips of celluloid from Utah, Omaha and Ohio, as a party of tourists watched them from their coach.

'It seems to me,' said the bishop, 'that the issue is whether or not this bush can be said to resemble a human organ.' He and Oliver stopped their pacing and stared up at it, providing Mavis Butler from Salt Lake City with a perfect shot depicting rural English eccentricity.

'I can see your point,' said Oliver, after consideration, 'but surely what really matters is what people think it is, even if, to you or me, it is a bush. If people believe it to be a human organ, then it is one. That, after all, is why it is bringing us profit.'

'An interestingly philosophical view,' said the bishop, resuming his pacing, 'and one to which, I have to say, my wife subscribes.'

Oliver shuddered at the knowledge that the bishop's wife knew all about it. Rose would not be pleased. 'I think perhaps I should pray for guidance,' he said, heading into St Jude's.

The bishop paused for a while, looking rather sadly at the bush. 'Alas,' he said to it, 'the fruits of human endeavour are not always those which we thought we planted.'

'Oh, sir!' called Mavis Butler, unsure how to address an English cleric. 'Could you smile and give a little wave?'

The bishop complied then followed Oliver into church.

After a while, Oliver went in search of Jacob. He now felt clear in his heart as to what should be done. The penis should be converted back into a church by the man who had designed it.

Jacob was enthusiastic, producing his shears and stepladder at once. It had not occurred to any of them that if a man has once, in trying to sculpt a church, created a penis, then to ask him to create another church out of the penis which he has made is a path fraught with difficulty. He did try. His spirit was willing and so, as the bishop said, the fact that it took several weeks of clipping and a progression through a series of penises of various shapes and sizes before Jacob achieved an even remotely church-like shape was immaterial.

During these alterations, the tourists came in droves, and one enterprising photographer produced a whole calendar of pictures of the Great Barking penis.

Few things go on for ever, and experience has shown that privet penises in country churchyards are more short-lived than most. The time came, therefore, when the privet bush resembled a church and not an organ, and Rose could at last breathe easily. The fact that the bishop's wife had already made as many penis jokes as she was ever likely to, had escaped her. The American tourists gradually reduced in number.

However, there remained a small but gratifyingly steady stream who came, as Americans often do, simply to look at the bush which had once been a penis. There was also an equally gratifying trickle who came because their guide book was out of date, and said that there still was a penis. Upon arriving and finding a church instead, they concluded that the English idea of what constituted a penis was actually rather quaint, so they photographed it anyway. This, as Oliver said, went to remind one of how mysterious are the ways in which God moves in the performance of His daily wonders.

Thanks to the tourists and the collection box, to the fête and to the generosity of Lady Sybil Ormondroyd, the dry rot was completely gone from the church, and the parochial church council's accounts were really very healthy, so healthy that, all in all, the church could be said to have had a very profitable year.

The bats, rustling gently and singing songs far beyond the reach of human ears, were now a listed colony. It made little difference to them. Their lives had been unchanged for many generations, but if they had been worried that their upside-down world might be under threat – and no-one could say for certain that they had not – then they no longer had cause for concern. Not only was there now a preservation order on the belfry, but Mrs Groat had forgotten all about them.

Things seemed to have calmed down nicely, all told, and if the place was not exactly normal, it was normal for Great Barking.

**THE END**

# JUST FOR THE SUMMER
## Judy Astley

'OH, WHAT A FIND! A LOVELY, FUNNY BOOK'
*Sarah Harrison*

Every July, the lucky owners of Cornish holiday homes set off for their annual break. Loading their estate cars with dogs, cats, casefuls of wine, difficult adolescents and rebellious toddlers, they close up their desirable semis in smartish London suburbs – having turned off the Aga and turned on the burglar alarm – and look forward to a carefree, restful, somehow more *fulfilling* summer.

Clare is, this year, more than usually ready for her holiday. Her teenage daughter, Miranda, has been behaving strangely; her husband, Jack, is harbouring unsettling thoughts of a change in lifestyle; her small children are being particularly tiresome; and she herself is contemplating a bit of extra-marital adventure, possibly with Eliot, the successful – although undeniably heavy-drinking and overweight – author in the adjoining holiday property. Meanwhile Andrew, the only son of elderly parents, is determined that this will be the summer when he will seduce Jessica, Eliot's nubile daughter. But Jessica spends her time in girl-talk with Miranda, while Milo, her handsome brother with whom Andrew longs to be friends, seems more interested in going sailing with the young blonde son of the club commodore.

Unexpected disasters occur, revelations are made and, as the summer ends, real life will never be quite the same again.

'A SHARP SOCIAL COMEDY . . . SAILS ALONG VERY NICELY AND FULFILS ITS EARLY PROMISE'
John Mortimer, *Mail on Sunday*

'WICKEDLY FUNNY . . . A THOROUGHLY ENTERTAINING ROMP'
Val Hennessy, *Daily Mail*

0 552 99564 9

# BLACK SWAN

# THE TENNIS PARTY
## Madeleine Wickham

'SHARPLY OBSERVED FIRST NOVEL ... LIGHT BUT LETHAL'
*Mail on Sunday*

It was Patrick's idea that they should have the tennis party weekend. After all, he had the perfect setting – the White House. Bought out of his bonuses as an investment salesman, it was complete with stable, cocktail bar, jacuzzi, shell-shaped bedheads, and, of course, the tennis court (towered over by an authentic Wimbledon-green umpire's chair).

He hadn't actually told Caroline the *real* reason for the tennis weekend. Caroline was brash, beautiful, tarty (he had met her when she was a busty promo girl at the Finance Exhibition) but she was also honest. If she thought he had set it all up to pressure the Mobyns into one of his investment plans, she just might cease to hostess the weekend the way Patrick wanted. The Mobyns were rich, or at least Cressida was. Charles loved her, not because of her money, but because she was discreet and aristocratic. It was just a shame she thought Patrick and Caroline so vulgar.

As the four couples gathered on the Pimm's-soaked terrace – Patrick and Caroline who were rich, the Mobyns who were even richer, Stephen and Anne who weren't rich at all and didn't have designer tennis clothes, and Valerie and Don who were just dreadful and who really *cared* about winning the tournament – it signalled the start of two days of tempers, shocks, revelations, the arrival of an uninvited guest, and the realisation that the weekend was about anything but tennis.

'IT'S EXACTLY THE SORT OF BRIGHT, HILARIOUS NOVEL YOU WANT TO READ WHILE FLOPPING ON A SUN-LOUNGER WITH A CHILLED SPRITZER TO HAND'
Val Hennessy, *Daily Mail*

'AS SHARP AND REFRESHING AS AN EXTRA-STRONG GIN AND TONIC'
*Living*

0 552 99639 4

## BLACK SWAN

# GUPPIES FOR TEA
## Marika Cobbold

'THE TOUCH IS LIGHT BUT ACCURATE AND
TELLING. HER AVOIDANCE OF SENTIMENT MAKES
THIS READER FEEL THAT SHE REALLY CARES FOR
HER SUBJECT – A REALLY GOOD ACHIEVEMENT'
*Elizabeth Jane Howard*

Amelia Lindsey was an exceptional young woman. She
had a grandmother whom she loved, a mother whom she
bore with patient fortitude (Dagmar spent much of her
time scrubbing the backs of wardrobes and wiping
clothes- hangers with Dettol-drenched J- cloths), and
Gerald.

Gerald had fallen in love with Amelia two years earlier,
when he was in his artistic phase, and had begged her to
move in with him. Now (no longer in his artistic phase)
he was showing signs of irritation.

And then Selma, the talented and much-beloved
grandmother who had given Amelia all the background
of family and home that poor Dagmar could not give,
suddenly became old. As life – and Gerald – began to
collapse all round Amelia, she determined that the one
person who would *not* collapse would be Selma.
Fighting a one- woman battle against Cherryfield
retirement home, against Gerald's defection and her
mother's obsession with germs, Amelia found herself
capable of plots, diversions, and friendships she had
never encountered before.

'AN ORIGINAL, PAINFUL, FUNNY, FRESH BOOK'
*Joanna Trollope*

0 552 99537 1

**BLACK SWAN**

# A SELECTED LIST OF FINE WRITING
## AVAILABLE FROM BLACK SWAN

| 99564 9 | JUST FOR THE SUMMER | Judy Astley | £5.99 |
| 99565 7 | PLEASANT VICES | Judy Astley | £5.99 |
| 13649 2 | HUNGRY | Jane Barry | 6.99 |
| 99648 3 | TOUCH AND GO | Elizabeth Berridge | £5 99 |
| 99537 1 | GUPPIES FOR TEA | Marika Cobbold | £5.99 |
| 99593 2 | A RIVAL CREATION | Marika Cobbold | £5.99 |
| 99602 5 | THE LAST GIRL | Penelope Evans | £5.99 |
| 99622 X | THE GOLDEN YEAR | Elizabeth Falconer | £5.99 |
| 99610 6 | THE SINGING HOUSE | Janette Griffiths | £5.99 |
| 99590 8 | OLD NIGHT | Clare Harkness | £5.99 |
| 99391 3 | MARY REILLY | Valerie Martin | £4.99 |
| 99480 4 | MAMA | Terry McMillan | £6.99 |
| 99503 7 | WAITING TO EXHALE | Terry McMillan | £5.99 |
| 99561 4 | TELL MRS POOLE I'M SORRY | Kathleen Rowntree | £5.99 |
| 99606 8 | OUTSIDE, LOOKING IN | Kathleen Rowntree | £5.99 |
| 99598 3 | AN ANCIENT HOPE | Caroline Stickland | £5.99 |
| 99607 6 | THE DARKENING LEAF | Caroline Stickland | £5.99 |
| 99620 3 | RUNNING AWAY | Titia Sutherland | £5.99 |
| 99650 5 | A FRIEND OF THE FAMILY | Titia Sutherland | £5.99 |
| 99130 9 | NOAH'S ARK | Barbara Trapido | £6.99 |
| 99549 5 | A SPANISH LOVER | Joanna Trollope | £6.99 |
| 99636 X | KNOWLEDGE OF ANGELS | Jill Paton Walsh | £5.99 |
| 99592 4 | AN IMAGINATIVE EXPERIENCE | Mary Wesley | £5.99 |
| 99639 4 | THE TENNIS PARTY | Madeleine Wickham | £5.99 |
| 99591 6 | A MISLAID MAGIC | Joyce Windsor | £4.99 |